Blue Skies
and
Dark Nights

The autobiography of an Airman

By

Bill Randle

Blue Skies and Dark Nights - by Group Captain Bill Randle

First publication in Great Britain

© WSO Randle 2002

First edition published in 2002 by:

Independent Books
3 Leaves Green Crescent
Keston
Bromley
BR2 6DN
United Kingdom

Tel: 01959 573360 Fax: 01959 541129

e-mail mail@independentbooks.co.uk

Edited and designed by Peter Osborne

Jacket illustrations by Tony Theobald

Special thanks to Air Commodore Mark Tompkins for his help with the
technical preparation of the original manuscript.

ISBN: 1 872836 40 2

CHAPTER ONE

Although it happened more than seventy years ago, I still remember the wonderful thrill of my first flight in an aeroplane. The noise of the clattering engine, the smell of burnt oil, and the excitement still come back to me. It was all very much of a surprise. It was my eleventh birthday and my father had combined this, my birthday present, with the idea that the trip would 'knock the nonsense out of my head' of wanting to be flyer. He expected me to be scared, perhaps terrified by the experience. Instead, it proved to be the time when I made up my mind that somehow, sometime, I would learn to fly.

The flight did not take more than five minutes and it cost the princely sum of five shillings. Together with a school chum, Ken Trueman, we had waited our turn in a long queue of those wanting to 'dare the devil'. We had to be helped into the large rear cockpit of a sky-blue painted Avro 504 with silver wings, one of the machines used by the Alan Cobham's Flying Circus that toured the country promoting air-mindedness. That afternoon they were operating from a small heather-strewn field on the edge of Woodbury Common, just a few miles from Budleigh Salterton, Devon. The skies were clear and blue, the wind blowing fresh from the sea and the only clouds to be seen were well away to the north, over the Blackdowns.

We sat together on a painted wooden seat, not even strapped in; there were no seat-belts. Ken was on my left and we could just about look over the side without straining up. My father and Zon, my elder sister, waved to us as we taxied away; we waved back. We were quickly into the air after a run of little more than a hundred yards or so. Then the pilot began a climbing turn to the left, up and around, levelling for a while as we looked out at Exmouth. Then, all too soon, he was throttling back and we were coming in to land. After a longish taxi back to the waiting queue, we were helped down from the aeroplane. I can still see the puzzled expression on my father's face as we both cheered our experience.

My father in 1917 in the uniform of the Machine Gun Corps

My parents never understood the obsession I had with everything to do with aeroplanes. No one in the family had ever been remotely connected with flying. The Great War had ended just fourteen years previously and I had been raised in an atmosphere dominated with memories of what happened in 'the war to end wars'. My father had served in the Machine Gun Corps and had been badly gassed at Passchendaele during the Third Battle of Ypres. I had grown up believing that Britain was best and that no matter how bad the odds were against us, we would always win in the end. We were of better stock than the others; we were part of a great Empire, spread across the world. We looked up to a respected Monarch and knew our places in the social scheme of things.

Our history was drummed into us at school. Our pride was supported by Empire and Naval Days. Battleships moored off the Devonshire coasts; sailors came ashore and paraded. The bands played and there were patriotic concerts and exhibitions. Everyone seemed to look forward to such events, and they thronged to take part.

It was no wonder that we youngsters knew about the heroes of the past, particularly those of the war just won. The military had always been my favourites, but not the soldiers and sailors. I admired the airmen such as Mannock, Ball, and Bishop; and knew their victory scores, together with the aircraft types flown by all the top British, French, German, Austro-Hungarian, Italian, Russian and American aces. I read avidly about them and kept well-documented scrapbooks of everything to do with flying; much was happening in those days. Just five years previously, Lindbergh had flown solo from America to Paris, others were now doing so regularly. The Royal Air Force had flown at over 400 miles an hour, winning the Schneider Trophy outright. And there was Amy Johnson: 'Amy, wonderful Amy, how can you blame me for loving you', as went the top popular song.

I reached a significant milestone that year by winning a scholarship to the Exmouth Grammar School. This caused great surprise in the family because I had kept the attempt a secret. My father was not happy because I would now be at school at least until I was sixteen, and would not start work at fourteen as I could have done had I progressed from the elementary Church School to the secondary Board School. We were not well-off, my father worked as a clerk with the Exmouth Urban District Council at a top wage of £3 a week. He was an excellent calligraphist and a reasonable artist, painting in oils. He played the piano and the mandolin, read a lot, and had many fanciful ideas that always came to naught. He displayed little initiative and was a dreamer. Mother was the opposite, the practical one, the leader and decision-maker, living in the hope of helping her children to a better life than she and father had led. There were four of us, two boys and two girls, and I was the eldest. She became adamant that if Bill was to go to a good school, then so should the others.

Myself with mother 1921

The shortage of money meant that something had to be done to augment Father's wage. Mother rented a small-holding of about six acres at Hulham, on the outskirts of Exmouth. There she went into business growing vegetables and fruit, and breeding hundreds of chickens, ducks, geese and turkeys, together with a few pigs. She undertook all the hard work and we children helped as best we could. I quickly picked up the skills of husbandry, and the knack of buying and selling, working with a will because of Mother's example. I undertook a weekly milk-round for which I was able to add two shillings and sixpence to the family income. It meant a start at five o'clock each morning, rain or shine, collecting a carrier-bicycle loaded with milk bottles from Thorn's Farm just down the road, and delivering the milk over a fairly wide area during the next two hours. Usually there was an inevitable last minute bicycle dash to school in Exmouth before Assembly that took place precisely at nine o'clock.

Exe View - our home for three years

*Christmas 1936. From left to right, my brother Peter, younger sister
Alynda, older sister Zonora (Zon) and myself*

The Exmouth Grammar School had a fine reputation, emerging as it had
from the private Grange School just after the Great War. The Headmaster
was the impressive D' Arcy Hughes, an Oxford MA, together with his
teaching staff, all of whom had good degrees and, with one exception,
were veterans of the war. For me, the change in my circumstances was
profound. So much was different and new, a decided step up in the world.
There was order and discipline, and a sense of purpose that was lacking at

the Church School. Prayers were said at Assembly; prefects curbed our natural wantonness and classes were held without interruption or any vestige of nonsense. We were disciplined by the prefect system, awards of order and conduct marks, detention after school and, as a last resort, by 'six of the best' delivered by cane on the rump by D'Arcy Hughes, and no one else. The curriculum covered many subjects, ranging from Divinity, Music, Latin and French, to English, Mathematics, Chemistry and Physics. We had large playing fields which encompassed two full-sized soccer pitches, a fine cricket ground encircled by an athletics track, and a first-class gymnasium. The school motto was our inspiration; 'Facta Non Verba' - 'Deeds Not Words', the same as that of No. 20 Squadron in the Royal Air Force.

I did reasonably well at the Grammar School, becoming a member of the School Junior Soccer team in my first year and, once I had gained a place, played regularly as left-half in the Senior Eleven. I didn't shine at cricket although once I carried my bat in a House match for a never-to-be-forgotten 51. I was not fast enough on the athletics track, much more of a plodder, shining only in a moderate way in the longer races. Academically I did better. My métier was History with Geography a good second. I was made a prefect when in the Fifth Form and obtained the School Certificate with Exemption from London Matriculation, surprisingly with Distinctions in History, Mathematics and Physics. I entered the Sixth Form to study History, Geography, and Physics for the Higher Schools Certificate.

I kept up my interest in aviation and, as there were others at school with the same intense search for knowledge, we formed an aircraft modelling club and had an exchange mart for pictures and material. I kept scrap-books of every notable event and development, and travelled around East Devon to wherever aeroplanes could be seen. I did extra work at weekends to raise money to pay for flights, a painstaking effort. The best I could manage for a morning's hard work clearing chicken coops or mucking-out sheds was sixpence. It therefore took a long time to accumulate the necessary five shillings for a flight but, when I had it, what a thrill it was to get airborne. In one year, I managed trips in an Airspeed Ferry at Exeter, a Puss Moth at Dunkerswell, and a Short Scion from the Haldon racecourse.

Devon Air Day 1937. Leaving a Short Scion with Peter Stovel

Financial disaster overtook the family in 1937 when the small-holding could not be made to pay its way. The rent was long overdue and it was clear that the venture had failed. Mother was distraught but nonetheless determined to hold on to as much as she could of her possessions. Before the bailiffs moved in, she directed the evacuation of the little that was left. Peter, my brother, and I, spent the whole of an autumn night, driving a horse and cart, back and forth between our house and a friendly farmer's barn, where we hid as much as we could. I learned a lot but not how to get a carthorse to go in reverse after it had deliberately headed into a pond to sit down and drink, and to stop working. Luckily, our friendly farmer came to our rescue in time for us to make the final journey of our 'moonlight flit'.

We were in such a financial mess that I had to leave school, either to find work to help support the family or to leave home and fend for myself. The hopes of higher education, possibly a degree, had been dashed. A post was being offered for an office boy with the Exmouth Council and my father, without telling me, had arranged that I should try for it. Half-heartedly, I attended an interview together with three others. My lack of interest must have shone through because I was turned down on the spot, very much to Father's disgust. As usual, Mother, came up with a solution. I would do much better if I tried for a position in a bank - a step up, so she said. It should be relatively easy because I had done so well at Mathematics in the School Certificate Examination.

She was right. I underwent a selection board at Lloyds Bank, Exmouth and, to my surprise, was offered a post as a junior clerk with an income of £80 a year. The only snag was that I would have to serve at any branch of the Bank's choice and, most likely, that would not be anywhere near Exmouth. Within a week, I received instructions to report to Lloyds Bank, Norbury, in South West London.

Leaving home was a terrible wrench, my world tumbled around me. Although I was fortunate to be going to live with relatives at Tulse Hill, not far from Norbury, I was, for almost a week, dreadfully homesick. I was incapable of doing any work and my uncle and aunt did their best to make me see reason. Only once before had I ever been away from home and that was on a day-trip to Southampton from school. It was all very silly on my part and, in the end, shame made me face up to reality.

The Norbury branch of Lloyds Bank was small with a friendly staff of just four which included me. I settled down quickly to learn something about the wide range of banking activities. Machines were not used in those days, all accounts, ledgers, balances and records were made up by hand. I had to improve my handwriting and soon became adept at scanning and casting-up columns of figures. I travelled to work by electric train from Tulse Hill and kept within a budget by always taking a sandwich lunch. My only real expenditure was a modest sum I paid to my relatives for food and accommodation.

I made many friends at Tulse Hill, joining a tennis club and becoming a member of the Congregational Church at West Norwood and even teaching in the Sunday school. Otherwise I was always out and about, Croydon, Redhill and Gatwick airfields were all within easy cycling distance, and I visited them regularly. Although the country was heading towards war with Germany, like most young people at that time, I paid little attention to the worsening situation. Even though there were many signs of hurried rearmament to be seen, including the introduction of air-raid precautions I, like most, chose to believe in Mr Chamberlain's policy of appeasement.

Without any warning I was transferred to the St James's Street branch in the West End. This I regarded as some sort of promotion because my salary was increased to £90 a year. I joined three other juniors in the Current Accounts department and began to see banking as a career. I applied for and easily passed Part 1 of the Institute of Bankers Examination and got down to deal with Part 2 in record time by undertaking a Correspondence Course. I liked the bustle and urgency of business in the big branch. In those days, the cashiers were the important people, next in line under the Manager, Assistant and Sub Managers. Two cashiers had served in the Great War; one had been a captain in the Royal Fusiliers and had been badly wounded in the final push at Amiens in August 1918; the other had flown Felixstowe flying boats on anti-submarine patrols over the North Sea and along the Belgian coast. I became good friends with two of them, both recognized my sheltered upbringing and each, in his way, introduced me to new things. I got to appreciate good food, particularly sea food, at Pruniers just across the street and best of all eaten at no cost to myself. I had also come to enjoy orchestral music and the theatre.

However my interest in aviation dominated my spare time, every day new military types could be seen flying over London. I went to Northolt to look at the Hurricanes of No. 111 Squadron, and to Hornchurch to see the new Spitfires. I cycled down to Brooklands where they were building the Wellington bomber. There was always something to do; life was full of interest; there was never a dull moment. I fully supported my church in its many activities, steadily improved my tennis game, and switched from playing soccer to the more robust game of rugby. Air raid precautions were being set up. Gas masks were issued; vital buildings were sandbagged. The Militia had been called to the Colours. We were beginning to doubt the effectiveness of Mr Chamberlain's appeasement policy.

CHAPTER TWO

At the moment war broke out I was having a drink with my uncle and his
friend, a sergeant airgunner in a Fairey Battle squadron, in the White Hart
at the bottom of our road in Tulse Hill. The wireless was switched on and
the volume turned up as we listened to the Prime Minister's fateful words.
As he finished, the air raid sirens sounded and we poured out on to the
pavement outside expecting to hear the sounds of anti-aircraft fire and to
see approaching bombers. The RAF sergeant calmed us, saying it was
probably a false alarm, 'Jerry has his hands full in Poland. There's not a
chance in hell that he can take us on as quickly as this,' he added.

I had been brought up to believe that there could never be another
Great War, yet another was beginning. Inevitably, I would be called upon
to serve and, when that time came, I was determined to do so as aircrew
in the Royal Air Force. The bombing of London seemed to be inevitable
as we could clearly see from the news-films in the cinema that showed the
destruction of Warsaw. We began to prepare for such horror: a pre-fabri-
cated Anderson shelter was delivered in a pile of metal bits to every house
in our road. I personally dug it in at the bottom of the garden, far enough
away from the house for us not to be covered by rubble if it were to be
blown down. At work, many of the junior and middle staff left to join their
Territorial and Royal Naval Reserve units. Each of us was questioned
about our intentions to serve and asked to delay joining-up for as long as

possible; otherwise the bank would be swept clean of staff. Most of us complied with this request, made the easier as danger seemed to fade into the uncertainty of the 'Phoney War'. All was quiet on the Western Front; the German Fleet was bottled-up in harbour, and the Royal Air Force was on guard in France. Bomber Command, however, had been driven out of the daylight skies over Heligoland and the North Sea, and was using its offensive capability to drop leaflets at night over Germany.

Nonetheless, there was hardly a person in the bank who was not ready to go. Another junior, Willy Parke, was also intending to join the RAF. We struck up a friendship and together made enquiries about how we should volunteer our services. We did not want any holding-back on our part to jeopardize our chances of becoming flyers.

The rundown of the staff meant that many of us had to double-up and take on additional responsibility. I began to learn something of the work of the Loans and Income Tax departments. There was an almost total collapse of the Lloyds Bank Rugby Union XV in which Willy Parke was a regular player. Somehow, he induced me, an absolute beginner, to turn out just to make up the numbers. The selectors must have been desperate because I became a steady choice, each weekend, throughout the winter of 1939/40, playing a very poor game as a wing three-quarter. We got trampled over and well-beaten every time we played, losing to much better endowed teams such as the Metropolitan Police and Rosslyn Park

The 'Phoney War' came to its abrupt end early in April 1940. First there was the invasion of Denmark and Norway, and then the Blitzkrieg through the Netherlands, Luxembourg, Belgium and France. It took a little while for us to comprehend the seriousness of these disasters as the full facts were kept from us by the Government control of the Press and the BBC. I did see a trainload of weary survivors from Dunkirk unloading at Clapham Junction but it was not until Mr Churchill made his famous 'Finest Hour' speech about the fall of France and the coming Battle of Britain that I realized we could be invaded and, most likely, defeated. Surely this was the time to join up.

German troops landed in Guernsey on 30th June and by the next day the whole of the Channel Islands had fallen without even token resistance. Portland harbour was bombed on 4th July and the first Victoria Cross was posthumously won by Leading Seaman Mantle as his ship, HMS 'Foyle

Bank' went down. I reasoned that all might be over before I could be trained to fly and, therefore, in such desperate circumstances, it would be best to join the Local Defence Volunteers in the expectation of playing a part in the defence of London.

Dad's Army. Sporting my LDV arm-band and my .30 Mod.1917 rifle which was superbly accurate

The Local Defence Volunteers, the LDV, renamed later as the Home Guard, was composed of a mixture of men over military age and youngsters like myself. I became a member of a platoon based in a private house just outside Dulwich College. Our only identification was an armband stamped with the letters LDV. We were armed with a Ross rifle and five rounds of ammunition. Our platoon leader was someone in the City and our NCOs all veterans of the Great War. There were attempts at first to impose old-style drill and for the NCOs to hector and shout but, very soon, our collection of so many different characters and talents, settled down as a very free and easy band of volunteers.

Our main concern was what we should do when the Germans reached Dulwich. The informed amongst us were certain that the invasion attempt would have to be made in the coming four months of expected reasonable weather in the Channel. By October the sea-state would make it virtually impossible for the enemy to motor or tow their boats and barges across. A fiery old major from battalion headquarters cheered us up no end by lecturing us on how to hold our ground. We would fight from trenches and ditches, from fortified buildings, and behind roadblocks. We would never acknowledge defeat and, if necessary, we would fight to the last man. Try as I could, I could not see myself making such a sacrifice, I was no hero and thanked my lucky stars that we had not been issued with bayonets. After my five rounds had been fired, I believed I would be on my way with many others, withdrawing and hoping to live to fight another day.

A healthy democracy in the platoon bound us together. We resolved to do our best and tried to come up with ideas of better tactics. We drew up a plan for building dead-falls and tank traps. We set up our own production of fire bombs; bottles filled with petrol and with linen fuses to be lighted before the gadgets were thrown under German tanks. Although most of us had jobs in London, we paraded every night and maintained a good guard.

For a while there was little evidence that the Battle of Britain was being fought in the skies over south-east England. The battle came nearer around the middle of August when the Germans began to attack the fighter airfields at Biggin Hill, Kenley, Croydon and Hornchurch. We knew little about how serious and effective these attacks were as the only news available was what we read in the censored newspapers or heard on the equally-muted BBC wireless. We were led to believe that the battle was being won while, all the time, our airfields were being battered almost to the point of ineffectiveness.

We did not realize the importance of the news that Bomber Command had raided Berlin in retaliation for a single German aircraft unloading its cargo of bombs, mistakenly as the Germans put it, over Croydon. Nor did we know that Hitler had ordered a change of strategy from the attacks on the RAF airfields to mounting attacks on London.

I was weeding in the back garden during the afternoon of Saturday, 7th September, a fine clear day with just some high cloud away to the north-east, when the air raid sirens were sounded and almost at once the anti-aircraft guns began to fire. To my sheer amazement, I then saw the approach of a veritable armada of German bombers escorted by Me 109s. They were in formation, layer upon layer, and there was not a single British fighter to be seen. I stood on top of the Anderson shelter and watched the beginning of the bombing of Silvertown and the East India docks. I let out a cheer when an escorting Messerschmitt Me. 109 was hit and went down vertically, minus its tail.

Dashing indoors I put on the uniform with which we had just been issued and ran most of the way to platoon headquarters. By now, dockland was ablaze and the towering columns of smoke could be seen in the distance arising from the burning houses, wharfs, and warehouses. All we could do, however, was to sit and wait for orders which never came.

I stayed on duty throughout that night, fully expecting the church bells to ring heralding the start of the invasion. The Germans kept up the attack on the East End until daybreak. The Blitz had begun. It was the start of night bombing that would go on without let-up, night after night, to the end of the year, and beyond. It soon became indiscriminate; there were seemingly no particular aiming points. Maybe it was because of the weather or the accuracy of the anti-aircraft fire but, more likely, that the Germans were ordered simply to destroy the Capital and so break the will of its inhabitants.

Bombs fell all over London and we got our full share in the south-west. Strangely, I found it exciting. The last thing I wanted to do was to take shelter and stay indoors. I joined in patrolling the streets and helping the rescue services whenever possible. I had to ring the changes between duty with the Home Guard and taking my turn as a fire-watcher on the top of the Bank's building in St James's Street. I always wore a steel helmet as protection against the red-hot bits of shrapnel that fell from the skies. Sometimes, but not often, I had to fling myself to the ground when bombs fell nearby.

We were certainly in the very frontline of the war. Most of the children had been evacuated leaving the rest of us resolved not to be beaten by a barbaric enemy; indeed, it was a fact that the constant bombing actually stiffened morale. It became difficult to get to and from work because of the constant damage to the roads and railways. The Underground railway still functioned well and, every night, it provided shelter for thousands who were able to sleep undisturbed deep down beneath the streets.

Most of us were building up a real hatred of the Germans; the bombing of London, the wanton destruction of our heritage, together with the killing of so many civilians, for what seemed to be little point. I remember well an incident that took place on Sunday, 15th September, the day the *Luftwaffe* made its last big daylight raid. I was on duty at platoon headquarters and in the late afternoon, to my delight and surprise, I saw a Heinkel 111, obviously in trouble, at about 2,000 feet with first one and then another crewman leaving by parachute. The aircraft passed overhead and went down to crash, some miles away, most likely near the Thames. I watched the second parachutist coming down to land on the far side of Dulwich College. I had a rifle but my five rounds had been taken from me for safer storage but I was determined I would be the person to capture the German. I dashed into the College grounds, across the playing fields, past some newly-dug allotments, to where I could see, about a hundred yards away, the collapsed canopy of the enemy's parachute. Other people were hurrying towards it from a nearby row of houses. When I got there, two women had already dragged the badly-wounded and terrified airman away from his parachute and were screaming and hitting out at him, one with a heavy piece of wood. Had I not restrained them at gun point they might well have killed the wretched man.

We still thought that the Germans would invade; not knowing that Hitler had postponed Operation 'Sea Lion' to a later date, and later cancelling it altogether. He must have known by then that bombing alone would not bring the British nation to its knees. For our part, we knew that we had survived a possible national catastrophe and would now have to face up to a long war. The signs were around us, strong rumours continued that the 18-20 year-olds would soon be called up. I gave notice to the bank that I would join the Royal Air Force before such conscription came into effect.

The Blitz went on almost every night right to the end of the year. Life was becoming more difficult. I now travelled to work on a bus because of the damage to the railways. Every night, I was involved either in Home Guard duties or in fire-watching on the roof of the bank in the West End. There was no pattern to where the German bombs fell. They were attacking London in the same way they had dealt with Warsaw; trying to destroy it. Fire-watching in the West End was becoming dangerous. On 17th September I kept well under cover as bombs fell around us on Burlington Arcade, Bond Street, Berkeley Square, and Park Lane. I was on duty when the Carlton Club in Pall Mall was hit and burned out, and the church next to Simpson's in Piccadilly was destroyed.

Then, on 16th November, I thought that my last moments on earth had come. We seemed to be the very target centre that night. I remember being terrified as bombs fell in St James's Street, St James's Square, Duke Street, and on our larger branch, just along the road in Pall Mall. Three incendiaries fell on the roof where we were sheltering. We quickly dealt with them.

That night a 250 kg bomb buried itself in the garden next door to our house in Tulse Hill without exploding, just a few yards away from where my aunt and uncle had been sleeping in the Anderson shelter. It was dug out and taken away the next day by the Army bomb-disposal people. My uncle's place of work at Hay's Wharf received a direct hit and was completely demolished, Then, on 29th December, I watched the horrific fire bombing of the City of London from the bank rooftop, just a couple of miles away.

One of my New Year resolutions for 1941 was to keep a diary and the first entries dealt with the chaos caused by this great incendiary attack. Other parts of London had also suffered: at Tulse Hill, gas mains had been ruptured and tram lines blown-up and the road to Herne Hill was blocked with the debris of houses. More tragically my uncle's best friend and drinking partner, together with the whole of his family, had been killed in their house no more than a hundred yards from where we lived.

The raids continued into January but they became less frequent and were not so intense. High-flying fighter-bombers made daylight hit-and-run attacks. They were not very effective but they were a nuisance. At first, each time they came, the air raid sirens were sounded and people would stop work and take cover, but they soon got used to it and after a while hardly anyone bothered. I no longer spent time fire-watching at the Bank and therefore had more to do with the Home Guard. There, much had changed: there was a very different attitude, the carefree spirit had gone as more and more of the younger people had left to join the Services. The diminishing possibility of invasion had removed the sense of urgency and we had many more parades, drills and lectures. We had at last been issued with bayonets and were now practicing how to parry, thrust, and withdraw the weapon from straw-filled dummies. I note from my diary that on Sunday, 19th January I was wounded in the head by a bayonet wielded by an old-stager, who lost his balance while trying to slope arms alongside me with fixed-bayonet.

There was a Royal Proclamation on 29th January instructing the 18-20 year-olds to register for service by 22nd February. I tried to join the Royal Air Force the next day but I was kept waiting for hours at the RAF Recruiting Centre at Euston and, in the end, had to return to the bank without seeing anyone. I went again the next day, this time with the sub-manager's blessing to stay there for as long as was required. I was interviewed by a middle-aged Pilot Officer who explained what was expected of me. After answering questions on my early life and my present occupation, he suggested that it would be best for me to join as a would-be navigator. I could always move on to piloting after gaining experience in the air. In any case, I would have to brush up on my algebra and trigonometry, and make sure I was in tip-top physical condition. Another medical examination would follow on 26th February. If all went well, there would then be a full RAF aircrew medical, together with an examination in mathematics, and an interview before a Selection Board.

I hated the time spent waiting. There was now only the occasional raid, the Germans were picking on easier targets than London. It was hard to understand why they even attacked my home town at Exmouth, broadcasting that the important docks there had been put out of action. The fact that they were little bigger than a large swimming pool and that nothing larger than a small coastal collier could squeeze through the dock gates, said little for German target intelligence but spoke volumes for the propaganda ministry.

My father, now a corporal in the Royal Army Service Corps, stationed at Perham Down, not far from Warminster, had also been a target of sorts. A lone German bomber had jettisoned its bombs in the fields bordering the camp. I accepted an invitation to spend a weekend with him but was not very impressed with what I saw and experienced. I slept in a smelly dormitory hut shared with about twenty others. The meals were awful: corned beef, beetroot, bread and Daddies' sauce was offered for breakfast, lunch and dinner. There was a lot of bugle-blowing and much shouting. The only redeeming feature was the pleasure I got from getting away from the camp and walking for hours with my father through the lanes and over the hills of Salisbury Plain.

I registered for service on 22nd February at the Labour Exchange in Coldharbour Lane, Brixton. I was asked a few questions about my education and which branch of the Services I preferred. I thanked my lucky stars that I was already committed to the Royal Air Force. I reported to the RAF Recruiting Centre in Endsleigh Gardens at Euston right on the dot at 09.00 hours on the 26th. My eyes, heart, lungs, and feet were examined by four different specialists. I spent a lot of time standing around in my birthday suit, and getting cold. At the end, I was pleased to be told that I was A1 but not at all happy with having to see a dentist to have five diseased teeth repaired before returning for other interviews on 4th March.

The final interviews took two days. With my teeth mended, I arrived early to find the place teeming with would-be aviators. I was given a written examination in mathematics and another on general knowledge. I was keyed up to begin with but soon relaxed when I found how easy it was to deal with the tests. Then there was a particular medical examination. I blew-up and held a column of mercury steady while my blood pressure was taken. I sat on a chair, blindfolded, and was whisked around and then, eyes uncovered, had to walk straight along a line chalked on the floor. I had to hold my breath for as long as possible, look at colour-blindness charts, and have my hearing checked. It was indeed a relief to be told that there was nothing wrong with me.

The next day, I was interviewed by the Selection Board that comprised an Air Vice-Marshal and two other officers, one a Wing Commander, the other a Flight Lieutenant. Naturally, I was nervous but I could not credit my good fortune when I realized I knew something about the Air Vice-Marshal from the wealth of information on the RAF I had accumulated over many years. His first words to me were, 'Do you know who I am?' 'Yes sir,' I answered in a flash, 'you flew Sopwith Pups with No 66 Squadron, Royal Flying Corps, in 1917.' A smile broadened his face. I knew I had made a comfortable start.

Questions were put to me by the two junior members, few of which had much to do with flying. Then the Air Marshal, who had been studying a form, took over. 'I see here that they have got you down as wanting to be a navigator, why is that? Most young men like you want to be pilots.'

I answered too soon, 'I was told that it would be best for me, sir. I do well with mathematics, but ...' I was lost; I now realized that, at my first interview, I had allowed the Pilot Officer to impose a solution which had not been of my choice. I looked despairingly at him. 'I was told that after a spell as a navigator, sir, and if all went well I could be considered for pilot training.' I knew it was the wrong answer but tried to flannel on, 'I suppose what happened was that I didn't think I'd be good enough to make a pilot, sir.'

The Air Marshal was smiling at my obvious distress. 'That's for this Board to decide, young man. We will know what you are made of. Just answer these questions,' he said as he looked me straight in the eyes. 'Can you sail a boat?' Having been brought up near the sea I knew a little about boats and how they should be handled. I had even managed a small clinker-built tub once or twice in the Exe Estuary. 'Yes sir,' I replied.

'Do you ride a horse?' Here he had me; I most certainly had never ridden the sort of animal he had in mind but ... I had often practised on cart-horses. I had even managed to get them to gallop. 'Yes sir, I do... but not often,' I said.

'Can you swim?' That was easy. 'Yes sir.'

'And do you dive?'

'Yes,' was my enthusiastic answer.

'Head or feet first?' he asked.

'Why, head first of course, sir; there's no other way.'

The Air Marshal was scribbling something on the form. He looked pleased with himself. 'I'm putting you down to be trained as a pilot, my boy. Don't worry about this navigating business, all pilots become reasonable navigators ... in time. It's not the other way round.'

I could not believe my good luck. I left the room as though walking on air. I could have shouted my exaltation to the rooftops.

CHAPTER THREE

I was thereupon attested and given the number 1385872 and the rank of AC2 (Aircraftsman Second Class), plus the sum of six shillings for some sort of expenses. I was told to report to No 1 Receiving Wing at Babbacombe in Devon in eight days and given a railway warrant to get there.

It took me just a day to clear up and leave London. First I said good-bye to my colleagues at the bank and received the blessings of the Manager together with his hope that, as a permanent member of his staff, I would return safely one day and renew my career. I said farewell to my relatives and friends at Tulse Hill, to those at the Church, and at the Home Guard. The next day, I travelled to Exmouth, stopping off on the way to see my father at Perham Down, arriving home just before midnight. I had to wake my mother, brother and younger sister, who were very surprised to see me, and then tearful when I told them I was off to learn to fly.

I spent six days at home, the weather was bad throughout, including three days of snow. I visited relatives at Colaton Raleigh, Newton Poppleford, Ottery St Mary, and Otterton and had a 'short back and sides' haircut. There was an air raid alarm on the fourth day which brought the town to a standstill for almost an hour. Nothing happened, although I refused an order by a policeman to take shelter. A German aircraft did come in just after midnight to machine-gun the streets near the docks

It was a sparkling day with blue skies and a fresh wind when I said goodbye to the family and boarded the ferry that took me across the Exe to Starcross where I took the train to Torre. From there I walked to Babbacombe, arriving at the Receiving Wing at about 2.30 in the afternoon. I signed some forms, was given a quick medical check and then ate a meal of kidneys on toast, bread and butter, and tea. I was sent to the Trecarn Hotel to share a room with three others: Bush from London, Bourne from Trinidad, and O' Sullivan, a former Merchant Navy man.

1a Flight, No. 1 Receiving Wing, Babbacombe, Devon, March 1941.
Second row, fifth from the left

The next day we were inoculated against a host of possible diseases. It was done most efficiently; we were paraded in a line with shirt sleeves rolled. While waiting my turn, I noticed that the person in front of me was getting agitated, and by the time he reached the doctor, who had the injection needle poised, he was shaking from top to toe. Before the injection could be made, he collapsed unconscious. I noticed that he had a strange blue tinge to his face as he was taken away and we never saw him again.

The next task was to get us kitted-out: I drew two pairs of trousers, a tunic, greatcoat, vests, 'long johns', which I never once wore, 3 shirts, 5 pairs of socks, 6 collars, 2 pairs of boots, and 2 kit-bags. We had to pack our civilian clothes which were taken away to be posted to our homes. In the afternoon, proud to be dressed in uniform with white flashes in our forage caps denoting that we were aircrew under training, I walked - or rather marched, with Bush and O' Sullivan, into Torquay where a War Weapons Week was in full swing. I saluted my first officer, a Flight Lieutenant pilot who was sitting with other wounded aircrew watching the crowds pass along the seafront. Some time later we walked slowly back to Babbacombe, each of us finding that our brand new boots were hurting.

We were kept at Babbacombe for two weeks, receiving lectures on *esprit de corps*, pride in uniform, why the Air Force could claim to be one of the best in the world, the Air Force Act and King's Regulations. We had a stirring talk on the various ways the death penalty could be imposed for treason and serious breaches of discipline. Then, inevitably, we were drilled at least twice a day, by corporals who seemed to take a singular delight in bellowing at us at every opportunity. There was also daily physical training but I was enjoying every moment, liking to a man my colleagues, all enthusiastic volunteers.

As a Devonian, I felt very much at home. When the visibility was good, I could stand on the cliffs at Babbacombe and see the Exmouth Pavilion and swimming pool across the bay. Twice in that fortnight I was able to sneak away, hitch-hike to Exmouth, spend an hour or two at home, and then be back in the hotel before 'lights-out' .

Our training began in earnest on 29th March. We packed our kit and, as a Flight, marched into Torquay, singing as we went, that repetitious song, 'I've got sixpence, jolly, jolly sixpence, I've got sixpence to last me all my life.' We joined No 5 Initial Training Wing and were housed in the Templestowe Hotel. The fifty of us became 'B' Flight of the No 2 Squadron of the Wing which was under the command of Air Commodore Critchley of golfing fame. After waiting around for some time for an embarrassing FFI (Freedom from Infection), we unpacked and settled into comfortable quarters. I roomed with Bush and O' Sullivan, Bourne had been left behind at Babbacombe, sick.

We spent the next two months learning the basics of flight training: drill and physical exercises every day and marching a lot, often into the fringes of Dartmoor and through the charming villages that surrounded Torquay. We generally sang as we marched, usually the same monotonous song, 'I've got sixpence ...' that I had grown to detest. I took up playing golf and turned out as left wing in the Flight's soccer team. On the academic side our studies were wide ranging; much emphasis was placed on mathematics and we were subject to regular tests, even one called an elimination examination. The standard was not particularly high. We studied the basics of navigation, and refreshed our scant knowledge of trigonometry. It was all well within my capabilities, and I managed good marks.

B Flight No. 2 Squadron, No.5 ITW Torquay May 1941
Front row, far right

The learning of the Morse code was another matter. It was new to most of us, apart from O' Sullivan and another former sailor. After a few weeks most of us were reasonably proficient at receiving five words a minute. We steadily improved and I reached my peak at ten words a minute without a single mistake, but failed badly at twelve.

We were paid every fortnight in the Army style, on parade. Each of us in turn marched up to the pay desk, came to attention, saluted the Accounts officer, then shouted the 'last three' of our number when our name was called. The sum of one pound, fourteen shillings would then be pushed forward on the table by the Accounts sergeant. Another salute, right turn, and march smartly away.

This sum of money was a bonus to me as I was still receiving a salary from the bank. However, for some time at first, our food was plentiful and reasonably well-served. As time went by standards began to fall until we were making complaints at every meal about the meagre quantity and poor presentation. There was never enough to satisfy our demanding appetites. It was then I began to use my pay. We resorted to buying extra food from nearby shops; usually Cornish pasties or newspaper-wrapped 'six penny-worth of fish and chips.'

My self-esteem received a boost when we began to study aircraft recognition. I was very surprised to find that I had the edge on almost everyone, including our kindly school-masterish instructor. Because of my earlier studies I could identify any British, German, Italian, French or American machine in a flash and then rattle off a fair description of its construction and performance. One day, after I had perhaps foolishly thought it necessary to correct a statement made by our instructor, he suggested that I might like to take over the class. This I did, and coped well. Afterwards he asked if I would do so regularly and agreed that I could tackle the job in my own way. I used a compendium that I had compiled over the years of photographs, sketches, and diagrams of more than 150 aircraft.

We were able to indulge in all the usual off-duty pleasures. I went to the cinema, the theatre, and to dances of which there were many. I disgraced myself by getting drunk for the first time in my life when Paddy O' Sullivan introduced me to drinking rum. I drank so unwisely that I became sick and nauseated by the smell and taste of the liquor. To this day, I have never again drunk rum.

More pleasantly, I was allowed three one-day Sunday passes that enabled me to go home to Exmouth. We had a good postal service and I received regular news from relatives in London, and from friends in the Bank. The latter had experienced a very heavy air raid on 21st April when the West End had been badly hit and Christies in nearby King Street was burnt out. An even heavier raid had followed during the night of 12th May, damaging the House of Commons and the British Museum. That was the day when Rudolf Hess, Hitler's deputy, made the news by flying a Messerschmitt Me110 to Scotland and parachuting down near Glasgow. We heard rumours that he had arrived to help us sue for peace. This made little sense when we were beginning to hold our own, particularly in North Africa.

'A' Flight left for training in Canada at the time we began our final examinations. We were each asked if we wanted to volunteer to be trained overseas. I said yes, as most of my fellows in 'A' Flight had and I had visions of enjoying myself in the peaceful surroundings of Canada or South Africa. We were then issued with flying kit, leather helmet, goggles, a Sidcot flying suit, silk under-gloves, leather gauntlets, and flying boots. We were inoculated against tetanus and yellow fever, and graphically informed of the nature and perils of venereal disease.

On 17th May, my 20th birthday, we were told that we would be going overseas to be trained, and that we would do so wearing civilian clothes. The more knowledgeable thought it meant that matters in South Africa had become touchy and that perhaps the authorities, particularly in Rhodesia, wanted us out of uniform to keep the peace. Others thought we were to be trained by civilian organizations in a neutral country; after all, the Empire Training Scheme was expanding by leaps and bounds as the demand for aircrew increased.

We were measured for civilian suits while the examinations progressed. I had another medical and, yet again, the dentist went over my teeth. The examinations went well, conducted as they were in a free and easy fashion, as though everyone was expected to pass. In the Aircraft Recognition test, many turned openly to me for the answers while the adjudicator turned a blind eye. I had a final interview with a Wing Commander and was told I had done well. We were then sent on embarkation leave.

I travelled first to London and spent a night with my relatives at Tulse Hill. I paid my respects to my friends in the bank and went on to look at the damage inflicted on the City of London by the great incendiary attack. There was little left except St Paul's which still stood, surrounded by the charred, broken and blasted shells of buildings; some of the streets had all but disappeared in a sea of rubble and charred timbers. As I walked around, sporting the aircrew white flash in my cap, more than once I was welcomed and told, 'They can't beat us, no matter how hard they try. Soon it will be your turn - go to it, young man!'

The next day I went by train to Salisbury, caught a bus to Warminster, and walked to Sutton Veny where my father was then stationed. We had a meal together and strolled around the camp, then it was back to Salisbury to catch a train to Devon. I arrived at Exmouth late that evening to be met by my mother who had just received a telegram recalling me to Torquay. I was just in time to catch the last ferry across the Exe, and so on back to my unit.

We were all promoted to LAC (Leading Aircraftsman) on 28th May with a rise in pay to 5/6 (five shillings and sixpence – 28p) a day. We left Torquay the next day with our belongings stuffed into our two kit bags, facing a long train journey northward to No I Personnel Dispersal Wing at Wilmslow. We arrived there in pouring rain and were wet through in the time it took us to march from the station to the camp. It was a wretched place, a sea of mud, crammed with hosts of airmen on the move.

The mystery of where we were going deepened when we were issued with sun-helmets, khaki-drill uniforms, blue overalls; our civilian suits, and a floppy black beret. This confounded our South African theorists who switched the whereabouts of our possible destination to a small, friendly, French-speaking colony somewhere near the Equator.

We spent three miserable days at Wilmslow and were greatly relieved to learn that we would be on our way by 1st June. We boarded a train that afternoon, each supplied with a packaged day's rations. We arrived in Manchester just before midnight in the midst of an air raid. The train was held in the station and we had no option but to sit tight in our seats. A stick of bombs fell on the station straddling our train. Glass was showered over our compartment, a small fire was started in the next carriage; no one was hurt but we were held up for hours while the track was cleared to allow us to proceed on our way. Fortunately, there were no more hindrances in our journey and we eventually reached Glasgow, finally stopping just beyond the city at the port of Greenock.

We had to take our place in the line of groups of airmen waiting on the quay side to board ship. When our turn came, we were taken by tender out to a fine-looking liner, the Windsor Castle, rigged as an armed transport. We were directed below to a small deck where I was counted in together with one hundred and forty-nine others.

The first night aboard was very unpleasant, cooped in a small area with hammocks slung in line above the mess tables; they were so close they touched. I couldn't get to sleep because of the noise made by excited men, the cold, and finally the oppressive atmosphere of tobacco smoke and human smells. I dressed and went up on deck where I stayed until dawn broke.

Breakfast could not be taken until all the hammocks had been taken down and stowed. Strangely, the greasy eggs, bacon and sausages went down a treat, helped along with chunks of newly baked bread and steaming-hot tea. Afterwards we had nothing to do so we roamed the decks, read, and visited the fine ship's canteen where we could buy cigarettes, chocolate, apricots and oranges, things that were almost impossible to get on-shore. In the evening we were issued with life-jackets and given boat-drill.

We weighed anchor at 21.00 hrs on 3rd June and steamed down and out of the Clyde Estuary in the company of four other liner transports. We slept better that night, warmed by the ship's heating systems, and ventilated by the wind of its passage. I was up early and went on deck to find that we were in the open sea, escorted by the battleship HMS Rodney and four destroyers. The other transports were nowhere to be seen. We were in the Atlantic, steering a westerly course. If that was to be maintained, then we were surely headed for Canada. There was another boat-drill that morning, but the rest of the day was spent lying on deck and reading in the fine weather.

That evening we had our first scare, we had just gone below for a meal when the alarm was sounded for 'Boat Stations'. As we quickly collected our life-jackets, we could hear the rapid fire of guns. By the time we reached our lifeboat positions the firing had stopped and the 'all-clear' had been sounded. What had happened was that Rodney had been firing away with its pom-poms at a Coastal Command Catalina that had been sent to give us protection. The amphibian stayed with us for almost an hour and then turned about to escort a twenty-one ship convoy back to Scotland.

We were given work to do the next day. The lucky ones got jobs on deck, some even being added to help the gun crews. Most of the rest of us had cleaning tasks, in my case, dealing with a string of lavatories and two bathrooms. It took just an hour to do a good job, which meant the rest of the time could be spent lazing on deck, or wandering around the ship, and eating. The canteen did good business, I had never before eaten so many oranges, apricots and apples.

That night we ran into a full-blown Atlantic gale and the Windsor

Castle did not sail well. Although she registered over 20,000 tons, she rolled, plunged and cavorted like a small trawler. Waves broke over her bow and regularly, at the top of huge swelling wave, her screws came clear from the water to make an alarming noise as they raced away. It was bedlam below in our mess-deck, almost impossible to stay in the hammock; some broke away, others became entangled. I got out of mine and tried to anchor myself to the mess table underneath but, by then, the situation was out of hand. Many were already desperately sea-sick, vomit was everywhere and the stench was awful. I decided that the only place for me was on deck where I went to wedge myself behind a bollard and hold on in the lashing rain.

As dawn broke, the only ship I could see was the Rodney, plunging even deeper into the waves than we were. There was no sight of the destroyers but we were being followed by a flock of sea-birds, no doubt regarding the ship as some sort of haven in the storm.

Order began to be restored below. Those, like myself, who had not been sea-sick had to turn to help the sick, but first we were rewarded with a breakfast of sausages, beans and fried bread. I most certainly did not relish the task ahead; I had never seen such sea-sickness. We began by getting the afflicted to rest and we tried to help them clean themselves. It was a beastly job, mopping-out the vomit-splattered lavatories and bathrooms but fortunately, in the end, we were helped by some of the ship's crew.

We sailed through the storm and into fairish weather the next day. I was still feeling fine and enjoying my food. A hearty breakfast of egg, bacon and fried bread prepared me for an extra long stint of lavatory cleaning duties. Most of the sick were beginning to recover. The strange sea-birds were still with us, and word was received from Rodney that we had detoured some 800 miles during the gale, to avoid a U-boat pack.

The following day the weather grew even calmer. We were holding a steady course in a ship that bore all the evidence of an ordeal. By now, most of us had enough of life on the rolling main, particularly so in my case by having to work in continuous filth. There were cockroaches everywhere, most of us stank for want of a good wash, and our clothes were filthy. Nonetheless, we knew the voyage would soon be over, confirmed when a Liberator aircraft appeared and gave us an hour or two of protection. We had the happy sight of a school of whales blowing just a hundred yards from the ship, and different kinds of sea-birds were out to greet us. I managed to wash some clothes; in the afternoon I played a game of deck tennis.

We sighted land at midday on 10th June and, a few hours later, steamed into Halifax harbour. It was grand to see Rodney drop anchor ahead of us and to moor alongside the battleship Ramillies and the battle-cruiser Repulse. It took quite some time for us to disembark and, when we did, we trooped across the dock-side straight on to a Canadian National Railroad train which was waiting for us.

We left Halifax that evening and travelled through the night trying to sleep in a most uncomfortable old tourist carriage. We bumped along, marvelling at the absence of a blackout and blessing our good fortune for a safe crossing. There was much washing and scrubbing in the train toilets and by dawn we were ready to tackle a truly tremendous meal. The food was wonderful: three kinds of meat, lashings of butter, real fruit juice, fruit and vegetables; all the things we were missing back home. Other meals followed and I estimated that first day we must each have consumed the equivalent of a fortnight's British rationing of meat alone.

Our first stop was Monckton, New Brunswick. There was time enough there to change our English pounds into Canadian dollars. We travelled on, stopping now and then at small towns with such interesting names as Mont Joli and Riviere du Loup. In most cases, the population seemed to know we were coming and they thronged the platforms to greet us. I practiced my schoolboy French on some which was answered in much better but accented English.

We got into Ontario on the second day of the journey and arrived at Toronto by midday. There we were rushed from the station in a motorised convoy to the No 1 Manning Depot where we received a great welcome. Again we were fed a feast and were interviewed by the Press and photographed. A few hours were spent on the formalities of booking-in, signing documents, and being given bed spaces. Then we were handed over to the most hospitable of Canadians who showed us around their city of which they were so proud. I went to what I was told was the biggest hotel in the British Empire, and I ate my first hamburger.

The next day we received the astonishing news that we were going into the United States of America. We were to be the first Britishers to be trained there to fly in what became known as the Arnold Scheme. An arrangement had been made at the highest level for the Americans to train two hundred of us at private flying schools in California, Texas, Florida, and Oklahoma. Our Flight of fifty from Torquay would be going to the Spartan School of Aeronautics in Tulsa, Oklahoma.

Our uniforms were packed away and we put on our standard grey-flannel suits. There was a flurry of activity with passport and visas, and the signing of documents that had something to do with disease and personal habits. We were lectured on how to behave in America and told something about conditions in the Middle West. All done, we were taken away to see a baseball match.

I was almost out on my feet when taken back to the Manning Depot remembering a final last gorge of loads of strawberries and cream. Before we left Toronto there was a last round of Canadian hospitality to be enjoyed. At the Black Watch Club we drank beer and sang songs, and left with a large Union Jack for us to take to the States.

———————————————

CHAPTER FOUR

We returned in a fleet of cars with police escort and were aboard a train by 9 p.m. Two hours later we were in Detroit, and then went to bed. We were met by a welcoming party when we arrived at Chicago early the next morning and, after breakfast, they took us on a conducted tour around their remarkable city. To a man, we realized just how fortunate we were to be setting out to be trained in a land of plenty, a country comfortably at peace. We were on our way again by early afternoon and travelled southwards without incident. The food was splendid: we had a vast, leisurely lunch, and then the American substitute for afternoon tea. By this time we had reached St Louis, Missouri and dinner was equally remarkable. Arriving at Tulsa just after 5 a.m. on 16th June we were rushed away from the station to the Spartan School on the outskirts of the city. Breakfast was taken and we were packed off to bed to sleep until midday. After lunch we again met the Press.

The rest of the day was ours. We washed, bathed, and cleared-up and settled into barrack-style accommodation. In the evening, we met cadets of the United States Army Air Corps who were also being trained at Spartan. We had drinks together and entertained each other with songs. Our best effort was the awful 'I've got sixpence', while the Americans did so much better with the Marines', 'Halls of Montezuma', the Artillery's, 'As the caissons go rolling along' and their own, 'Off we go into the blue out yonder, off we go into the sun ... atta boy give her the gun' .

The Spartan School of Aeronautics, June 1941

Training began the next day but first we had to meet the Press once more and have our photographs taken. We made a start with parachute drill and then were introduced to our instructors. I took to mine at once. James C. Lowe was a somewhat overweight Texan extrovert, with a great sense of humour. He showed me over the aeroplane I would fly, a Fairchild PT19 monoplane, the Cornell, fitted with a Ranger in-line engine, painted blue on the body, with yellow wings marked with the insignia of the US Army Air Corps. I was shown how to start the engine and then allowed to do so myself.

We flew from a former cornfield about three miles outside Tulsa, to which we travelled by bus. The next day I was taken on my first flight. It was a great thrill in a machine that, 'Almost flew itself,' so Lowe told me. Demonstrating his ability, we flew loops, stall turns, and finished with a spin; it was all an absolute wonder to me. From then on I flew every day in perfect weather; blue skies, unlimited visibility, and gentle winds. I progressed from 'straight and level', to gliding, stalling and spinning. We practised forced landings and then concentrated on work in the circuit, on take-offs and landings.

Flying was interspersed with Ground School, conducted in barrack accommodation back at the Spartan aerodrome and under most uncomfortable conditions. Every day the heat was terrific; inside the stifling classrooms there was no air conditioning. At times, it became difficult to concentrate on what was being said and it was often a fight to stay awake. We were permanently dehydrated and, perhaps foolishly, drank and drank bottles of ice-cold Coca Cola which was on sale everywhere at five cents a bottle. There was even a dispenser just outside our classroom.

On 27th June, after a repetition of what I thought were poor landings, and after I had taxied back to the take-off point to prepare for another circuit, I was dumbfounded to see Lowe unstrapping his harness and getting out of his cockpit. He lent over me, patted me on the head, and said, 'It's

First solo in the Fairchild PT 19

all yours - just do me a circuit and bring her in.' I simply could not believe it, but I was ready to go and did not feel nervous.

I checked that there was no one on the approach and carefully lined-up. I was absolutely delighted as I took-off, flew around the circuit, came in and made a good three-point landing. Full of myself at being the first on the course to fly solo, I taxied across to the flight-line, and switched off. For a while, I sat in the cockpit relishing my achievement but I was brought down to earth with a bump when the Chief Instructor stormed out to the aircraft and told me what a fool I had been; he had watched my performance and was furious. First, I had waved during the take-off run; then I had forgotten to raise my flaps before taxying-in and, worst of all, I had left my instructor at the other end of the field to walk back in the sweltering heat, with his heavy parachute over his shoulder.

In the next week thirty-one of the fifty of us flew solo. Amongst the unlucky ones was my friend Bush for whom I really felt sorry. It was strange however that he had got this far because of his obvious lack of coordination, he even had difficulty in marching in step. With the other failures, he was sent back to Canada to train as an observer. The thirty one successes were however reduced by one when someone I thought to be amongst the best, unfortunately too fond of the bright lights and the ladies, was sent home because he had contracted syphilis.

There was so much to be enjoyed in Tulsa. Although we trained along-side the American cadets, our differences were marked. So many locals just wanted to hear us speak, the girls were attracted by our manners and behaviour and we were fêted whenever we went out in a group. Our attendance at a baseball match between Tulsa and Fort Worth meant a police escort all the way to the ground with sirens wailing. We were often interviewed by the Press and the first three of us to fly solo made headlines in the Tulsa daily newspaper. Within a week, I had received letters from three American William Randles who had seen the write-up and my photograph. One from Oklahoma City wanted to know if we were related because he

Jimmy Lowe's three students, left to right, Tony Payne,
Eric Francis and myself

alleged he was descended from a family that came across with the Pilgrim Fathers.

There were many things we found hard to understand. We had no officer in charge of us; we managed and disciplined ourselves. The American cadets, on the other hand, were subject to the strictest rules, one of which was the custom of 'hazing'. They had upper and lower-classmen, very much in the West Point fashion. The lower-classmen were always moved at the double and given strange extraneous tasks to perform. At meals, which we shared with them, an upper-classman only had to tap a glass and say, 'Square meal, mister', when the lower-classman was bound to sit, bolt upright, eyes fixed straight ahead, and fend with his fork for the food he was unable to see on his plate. His arm movements had to be rectangular in bringing the food to his mouth; he was not allowed to speak, smile or look down. If he was unable to perform, then he would have to recite gibberish until told to stop. Naturally, all our sympathy was with these lower-classmen. We thought that 'hazing' was ridiculous but were careful not to air such undiplomatic views.

Most of us had never before seen such numbers of black people as were in Tulsa. Segregation, in the widest sense, was imposed everywhere. The blacks did not mix with the whites; they lived 'on the other side of the tracks'. Some of us unwittingly broke the segregation rules and were corrected, time and again, by white people, some of whom were most annoyed. It was usually a case of sitting in non-white sections of public places, or using toilets that were for blacks only. However we soon learned how to avoid trouble and adjusted to the American way of life.

Self with Jimmy Lowe in front of our trainer. (It is interesting to note that Bill was already getting people to sign things - Ed.)

The local population treated us as heroes. The Battle of Britain had been won only a few months previously and we were not inclined to spurn the reflected glory that had been won by others. Most of our new-found friends were decidedly pro-British, but there were some of recent German and Italian extraction who did not like having us amongst them. The local chapter of the German-American Bund considered that President Roosevelt had no right to disregard international neutrality laws by allowing us be trained in the United States.

There was never any lack of invitations to social events, attracting as we did girlfriends who took control of much of our sight-seeing and entertainment. We were taken to baseball games, rodeos, open-air cinemas, on boating trips and to such places as Will Rogers' birthplace and the Osage Indian reservation. We lived 'the life of Riley', and thoroughly enjoyed it. However, the hectic pace must have affected our work. The Chief Instructor held that in future we were to be back in camp by 21.30 hrs to get a good night's sleep.

Les girls, Mohawk Park
4th July 1941

My flying progressed reasonably well but, unfortunately, I was beginning to show signs of certain limitations to my ability. I was good at instrument flying, having no trouble at all co-ordinating the readings of the turn and bank, altimeter, and air speed indicators, but when it came to aerobatics, it was a different matter. I could cope with spins and loops because of their set pattern, but with rolls and instinctive manoeuvring, I was hopeless. In fact, I had the greatest difficulty in rolling to the left at all, my co-ordination with stick and rudder was poor. Already my instructor was marking me down, saying that I was not very good at analyzing what I was doing. He hinted that I might not have the makings of the fighter pilot I wanted to be.

With a car made for ten - Mohawk Park,
4th July 1941

We had our first fatality on Friday, 11th July. Denis Harrison was flying solo around the circuit when he lost control of the aircraft, stalled, and spun into the ground. This accident coincided with the arrival of Squadron Leader A.C. Kermode who came to take control of us and move us to Miami in Northern Oklahoma where No 3 British Flying Training School was being built. He was a gifted officer; his book 'Flight without Formulae' was required reading. His impact was immediate, we were back in the Royal Air Force and were organized into two flights, each with its cadet leader. He brought us back to reality, our carefree existence was over, reminding us that we were in America to learn to fly in the shortest possible time. Soon we would be going back to play a part in a war that had to be won. We moved to Miami two days later, travelling in a convoy of cars and buses. The contrast with Tulsa could not have been more marked, it was a typical mid-Western country town with a single main street containing a bank, cinema, business offices, filling station and a drug store. Its finest asset was the College of Northern Oklahoma in which we were to stay until our barrack accommodation was ready at the airfield being developed on the northern side of town. We resumed flying the next day, watched by scores of local inhabitants.

Students with Squadron Leader Kermode, Miami, July, 1941

Flight Control

The small unfinished airfield was ringed by many noticeable landmarks: zinc mines, an old cemetery, and the winding Neosho River that stretched away into the far distance. I still had my instructor, Jimmy Lowe, and we got on very well together. There was none of the 'crash-bang-wallop' on the controls when a mistake had to be corrected, his criticism was always kindly and constructive. On the other hand, whenever I flew with another instructor, particularly on the regular progress checks, I seemed to run into trouble. I became very tense, and made silly mistakes and reacted particularly badly when flying with Al Scarlatta, a very experienced pilot of Italian extraction. He made no secret of the fact that he did not like me, trying to put me on edge from the very moment I was told to start up. He was always over-riding me on the controls and correcting me in a very heavy-handed way. On one occasion we finished a check ride with him telling me that I was so bad, I was on the verge of being 'washed-out'. I had to ask Lowe if indeed that was so, and why had he not told me. 'You are doing all right,' was his answer. 'The only problem you have is one you have made for yourself. Did you not know that you have been going out with Scarlatta's girlfriend?'

We were issued with official RAF log books at the beginning of August and had to make them up for the previous seven weeks of flying. They were then checked and signed by our instructors, and blessed with an interim written assessment that followed a check ride with the Chief Instructor, R.P. Tucker. My flight was a disaster: I knew that I had performed badly and was dismayed when he told me that I was wasting time in Miami and would be better off back in England, where I belonged. Nonetheless, my log book received an Assessment of Flying Ability as average, with the following points of flying and airmanship to be watched: 'Power-off work weak - Analytical ability only fair.'

I did much better with my ground studies. I again undertook instructing in Aircraft Recognition, using my large collection of photographs, facts and figures. We sat the mid-course examination in a wide range of subjects and I came out top of the course with high marks in every one. In the middle of August, we progressed to the basic trainer, the Vultee BT13 Valiant and I had my first flight on the 13th with a new instructor, E.V. Adair, middle-aged, expert, and kindly. Most of this first sortie was 'under the hood', flying on instruments. I was pleased that I seemed to cope reasonably easily.

A few days later I became ill during an aerobatic sortie. I was flying with Adair at 6,000 feet when I suddenly found my eyesight going and a splitting headache developing. On landing, I was taken to sick quarters where I stayed for the next seven days. There was concern at first that something dramatic had happened to me but, after the twenty-four hours, it was diagnosed that a virus had caused my ears, nose, and sinus to become clogged with mucus. I was alone in sick quarters for the first three days, responding to medication and fending off swarms of flies that inhabited the place. Late in the evening of the fourth day, I was joined by a member of No 2 Course brought in with his head covered in blood. He had argued with some German-American Bundists who had beaten him up and thrown him into the Neosho River.

I began to fly again on 2nd September, way behind the other cadets of No 1 Course, all of whom had soloed on the Vultee. I now had another instructor, Hank Duncan, whom I liked from the start. He was a no-nonsense man who believed that anyone who had come so far - I had 70 hours on the Cornell by then - should have little difficulty in graduating. I had two flights with him and was then sent solo. I liked the aircraft and soon made up lost ground.

Hank Duncan and his three students

One evening, I was formally interviewed by Squadron Leader Kermode on the suitability of being commissioned. He said that the competition for the limited number who would graduate as Pilot Officers, was very keen. I was nervous from the very start and made a complete hash of the interview. Kermode tied me in knots with questions I could not even begin to answer. I very soon knew that I had failed and will never forget his parting words, 'You will never become a pilot, Randle, until you can properly explain what the force of G really is.'

We began to fly cross-country, first dual, then on our own. Our instructors were doubtful as to whether we could find our way around the Middle West. They saw problems that never occurred to us. It was strange because the weather was constantly good, and visibility so remarkable that at 5,000 feet the turning points of the whole triangular course could be seen from quite close to Miami. Our flights took us to Parsons, Coffeyville and Wichita in Kansas and then on to Springfield, Pittsburg and Joplin in Missouri. Only the odd person got lost and the only real problems that later arose came from the autumnal break-up of the weather. Occasionally, there were sudden build-ups of cumulo-nimbus into line squalls. If we encountered them, the drill was 'about turn' and back to base or to land until the storm had passed.

Rollo, Scotty and myself in front of the Miami Country Club
August 1941

Basic stage - Vultee Valiants

Vultee cockpit

*Miami with Michael Glover
and George Westhorpe*

Air to air with Michael Glover

Early formation flying

*Maintenance inside No. 1
Hangar Miami*

We were then taught formation flying and passed on to flying at night, something I found easy to do. The whole countryside was ablaze with light in any case, the horizon always easily seen in the reflected lights of cities and towns and there was little turbulence. We now had a Wing Commander in charge as the BFTS had grown in size with a second course of fifty already at the elementary stage, and a third course on the way.

There was never a dull moment off-duty, I made some good friends both locally and in Tulsa and seldom spent an evening in camp. American hospitality was extraordinary, often more than we could easily accept. A favourite invitation was the progressive dinner where we went from house to house, eating each course at a different place and meeting fresh hosts on the way. A millionaire regularly held steak fries at his ranch where the T-bones were enormous and the waste of meat unbelievable. We attended a number of formal occasions, one of which I shall never forget; a mayoral reception at Coffeyville, Kansas, the small mid-western town where the notorious four Dalton brothers were shot dead in the main street. We were met by the Mayor, Sheriff and his Deputies, on the steps of the City Hall and were immediately led along Main Street to be shown the bullet holes in the sidewalk where the Daltons had met their fate. We returned to City Hall to meet more of Coffeyville's dignitaries, after which we sat down in an auditorium to eat a typical Western meal of huge steaks, beans, and fried potatoes, followed by as much ice-cream as we could manage. Speeches were made and Squadron Leader Kermode replied on our behalf, thanking everyone for such wonderful hospitality.

It had been a very pleasant occasion and we made ready to leave, but the reception was not over. Someone wearing a Stetson hat got up on to the stage, called for attention, and said that the British boys were about to be entertained. On came a stout, middle-aged lady who sang patriotic songs and finished with a full-blown, 'God Bless America'. A barber-shop quartet gave an excellent rendition of Western songs, 'Red River Valley' , 'Home on the Range', 'The Trail of the Lonesome Pine', and the top popular song at that time, 'The Hut-Sut Song'. All was quiet for a while until, surprisingly, a dozen young women ran on to the stage dressed as Indian squaws. They didn't sing or dance, they just whooped, jumped up and down, and made noises. It was hard to see the point of it all as was reflected in our polite applause when they left the stage. The man with the

Stetson jumped up onto the stage, adopting a theatrical downcast expression. 'It sure looks as though you British boys don't like our Western gals,' he shouted. Some of us shouted back, 'Oh yes we do!' That seemed to cheer Stetson a little, 'It didn't sound like that from where I was. Next time, let's hear a bit more appreciation.'

The girls came back and repeated their routine, waved to us, and left the stage. There was some better applause from us this time and they quickly returned on stage. It was immediately noticeable that each had slightly changed appearance; a little something had been discarded here and there; a piece of clothing, some beads, or feathers, or moccasins. They pranced about as before and went off, this time to much greater applause. Back they came, appearing even more undressed. Their antics on the stage became enlivened and uninhibited. Off and on they came; our applause getting louder and louder until they finished running around the stage, stark naked!

Stetson held up his hands. 'Now you will see just how friendly we have made these Indian gals.' He got down from the stage, grabbed Squadron Leader Kermode by the shoulder and almost dragged him on to the stage. 'The gals want to dance with you British boys,' he yelled. We were suddenly quiet; embarrassed both for ourselves and our commanding officer. Kermode said not a word, well aware that he could easily embarrass our hosts. He allowed himself to be grabbed by a buxom naked woman and I watched open-mouthed as, keeping her at arms length, he completed a few turns of a waltz. Our utter silence brought the performance to an end and many of the Westerners had the sense to realize that they had overstepped the mark. We made our apologies and gave our thanks for an interesting evening and withdrew slightly embarrassed to our waiting coaches to be driven back to Miami.

The next day, I flew solo to Coffeyville and indulged in some low-flying around the town. I was soon joined by two others who had the same idea of letting the good people of Coffeyville know that some of their hospitality had been appreciated. Thereafter, Coffeyville became the centre for reckless low-flying, and there was never a complaint made by the inhabitants.

By the end of September, No 3 BFTS was operating at full capacity. There were now two hundred cadets as Numbers 3 and 4 Courses had arrived. I had flown 43 hours on the Vultee BT13 and had begun conversion to the North American AT6, the Harvard. I considered myself lucky still to have Hank Duncan as my instructor. The fine weather had gone with the summer. Five days of heavy rain flooded the airfield making it difficult for the heavier AT6 to taxi through what had now become a quagmire. Many aircraft became bogged down and there were many landings away from base because of squalls, heavy rain and bad visibility. I had my first forced landing on 8th October when flying with Duncan in the rain, under a 1,000 foot cloud-base. The engine suddenly stopped and Duncan took control, with me lowering the undercarriage while he dealt with the flaps. He saw a small patch alongside the railroad and side-slipped off the last 50 feet of height, arriving with a thud on all three points, running on to stop with the propeller caught in a chain link fence.

We were now having more than our share of accidents. Most were due to our lack of experience and downright carelessness. We indulged in far too much low flying and I was caught out by the Chief Instructor who saw me fly between two factory chimneys at Coffeyville. I feared the worst, an early return to England in disgrace at the very least. Instead, I was let off with a twigging and promised never again to break the rules. On 18th October, Paddy O' Sullivan and Ted Hartnell collided while formation flying. Hartnell baled out just in time, his parachute opening fully just a few feet from the ground and O' Sullivan landed his damaged machine safely.

George Westhorpe wiped-off his propeller and a wing tip in a heavy landing and, the next day, landed with his wheels still retracted. On 27th October Freddy Tuft, our student 'B' Flight commander, was killed when he walked into a propeller during night flying.

The wreckage of Hartnell's plane after he'd had the tail sliced off

Taking off from Miami

*Like most young students we went in for a lot of
unauthorised low flying - sometimes following
the instructors!*

George Westhorpe landed with his wheels up

Another view of the same incident

*The result of a student taxiing into
another aircraft*

WSOR landing at Miami

'B' Flight Miami September, 1941
Close to our 'Wings' time

We sat our final examinations and flew our last check rides. On 31st October, I was told that I had qualified for my wings and was promoted to sergeant, as were most of No 1 Course. We didn't linger long in Miami, we said goodbye to our friends and attended a farewell dance laid on for us at the College. I bought things that I knew would be in short supply in England: trousers, a shirt, and cotton underwear for myself, cigars and cigarettes for my uncle at Tulse Hill, and perfume and nylon stockings for my sisters.

We left from Afton at midday on Saturday, 1st November, seen off by our officers and instructors. Hank Duncan presented me with a strip of parachute silk on which he had written, 'Good luck to the best student I have ever had.' Later, I discovered that he had given identical pieces to his other two students, Eric Shackleton and Bill Sheehan. Squadron Leader Kermode seemed withdrawn and strangely moved as we waved goodbye. Perhaps he realized something of what lay ahead for us, and how few of us he would ever see again.

CHAPTER FIVE

Our first stop was at Springfield, Missouri, where we exchanged ribald greetings across the platform with No 5 Course on their way to replace us in Miami. The journey northwards on the Frisco Line was slow; there were no sleepers so we dozed sitting upright in our seats. Arriving in Chicago early on Sunday morning we were given time to stretch our legs and walk around the streets. We reached Montreal on 3rd November and Monckton, in New Brunswick, the next day. The first things we did were to change into uniform, purchase our wings and stripes, and have them sewn on.

We spent nine days in Monckton, thankfully kept on a loose rein with little to do, living in a half-built camp, way out of town. There were many failed would-be pilots from the BFTSs in the States who told us that in some places as many as 50% of each course had been eliminated. Many had been subjected to the 'hazing' we had seen in Tulsa, and many had been waiting for months in Canada hoping for transfer to other aircrew duties. There was much resentment and very little discipline amongst them.

On Sunday, 9th November, we took part in an enormous Church Parade and received a powerful sermon from a fiery Canadian minister who seemed to consider that we were already damned and spent ages warning us of the perils of the flesh. On Armistice Day, we endured a wretched march around Monckton in the rain. At our head was a RCAF drum and bugle band, repeatedly blowing 'Reveille', while, at our rear, and within earshot, was the Monckton Concert Silver Band, playing 'Poor Old Joe' in swinging New Orleans style.

We were happy to leave Monckton on 12th November, but after just half of an hour our train collided with a lorry at a level crossing, the driver of the lorry being killed and our engine damaged. Our carriages were shunted into a siding for about two hours until another engine was found and we continued our journey. Arriving in Halifax late that evening, we were directed immediately aboard the Warwick Castle. Fortunately for us, we had been promulgated as sergeants and pilot officers, whereas other BFTS returnees were travelling as Leading Aircraftmen. It meant that we were allotted four to a cabin, not to the mess decks as were most of the others.

The Warwick Castle was a sister ship of the Windsor Castle, although a later model. She was packed with Air Force personnel of all descriptions and in addition to hundreds of British there were Australians, New Zealanders, Canadians, Norwegians, and Americans who had joined the RCAF. We had two boat drills early the next morning and the four of us in our cabin were allotted places on a life raft with twenty-eight Norwegians. The ship sailed during the evening of 13th November in the company of many other large ships, escorted this time by warships of the United States Navy, led by the old battleship, Colorado. The convoy included the liners, Athens, Duchess of Atholl, Durban Castle, Orcades, Rena del Pacifico, Orama, together with both a Dutch and a Polish liner.

The U.S. Navy handed over its duties to six British destroyers on 18th November, probably in the mid-Atlantic position, and no sooner was this done than we ran into another Atlantic gale. Again, most were sea-sick, including the other three in the cabin. I spent much of the time on deck in the fresh air watching the great convoy wallowing its way towards home. The destroyers were having a bad time, often disappearing beneath the waves, yet always holding their station. The Durban Castle was noticeable because she rolled so alarmingly, while the Polish liner could not make the required speed and had dropped a long way behind. It was a repeat of the storm on the outward journey only, this time, because I was now a sergeant, I had no lavatorial duties to perform.

The gale took a day and a half to blow itself out by which time we were steaming into the Clyde Estuary and passed Ailsa Crag on 21st

November, anchoring at Gourock that evening. We were kept on board for all the next day, the only distraction being a pep-talk by an Air Commodore who finished by telling us we were all to receive fourteen days leave after we had been processed at a Receiving Wing. It was a long and uncomfortable journey to Bournemouth where I was billeted for six days at the Christchurch Hotel on the seafront. We were kept occupied with daily parades, a little drill, and various medical tests which included one for night vision. I was issued with another kitbag, a steel helmet, gas mask, another pair of 'long-johns', and ration cards. Finally, I was given a return travel warrant to Exmouth.

It was great to be back at home. My father managed to get a few days leave from Sutton Veny, and my elder sister came in from Exeter where she was now a State Registered Nurse. My brother and younger sister were still at school. I spent three days of my leave in London where I stayed with my relatives, visiting the Bank and touring around London, noticing how well every bit of damage had been cleared away, and how the siege-like atmosphere I remembered from earlier in the year, had disappeared. Returning to Exmouth I was back in Bournemouth on 6th December.

I was surprised and delighted when told I had to report to No 5 Flying Training School at Ternhill in Shropshire for a refresher course on Miles Masters and Hawker Hurricanes. I had long ago given up hope of ever becoming a fighter pilot but it now appeared that I was to be given another chance to prove myself, however, things did not start well at Ternhill. I expected that now we were sergeants and on the verge of going into action, I would notice a marked change in our circumstances, it was not to be. We were housed in an old dormitory block, thirty beds to a room with a locker each for our possessions and kit. The furniture was aged, and the beds were relics but worst of all, we were not accepted in the Sergeants' Mess. From the moment we arrived, we were resented by the old-stagers of the Regular Air Force, who made it clear they considered that we didn't deserve our stripes; in their view we had not served long enough. Their opposition meant that we ate our meals in a makeshift Aircrew Mess, some distance from our true Mess. It seemed to be grossly unfair and we made our objections known to the Station Commander, but all to no avail.

December 1941, RAF Ternhill, Advanced Training Unit.
Second row from the front, fourth from the right

The station was an old training establishment in the process of changing from a Flying Training to an Advanced Training Unit. We quickly became aware of the vast differences there were between flying in England and in the United States. My instructor was a Sergeant Woodcock, an accomplished pilot, with a manner so matter of fact and different to that of the Americans. The flying regulations, wretched weather conditions of low cloud, limited visibility and almost continual rain, made us realize how much we had not learned in the blue skies and unlimited horizons of Oklahoma. We had many rough edges to be polished, and much to learn. I had flown 145 hours and 33 minutes in the States. Now I would add another 22 hours on Masters and Hurricanes before moving on to a Fighter OTU. This had to be done on an airfield cluttered with the work of building new runways and the repair of a hangar that had been badly damaged in a German air raid. An additional hindrance to training was the presence of a MU (Maintenance Unit) repairing Defiants, Hampdens, Halifaxes and Spitfires, all of which had to be air-tested.

On 19th December I began conversion to the delightful Miles Master 1 with its Kestrel engine, flying the radial-engined Mark 3 before I went solo on the Mark 1 on 1st January, 1942. The Master was a decided step-up from the Harvard and, oddly enough, I found I could fly it well and with confidence. My aerobatics were greatly improved, I could even do an accurate slow roll. The problem however was the weather, I had to work hard at map-reading and mental navigation to cope with the hazards of the Shropshire and nearby Welsh hills, often hidden by fog, drizzle, and low clouds.

All my hopes of a bright future as fighter pilot were dashed on 10th January. I had flown just 10 hours on Masters and was hoping soon to fly the Hurricane when, right out of the blue, I was sent to No 1517 Beam Training Flight at Ipswich airport. My earlier assessments must have caught up with me for now there was no doubt that I was headed for some place other than Fighter Command.

There were only a small number of us on the Beam course. In just a week, I flew 12 hours dual in the Airspeed Oxford, 11 hours and 20 minutes of which was 'under the hood'. There was no instruction given on how to fly the aircraft so, of course, we didn't fly solo. All our time was spent learning how to use the Beam Approach system for homing overhead the airfield and letting-down to land. All our flying was from a civilian, grass-covered airfield and we were billeted in Ipswich. I shared lodgings with a shortish, ginger-haired sergeant named Carrick Lock with whom I struck up an instant friendship. He was much better educated than I, a public school - I believe he went to Stowe – and had all the trappings of a middle-class upbringing. He spoke with authority in a well-modulated voice, and was better composed and assured. He read a lot, and wrote well; he even composed poetry. I couldn't understand why he had not been commissioned.

I flew every exercise in the company of Lock, taking it in turns at the controls. I found it relatively easy to understand and read the beam signals, and to anticipate the approach markers. Lock did not do so well, his basic instrument flying was lacking and I could often see that his concentration on the instruments was interfering with his interpretation of the beam signals. Nonetheless, we both returned to Ternhill with average assessments written into our logbooks for both the completion of a General Instrument Flying Course, and our ability in the Link Trainer.

I didn't fly the Master again, but spent the whole of February waiting for a posting. We were told that all those who had gone to Ipswich were destined to fly in Bomber Command. I must admit that I was not too happy with this news, we knew things were about to change in that Command, a new Commander-in-Chief, Air Marshal Sir Arthur Harris, had just been appointed to lead an all-out offensive and I was worried because of my single-engined upbringing. I had never handled an aircraft with more than one engine and nothing bigger than a Miles Master; I already felt inadequate.

While we waited, my friendship with Carrick Lock grew. We found we had a lot in common: we both loved the countryside and knew much about flora and fauna. We liked the same sort of music and, when we found it, the value of decently-prepared food. Walking around the neighbourhood, we discussed most every subject under the sun. Lock, however, was a fatalist: one dreary evening, after a long walk, we sat drinking beer in a pub on the outskirts of Market Drayton when he stunned me by saying, 'Have you ever wondered how you're going to die, Bill?'

It took me a while to answer, 'No, I haven't, the thought has never crossed my mind.' Nor had it. 'All I can think of is that we are supposedly fighting to save the world for democracy, and that, one day, we will win and I will still be there, Heaven knows how.'

'Then, if that's how you see it, you ought to wake up and face the facts. This is going to be a long war and from what I can see, the only people who will be getting at the Germans will be Bomber Command. Do you think you can last the course? I most certainly don't, I've already written my will, I know my number will come up in due course. You should do the same.'

I could only joke in reply. 'Not a chance, old boy. Not for me. In any case, I'm broke.'

Lock and I were posted to No 12 Operational Training Unit at Chipping Warden, not far from Banbury in Oxfordshire. We arrived there late in the evening of 12th March in a downpour of heavy rain. As we struggled from the guardroom to our accommodation, weighed down with soggy kit-bags, we heard the approach of a heavy aircraft. We instinctively ducked as it passed over to crash into the ground a few hundred yards ahead, bursting into flames and exploding. The next morning, after a wretched night of trying to sleep, we were told that the crash had been that of a Hampden bomber and, at the controls, had been Ken Farnes, the Kent and England fast bowler.

Pilots and Navigators of No. 29 Course, No 12 Operational Training Unit at Chipping Warden, not far from Banbury in Oxfordshire. I am second row from front, second from the right. On my left is Jock Brazill who, although neither of us knew it at the time, was to become my navigator and on my right Carrick Lock.

I was included in No 29 Course to be trained to fly the Wellington medium bomber. After about three months, during which I was expected to fly about 140 hours, I would pick up a crew of a navigator, wireless-operator, bomb-aimer, and rear gunner and be posted to a front-line Wellington squadron in Bomber Command. I most certainly had doubts about achieving this goal with just 170 hours in my log-book, and all of that on single-engined aircraft. My first flight in a Wellington Mark 1A did not go well. I have to admit that I was daunted by the size and complexity of the machine. A short spell of ground instruction had been followed by explanations of the controls and the many instruments in the cockpit. My instructor was a Flight Lieutenant with a DFC who made no bones about his dislike of being 'screened' from operations. 'I don't know much about this instructing lark,' he told me as we sat together in the cockpit, 'Only a few more weeks and then, thank God, back on ops!'

I settled into the left-hand seat feeling completely at a loss. We spent a while going over the controls and instruments, and discussing the vital actions to be taken before take-off. 'All I want you to do, is to follow me through on the controls,' explained my instructor. 'We'll fly around for a while, and you can handle her. Anyway, just relax and watch me.'

As we taxied slowly out from our dispersal, I was allowed to try the brakes and have a stab at using the engines for turning and changing direction. We got permission to line-up on the runway and the instructor opened the engines and checked the switches against the brakes. 'All right, now just put your hands on the throttles and follow me through on the controls,' he said.

He gradually applied power and we began to move. 'See how I'm correcting direction with the throttles ... see the speed building up ... I'm not using any rudder ... tail's coming up, now full power ... Oh! ... Jesus Christ!' he shouted, something was wrong. He reached up in a flash and cut the magneto switches, jammed on the brakes, and pulled back hard on the stick. The starboard engine cut first, and then, a few seconds later, so did the port, but by then, we were already off the runway on to the grass. A wheel collapsed, and the wing went down, the other undercarriage leg then gave way and we were slithering along on the aircraft's belly. The instructor had already thrown open the escape hatches above our heads. 'Out! Out!' he yelled as we came to a stop. 'She'll burn for sure!' I was out of my safety harness, through the escape hatch, and down the side of the aircraft in a trice. Together, we ran to a safe distance and turned to watch. Luckily, the wrecked machine did not burn. 'The bloody throttles just came away from the quadrant,' he said, 'That's what comes from using these bloody old aircraft.'

For some reason I did not fly for the next three days, then I began conversion on a Mark 1C with another instructor and always together with Carrick Lock. We each had a spell at the controls and could watch the other perform. There was always a makeshift crew of gunners and wireless-operators on board, together with someone in the rear turret. I flew solo on 4th April after 5 hours and 15 minutes of instruction with Lock sitting in the instructor's seat. I didn't feel at all in command of the aircraft and, looking back after years of instructing on the Wellington, I have to admit that much of my dismay was due to the poor standard of instruction I had received: I had no idea how to fly on one engine; or what the adverse effects of attitude, thrust and drag could be; and I was not told that the machine would not fly on one engine because of the drag caused by the windmilling heavy metal propeller of the dead engine.

I was quicker to fly solo than Lock who became downhearted at his slow progress. He admitted to me that he found the Wellington almost too much of a handful to manage. He did however fly solo on 5th May, and I flew with him. Even with my inexperience, I could recognize his lack of skill and confidence.

We had by now attracted the makings of a crew. The only one that I remember was Sergeant Bob Frost, a 17 year-old rear gunner. We flew every day, working towards the point when each pilot would be given a crew of his own to fly with during the second part of the course, the day and night cross-country flights.

I was excused from flying with Lock on 20th May because I had been selected, together with Frost, to play soccer against a team in Banbury. Lock, with the remainder of the crew and a student navigator was authorised to fly a map-reading exercise around Oxfordshire. After completing part of the exercise, he flew to Henley-on-Thames where his parents lived. From what I learned later, he had flown low over their house, attracting his mother into the garden. He circled and came in to make another low pass, completely misjuding the approach and hitting an elm tree at the bottom of the garden. His mother watched in horror as the Wellington reared up with flames coming from the wing, exploding at about 500 feet or so. When I acted as pall-bearer at his funeral in Henley, I could not help remembering the morbid predictions he had made at Ternhill, but it had not been as he had thought, losing his life on operations. He had thrown his life away and, in the process, accounted for those of four others.

I was teamed up with another sergeant-pilot to finish the first part of the course. I have his name in my log-book but will not disclose it because, after just five flights together, he decided that service in Bomber Command was not for him. He reported himself sick and unable to continue with flying. It had nothing to do with my inexpert ability, but rather that he had taken note of the many crashes and fatalities at Chipping Warden, together with the steadily increasing operational losses in the Command. He was off the station within hours on his way to Uxbridge with the stigma of LMF - Lack of Moral Fibre. I believe that he survived the war as a private soldier in the Pioneer Corps.

We did not know at the time that preparations were being made for OTU crews to take part in Operation 'Millennium', the first 1,000 bomber raid. I flew as second pilot in an Anson on four occasions between 27th and 30th May to various stations where we collected freight and items needed to make the OTU Wellingtons operational. Many student crews from 12 OTU, with 'screened' aircrew on board, took part in the attack on Cologne during the night of 30th-31st May.

After the completion of my night flying instruction which ended the first part of the course, I found my crew. There was no allocation or selection, we were allowed to make our own choices. We assembled in the briefing room one evening after a day of 'behind the scenes' bargaining. Already, pilots' abilities, such as they were, had been evaluated, and navigators, wireless operators, bomb-aimers and gunners sought out those to their liking. I already had a rear-gunner in the form of Bob Frost. A couple of Canadians, Sergeants Norman Graham and Walter Dreschler wanted to fly together and asked if they could be my wireless-operator and bomb-aimer respectively. However, there was difficulty in finding a navigator. At the very end of the evening, I had the good fortune to be introduced to Sergeant 'Jock' Brazill, a Scotsman born in India. He was older than the rest of us and I asked him to join us as I thought he would bring a balance to the crew, of which I was the second youngest.

We made a start as a crew on 6th June, flying cross-countries, both day and night, with a 'screened' pilot and navigator. Three days later we were off on our own, on a trip across to the east coast, then back to the Isle of Man, with the return leg direct to Chipping Warden. There was much cloud over most of the route. I flew under it to Norwich which we reached dead on time. As the second leg would take us over the Welsh hills and Mount Snowdon, I climbed to 5,000 feet and settled down in the cloud to show my new colleagues how good I was at instrument flying. We were now on dead reckoning with the navigator passing estimated positions to me that had been checked with cross-bearings from the wireless operator.

It began to get turbulent in the clouds. The navigator reckoned that we were over the Welsh mountains and would soon be able to let down for a visual approach to Jurby on the Isle of Man, our turning point. I then noticed the engine speed beginning to fall on the starboard engine's old-fashioned pillar rpm counter. The rpm fell to zero, the engine had apparently failed. In the turbulence, within the clouds, and with my only reference being the blind-flying panel, I had little feeling at all of the loss of an engine. I hurriedly carried out the vital actions for such an emergency, and warned the crew, while struggling to keep the aircraft on a steady course and even keel. I was losing height despite applying full power on the other engine and aware that Mount Snowdon was probably somewhere ahead as we descended. Then, mercifully, we broke cloud at about 3,000 feet to the south of the mountain and, away to the port side, I could see an airfield. Only by guess and by God, did I manage to land at Llanbedr with only slight damage to the aircraft, caused when I ran off the end off the runway.

Our next cross country was flown without fault or incident. We flew our first night cross country on 10th June, and got horribly lost. The planned route should have taken us across England to the east coast, north to Newcastle, then to the Isle of Man, on to Bristol, and back to Chipping Warden. I don't know where the navigator's plot went wrong. He passed reassuring estimated positions as we flew above cloud for most of the flight and it was just beginning to get light when I was given a position from which I could begin to let down for the approach to the Isle of Man. We broke cloud and I was pleased to see the sea below and I was told that I would soon see Jurby's red pundit ahead, but it did not appear. I began to worry as we flew on, now fairly low over the water until, to my relief, I saw a misty coastline ahead but, strangely, with lights shining along it. We were soon across it not knowing where on earth we were and so I began a square search, soon seeing the lights of a large town, straight ahead. Before I reached it, I flew low over an airfield with the words Dun Loghaire etched bold in its grass surface. Needless to say we left Ireland in a hurry, estimates of remaining fuel told us it would be a close thing to get back to base before running out of petrol. We again became unsure of our position and, after nearly six hours of wandering around in the sky, I landed at Church Lawford, a small airfield only a few miles from Chipping Warden.

A week later, it was my turn to show incompetence: we were on a day cross country, again taking the Isle of Man as a turning point, the skies were clear and there was good visibility, I could already see the Isle of Man ahead when, suddenly, the starboard engine began to backfire alarmingly, and to lose power. I alerted the crew and the backfiring continued as I nervously went through the vital actions for engine failure. I reached down with my left hand to pull up Balance Cock A to transfer fuel from the bad to the good engine. I should have looked at what I had done because, in my panic, I had mistakenly pulled up the wrong Balance Cock thereby cutting off the fuel to the good engine.

I had both throttles fully open. The backfiring engine was making a dreadful noise and, unbeknown to me, the port engine was beginning to fail through fuel starvation. We began to lose height and staggered round the town of Douglas which lay directly in our path and then, to my intense relief, I saw Jurby straight ahead with many small training aircraft in its circuit. I was now flying very low and almost at the point of the stall and had no other option but to try to land from a straight-in approach. We got the wheels down just in time and, amidst a scattering of Tiger Moths, I landed downwind and flapless, spinning around to a stop just short of the edge of the airfield.

I thought that I had done well in making such a fortunate forced landing but my confidence was short lived when a sergeant mechanic asked me why I had shut down a perfectly good engine by pulling up Balance Cock B. I immediately realised the gravity of my stupid mistake, that I had jeopardised the lives of my crew and had only survived because the ailing engine had managed to produce enough power to get us to the airfield. I was in an absolute panic but Jock Brazill, who was with me at the time, took over like a brother. I do not know what he told the sergeant or what was arranged but, when we were collected and flown back from Jurby, I left behind a Wellington that needed an engine change for some reason that I never knew.

We flew three more cross countries, two at night. I could sense that the crew, like me, had developed a nervousness that made us check and double-check all we did. This stood us in good stead during the night of 21st June when we were over East Anglia, at about two o' clock in the morning, on the last leg back to Chipping Warden. I was flying at about 1,000 feet above a blanket of thick fog. All of a sudden, there was a loud bang, the starboard engine raced away and burst into flames. What I did not know was that the propeller had dropped off.

We all knew our emergency drills. I operated the Graviner (fire extinguisher) system to put out the fire and gave the order to put on parachutes. Graham, who was working base (in contact with) at the time, tapped out an S.O.S. and that we were on fire. He then clamped down the key. Dreschler unbuckled my Sutton harness and clipped on my chest-type parachute. The engine was still burning so I gave the order to bale out. Brazill shouted on the intercom that we were too low to parachute safely; only too true because we were now down to 800 feet and descending into the fog bank. I therefore gave the order for the crew to take up crash positions. This meant, with the exception of the rear-gunner who stayed in his turret, that the others had to lie on the fuselage floor behind the protection of the main spar.

I really didn't know what to do or if, for that matter, there was anything that could be done to avert disaster. In my ignorance, I could only think of holding the machine at the lowest possible speed until it hit the ground. I did not know that by doing so I had set up the dreaded drag curve that made it impossible to fly level on one engine. As we went lower into the fog, I checked that the crew were in position behind the main spar and that Frost had his turret turned with its doors opened. I was now not strapped in but realized it was too late to call someone forward to help me to do so. I switched on the landing lights but quickly switched them off because of the glare they made in the fog. Someone had his microphone switched on and was praying to the Lord to save our souls. I told him to switch off, at once.

I spent the last few moments of the descent with my eyes fixed on the airspeed indicator which showed a steady 70 mph. I remembered Carrick Lock's mournful predictions and wondered just how I would meet my death. Would I hopefully be knocked unconscious first? Would I be smashed to pieces? Or would I be trapped and then burned alive?

I felt an enormous wrench at the controls, in the fog I had flown, tail down, through a row of trees. This dramatically reduced our speed and we slapped down on a village green, careered across it, and smashed into a farmhouse. By then, I had my head down, clutching the parachute on my chest, then I knew no more.

My awakening was frightful; I thought that I was dead and in hell. There was a dreadful smell and I was covered with viscera which I thought were parts of my body. I felt no pain and only gradually regained consciousness. I then heard the sound of an axe on metal. In an absolute fury, Norman Graham was hacking through the geodetics to get at me trapped in the nose of the Wellington, half-buried in the remains of a cow. His strong hands grabbed me and pulled me away from the stinking mess and out from the wreckage just before there was an explosion and it became enveloped in flames.

We had landed in the middle of the little village of Dittington, just off the Great North Road. Many of the inhabitants were on the scene quickly and were trying to help. Fortunately, no one had been killed, although an old lady asleep in the farmhouse had fallen through the bedroom floor into the kitchen below, still asleep in her bed. We had, however, accounted for one cow and a lot of chickens, together with the demolition of a barn and half of a farmhouse. The crew were miraculously unhurt. We had our fair share of cuts and bruises, and I had strained both my ankles which had been caught in the rudder bar when I was catapulted into the nose of the aircraft.

We sat watching for quite some time. I was badly shocked and although I did not smoke, I puffed away at cigarette after cigarette offered to me by bystanders. After the best part of an hour, an ambulance arrived and took us away to RAF Wyton.

Two days later we were released from sick quarters and flown back to Chipping Warden by our Course Flight Commander. We were told that there had been some confusion caused by our crash. At the very time that Graham had sent the S.O.S. and the news that we were on fire, another Wellington had crashed in flames on the airfield, killing all on board. For a while, it was believed that we were the dead ones, and steps had been taken to record us as fatalities. Fortunately, the true position was disclosed just before telegrams were due to be sent to our relatives.

On 25th June, we flew again, on an air test with a Warrant Officer instructor. I was still feeling pain from my strained ankles and the crew, to a man, were bundles of nerves. Later that day, I was astounded to be told that we were to fly that night on the third 1,000 bomber raid. I simply could not believe it. Just four days previously, we had survived a horrendous crash. More important, we were by no means fully trained.

We went to see our Course Flight Commander and I told him that we considered we were in no condition to fly on operations. He said that we were, he had already checked with the Medical Officer who considered we were all fit and well. He would not accept any argument and bluntly told us we were in grave danger by refusing to obey an order.

I went on my own to see the Chief Instructor, a Wing Commander, and he came straight to the point by saying he thought we were cowards. He inferred that the limp caused by my strained ankles had only appeared after the air test that day and was not prepared to accept any argument. The OTU had to make a maximum effort and if we refused to fly we would be deemed lacking in moral fibre. I tried to explain that I was having difficulty in flying the Wellington, as well he must have known, and that we were most inexpert in finding our way, but he just cut the interview short. The upshot was that, together with my crew, I was confined to camp and technically put under arrest. We felt shattered, misunderstood and abused. I had no idea what next to do, only that I had no intention of changing my mind. I couldn't sleep that night, spending most of it on the airfield alone with my thoughts while waiting for the aircraft to return. What I didn't know was that Graham and Dreschler, the two Canadians in my crew, had disappeared from camp.

That night, most of the student crews of No 12 OTU took part in the 1,000 bomber raid on Bremen. It was claimed to be a success, much better than the second such attack on Essen but not as effective as the first on Cologne. Bomber Command lost forty-eight aircraft; the heaviest casualties being suffered by the OTUs in our Group. A later evaluation indicated that the reasons for these losses, as high as 12%, were that the OTUs were equipped with old aircraft withdrawn from front-line squadrons, and that the trainee crews had to fly a round trip 200 miles longer than the two earlier raids.

I was ignored the next day as the important tasks of recovering from the raid were dealt with. The following morning I was again paraded before the Chief Instructor and he was in a furious mood. 'I'm fed up to the back teeth with you and your blasted crew, sergeant. Not only do you refuse to fly but you blatantly disobey orders.' I had not the foggiest idea what he was raving about, and I told him so, I considered I had nothing more to lose and therefore should stand up for myself. 'Don't tell me that you do not know what your Canadian friends have been doing?' he fumed. I honestly didn't know and shook my head. 'I don't believe you, sergeant, you're a conniving bunch.' He was now red in the face. 'Those two have had the nerve to go over my head. They broke out of camp and went to Canada House with your cock and bull story. They've dropped me right in it with Group.' I was dreading what he would say next but, having vented his spleen somewhat, he looked resigned and calmed down. 'I have been told to get you and your crew trained and on to a squadron as quickly as possible. I shall give you a check ride this afternoon. You will fly tonight, and every night until, thankfully, I can see the back of you lot.'

I could not find the right words for my diary which would express the intense relief at escaping the indignity of being labelled as a coward. I couldn't thank Norman and Walter enough for their inspired initiative that had saved the day. We felt renewed as we completed four more cross countries, three at night, determined that nothing would now stand in our way of leaving Chipping Warden. My log book was stamped with an average assessment as a Heavy Bomber pilot and I could only guess at what had been written into my Service records. On 6th July, we were posted to No 150 Squadron at Snaith in Yorkshire equipped with the Wellington Mk 3.

_____

CHAPTER SIX

We travelled up to Yorkshire by train on 8th July, carrying all our possessions in the usual two kitbags, pleased to get away from Chipping Warden, having suffered more than our fair share of misfortune in a place that had become something of a battlefield. Many crews had fallen by the wayside; only four of the original ten crews on No 23 Course had made it to a squadron.

Arriving in the rain at Heck, the small station that served Snaith, we found there was no transport, so we hefted our loads and set out to walk the mile and a half. It is strange how certain things stick in the memory, but I remember after we had asked a man the way, the wretched youngster with him had cheekily added, 'Don't worry, you'll soon be dead.' On arrival we reported ourselves to the Station Warrant Officer and were taken to our billets to unpack. I was told to report to a Squadron Leader, a Flight Commander, who greeted me warmly and surprised me greatly by saying that I would be flying on operations that night as a second pilot with an experienced crew. Within the hour, I had joined the crew on an air test and the pilot, Flight Sergeant Caldow, began showing me the differences between the Mark 3 and the Mark 1C.

Caldow was an accomplished veteran and had already been decorated with the Distinguished Flying Medal. His flying was sure and polished, and I noticed, at once, how his crew responded in a most disciplined way. There was no banter between them, they didn't waste words. Each got on with the job of testing his equipment: the navigator checked the GEE set; the wireless operator, his radio; the bomb aimer, his bombing panel and bombsight and, together with the rear-gunner, the turrets and guns. There and then I decided my crew would fly in the same disciplined way.

I sat with the crew at briefing very much like a new boy at school. The target was the docks at Wilhelmshaven, as Caldow put it, '... a pretty straightforward raid.' Most of the force would be made up of Wellingtons, although there would be some Lancasters, Halifaxes, Stirlings and Hampdens. My first time in action was an amazing revelation to me. Being a second pilot was a misnomer because there were no dual controls. I sat on a collapsible jump-seat, alongside Caldow, which had to be folded down whenever anyone wanted to pass up to the front of the aircraft. I soon found it best to stand in the walkway as I had nothing to do but to watch and learn.

The visibility was good and the skies were clear. We climbed to 16,000 feet and clearly saw the activity of the searchlights and anti-aircraft guns over the target from some considerable distance. Caldow made a straight-in approach, the bomb aimer giving only minor corrections. As the load of nine containers of incendiary bombs dropped away, we became held in a dazzling blue searchlight. Caldow held the aircraft straight and level with bomb doors open, while the bomb aimer watched below, timing the automatic taking of a photograph of the bombs bursting. The blue searchlight was joined by others that now held us in a cone of blinding light. The photograph taken, it was 'Bomb doors shut,' and Caldow did a wing-over just as the heavy flak began to be heard. He dived down some thousands of feet and got out of the searchlight cone, leaving the flak way above us. Our only bother now was the light variety that came up in visible streams but fell away a thousand or so feet below us.

I was fascinated with everything and as I had nothing to do, I felt detached from Caldow and his crew. It took me a while to realize that German soldiers down below were trying to kill us, and that we were undoubtedly killing some of them, also civilians, women and children, who would be huddled in shelters, just as we had done in London during the Blitz.

We flew back to Snaith without incident, only five aircraft were reported lost that night and Caldow had got a good photograph. I spent the next three days getting used to the Mark 3 and found it to be a so-much better machine than the Mark 1C. It had more powerful Hercules engines and wooden fully-feathering propellers. I impressed on my crew that we were going to fly as did the experts. No unnecessary chatter, microphones on only when there was something to say about the operation of the aircraft, and each message prefaced by the originator's function e.g 'Navigator to Skipper.'

I flew again with Caldow on 15th July, this time to Duisburg, the first of a series of raids on this industrial city on the edge of the Ruhr. We again carried a load of incendiaries. There was thick cloud for most of the way and we flew through electrical storms which often enveloped the aircraft in St Elmo's Fire. There was great difficulty in finding the target and the bomb aimer could not identify any particular aiming point. In the end he dropped his bombs on the biggest concentration of fire be could see through the clouds.

During the following week, I flew both solo and dual on particular exercises, pleased to find how relatively easy it was to fly an unloaded machine on one engine. We made a simulated bombing sortie to Spaldington and dropped 65lb practice bombs on the range there.

I flew my third operational sortie as second pilot, on 22nd July, with Warrant Officer Percy Gainsforth, a New Zealander. It was the second attack on Duisburg and most of the aircraft taking part were Wellingtons. This time there were aircraft of No 3 Group leading the way to drop marker flares over the target area. It was a very dark night and, as we crossed the enemy coast into the night fighter belt, the rear-gunner was warned to be extra vigilant. Gainsforth set up and maintained a weaving pattern of flight all the way to the target. He held a mean course, but cork-screwed down to port through thirty degrees, then climbed up to starboard through sixty degrees, then down again, and so on. The navigator easily kept a check on our true position using the GEE set. When we got to Duisburg the town was obscured with cloud. We could not see the ground and bombed on the best concentration of marker flares we could see. There were many smaller groups of flares scattered around, and many of the fires we saw could well have been dummy.

On 23rd July the great day arrived: I was briefed to fly my first operational sortie with my own crew. With three operations to my credit, I knew that they regarded me as something of a veteran. I felt proud having them around me at briefing; the target was again Duisburg. The weather was not expected to be good and we were told to drop our load of incendiaries on a concentration of marker flares that would be put down over the city centre.

I remember the take-off well; no sooner had I retracted the undercarriage and set the engines at 2,400 rpm to climb, than we were in cloud. I comfortably settled down to fly on instruments and remained on them for a very long time until we broke cloud at 18,000 feet. The enemy coastline was marked with searchlights shining up through the clouds and bursting flak. I could sense the excitement in the crew although each and everyone was performing just as we had agreed. I told them what I could see ahead and that I would soon be letting down to fly in the safety of the clouds. Jock Brazill was doing well with the GEE box and he gave accurate positions right across Belgium and into the Ruhr. When we got to the GEE limit, he switched back to dead reckoning and I began to let down, hoping to see the ground and the target. At about 12,000 feet, and still in cloud, it was estimated that we were very near to Duisburg. We could see below us the glare from searchlights, fires, and, as we had to suppose, marker flares. I went even lower as we approached but could not break cloud. We had little option but to make our bombing run on the concentration of light below and ahead of us. We dropped our nine containers of incendiaries and held steady for a forlorn attempt at a photograph. I then turned about and made the return flight almost entirely within cloud.

To my great surprise, the next day, I was allotted my own aeroplane, 'Z' for 'Zebra', a rather special Mark 3 that had been modified to carry a single 4,000lb bomb, a 'blockbuster'. Why someone as inexperienced as I had been chosen for this honour, I could never fathom. It was the first, so modified, to arrive at Snaith. The huge canister-like bomb was held by a single shackle in the space from where the bomb racks had been taken away. A fifth of it hung clear of the aircraft. If anything were to go wrong on take-off, causing the aeroplane to crash, then the effect on Snaith would have been catastrophic.

The target that night was again Duisburg. We were warned that there would be cloud in the Ruhr valley. The point was most emphatically made by the Squadron Commander at briefing was that as I was to be honoured with the dropping of the squadron's first 4,000 pounder, I would also be the last to take-off, for safety's sake.

I knew that I was exploring the unknown as I lined up and told the crew to 'prepare for take-off.' I allowed for the feel of a heavier aircraft, and all went well. The bomb, part-exposed to the slipstream, induced drag and slowed us a little. We climbed up into cloud and away and out over the North Sea. Then, after about an hour, disaster struck. A startled cry from the rear-gunner said that he could not rotate his turret; it was jammed. I sent Dreschler back to see if he could help. He was quick to report that there was oil everywhere and, as far as he could see, it had come from the piping to the rear turret. I didn't know whether to press on without effective defence or to turn back. The crew was unanimous on the latter. I abandoned the sortie and, because I could not take a chance at landing at Snaith with a 'blockbuster' on board, I jettisoned it somewhere off the Dutch coast. We were a very crestfallen and upset crew when we got back. My flight commander, Squadron Leader Kirwan, said I had done the right thing by not risking the aircraft and crew by pressing on.

'Z' for 'Zebra' was worked on at once. The oily mess was cleared away and the hydraulic piping replaced, but no reason could be found for the fracture. I air-tested her during the afternoon because we had been put on standby for ops that night.

We were briefed for a heavy raid on Hamburg. There would be some cloud along the route but it would be clear over the target. I was last away without any trouble and climbed out over the Humber where the Royal Navy fired at us, as was the custom, until we fired back the 'colours of the day'. I made a steady climb towards our operational altitude but, before I reached it, the unbelievable happened again. Both turrets became unserviceable this time and the pipes had broken again. Another 4,000 pounder had to be thrown away into the North Sea.

This time, I felt deeply ashamed. It was as though my bad luck had returned to haunt me. I had every reason to believe that there was something drastically wrong with 'Z' for 'Zebra'. A most thorough examination was made and the Engineer Officer thought that the removal of the bomb beams, together with the weight of a single heavy bomb held at a central point, might have put the fuselage under unusual stress. He had the piping strengthened and replaced in such a way that it was more flexible. I kept my fingers crossed hoping that the repair would be successful. While we waited, we flew a dinghy search over the North Sea looking for survivors of the Hamburg raid.

I air-tested 'Z' for 'Zebra' on 29th July having been warned for operations that night. The attacks on Duisburg had finished, this time we were going to Saarbrucken. The defences were not expected to be strong and we were given a low bombing altitude for better accuracy. I was instructed not to descend below 8,000 feet to drop the 'blockbuster'.

The weather was good. We climbed to 15,000 feet without incident, all the time wondering whether the guns and turrets would continue to function. All went well. Brazill gave us accurate GEE fixes right across Belgium and I kept up the weaving, cork-screwing cruise that Gainsforth had shown me. We approached the target area which had been well-marked by the 3 Group flare-droppers. I let down to 9,000 feet and the bomb was dropped after a short, undisturbed run-up. We actually thought we saw our bomb explode in the midst of the chaos below and it was then, that night, I first felt some remorse over the brutality of my duty.

Two nights later we took part in a large raid on Dusseldorf. It was revealed at the briefing that the numbers of aircraft taking part had been made up from the Bomber Command OTUs. There was no cloud over the target. The flak was heavy and time and time again aircraft were held in cones of searchlights and shot down. I saw one go down in flames and another explode. I made a straight-in approach and we dropped our bomb from 18,000 feet. That night, we suffered our first operational damage, a tearing hole in the fuselage fabric and another in the starboard wing. Twenty-nine aircraft were lost, again many from the OTUs.

Next came the strangest of sorties to Essen on 5th August. Very few aircraft were involved and the weather was atrocious. Whether we were sent just to make a nuisance of ourselves we were not told, but it was a night when accurate navigation and bombing were almost impossible. We reached the area around Essen on GEE fixes, but could see nothing in the murk below us. We believed that we had dropped our bomb on Essen but could not be sure. Only seventeen aircraft flew on this unfortunate raid; five did not return.

The next night we flew to Duisburg, but in a different machine. There was no call for big bombs this time, the squadron carried nothing but incendiaries. Yet again the weather was bad over the target. We could not see below us because of the thick cloud nor could we see anything of the parachute marking flares. We hunted around for a while but had no option but to drop our load on the biggest concentration of fire that could be seen reflected through the cloud cover.

On the 9th August the target was Osnabruck, again in a standard Mark 3 carrying incendiaries. Bad luck stalked us this time, we could get nothing at all from the GEE set, the signals seemed to be jammed. Brazill resorted to dead reckoning but, despite the good visibility, we found it difficult to find an aiming point. Then the marker flares, when we at last saw them, were all over the place. Furthermore, we must have received a hit when over the target because on the way back the port engine packed-up. I was at a good altitude and found it relatively easy to manage with the propeller feathered. All went well as we slowly lost height and I then held it at about 5,000 feet. We had warned Snaith of our trouble by wireless and I made a surprisingly easy approach and landing with the airfield alerted to receive us.

We were back in 'Z' for 'Zebra' for the two attacks on Mainz made during the nights of 11th and 12th August. There was something special about having my own aircraft, I felt more confident when flying her. There was just the single worry about the take-off and the possibility of an undercarriage collapse but then, if that were to happen, we reasoned that we would be in the next world before we felt anything.

Both raids went well and the ancient city took a dreadful battering on the first night. We could clearly see the target below and bombed from 15,000 feet and got a good photograph. On the second raid, there was a fair amount of cloud over Mainz, but it was well marked with flares when we arrived and we could see large areas ablaze. On the way back we received instructions to divert to Harwell, a Whitley OTU. There we spent a truly miserable time trying to get some sleep on the crowded floor of the Sergeants' Mess.

For some reason, the Squadron did not fly operationally for the next twelve days. We had lost several crews and had, perhaps, been taken off the front line to rest and recover our strength. I was given the task of flying with newly-arrived pilots, something not very much to my liking because of the absence of dual controls. After an initial demonstration, it was a case of sitting beside the new boy just hoping that he did not make a mistake.

Although it was now almost two years since the end of the Battle of Britain and the cancellation of the German invasion plan, there was another duty given, a strange one: we still practised Bomber Command's part in the plan to repel the would-be invaders and I flew two low-level cross-country sorties, in a formation of three Wellingtons, along the East Anglian coast where we simulated the spraying of poison gas over the beaches supposedly invaded by the Germans.

Other highlights during this lull were two funerals of aircrew who had died in sick quarters after being wounded, our crew acting as pall-bearers. Then we were ordered, together with two other crews, to witness what I suppose was the result of a drum-head court martial. We paraded in a hollow square at nearby Burn to watch three sergeants being stripped of their rank and flying brevets. They had been found guilty of raping a WAAF during a flight in a Liberator. We could not understand the logic of this imposition on us and we were resentful at being included in another station's parade just to make up the numbers.

By now we were included amongst the senior crews of the squadron and lived well. We were housed, very comfortably, in a wooden hut on the east side of the airfield, only a few hundred yards from 'Z' for 'Zebra's dispersal at the end of the main runway. I shared a room with Wally Dreschler, the others were in rooms either side of us.

When on duty, we took our meals in the Sergeants' Mess, a place with a dismal atmosphere, totally lacking any sort of camaraderie. There was an ever-changing population as the squadron lost crews and new ones arrived, often to stay for just a short time before joining the casualty lists. We consequently made no friends, seldom met officers and I only spoke to my Flight Commander when I flew. The Station Commander and Squadron Commander were only seen at briefing. We lived in our own cocoon as a crew, and kept up our spirits with our strong friendship. Our duty was clear: we were operational and had thirty sorties to complete before we would be rested for six months as 'screens' at an OTU.

Our existence took on a set pattern. If warned for operations then there was an air test to be done followed by a long wait until briefing. If there was a stand-down then, as a crew, we were up and away from the station.

There was nothing to hold us at Snaith which had been functionally built in a hurry as a heavy bomber station and had few amenities. There was a small village, Pollington, just down the road; its only attraction being a pub. The nearest town was Doncaster, where we spent most of our time. I usually shared the company of Bob Frost and together we sought the ordinariness of civilian life, so very different from the unnatural business of facing death and bombing Germany. We regularly visited cinemas; sometimes, but not often, we went to dances. Most of the time we walked and walked around the countryside; when the pubs were open, we drank beer. We gave up returning to Snaith to sleep when we had the good fortune to find bed and breakfast accommodation in Doncaster. A retired railwayman, living alone in a terraced house near the railway station, became a second father to us. We would drop in on him without notice and sleep most comfortably in feather beds. He would wake us with a cup of tea in the morning and feed us with a breakfast of egg, bacon, and fried bread - we had no idea from where he obtained this food. He charged us not a penny. As he said, he was proud to have us with him, making it possible for him to do his bit to help those who were fighting.

During this break in operations, Jock Brazill developed an enormous boil on his neck which made it impossible for him to fly or, for that matter, for him even to speak. I was given a new navigator, a Flight Lieutenant, whose name does not appear in either my log book or my diary. He was experienced, quiet, and self-effacing in our crew of young sergeants.

He made his first trip with us to Frankfurt-on-Main on 24th August and which began in a most dramatic manner. As usual, we were last to take off, I had received the green Aldis light from the runway control caravan and was well committed to take-off with throttles fully open, when suddenly, directly ahead of me, there appeared a huge ball of flame. The Wellington flown by Flight Sergeant Baxter had crashed but there was no possibility of aborting the take-off: I had to concentrate in getting my aircraft, with its 4,000lb bomb, off the ground and through the towering inferno ahead in which bombs were beginning to explode. My muttered prayer was heard by the crew as we flew through the flames and smoke. Luckily for us, Baxter had been carrying a load of incendiaries and we were able to climb away without any damage.

The raid was the second led by the newly-formed Pathfinder Force, and we expected great things. Unfortunately, Frankfurt was completely covered in cloud and the Pathfinders had great difficulty in marking the targets. The anti-aircraft and searchlight defences were good and I saw at least two aircraft go down in flames. We bombed through cloud on to the biggest concentration of fire that we could see.

The next raid, three days later, was to Kassel. The weather was good almost all the way to the target. We arrived over the city in excellent visibility to find that the Pathfinders had illuminated the area well. As we began our bombing run, I was surprised to see a Junkers 88 going in the opposite direction, clearly silhouetted just below us. Then our troubles began, we couldn't drop our 4,000 pounder, something had gone wrong with the bomb release mechanism.

I knew that we would have to jettison the bomb, but I was determined that it would be done over Kassel. As I turned to make another bombing run, we saw one of our aircraft shot down by a night-fighter. There was very little flak, possibly ordered to hold back to allow the German fighters to attack in the almost daylight-like conditions above the burning city. We made another steady run-up and this time, on Dreschler's command, I pulled the jettison toggle; nothing happened, our 'blockbuster' would not leave us.

I knew it would be dangerous to try our luck in making more careful bombing runs until the bomb could be got away but, even so, the wretched thing was going to be dropped on Kassel. I ordered Graham to take up the fuselage floor above the bomb release and then to try physically to actuate the mechanism. I began a tight circle above the city while, with the help of Dreschler, he hacked away with the aircraft axe. Somehow he managed to smash the mechanism so that the bomb fell away. I levelled the aircraft and held it steady hoping that the camera would work to take a photograph of where the bomb had dropped.

The enemy night-fighters were very active that night. There were no clouds in which to hide and I worked hard at the cork-screwing procedure all the way back to the coast. We reported our woes at briefing and apologized for the mess we had made of the fuselage floor and the damage to the bomb release. The next day, I was called to see the Squadron Commander who passed on the congratulations of the Air Officer

Commanding No 1 Group for a first-class photograph taken of our 4,000 pounder demolishing a large building not more than 200 yards from the main Kassel railway station.

The pressures on the Squadron were now very strong. We were operating on almost every possible occasion and losing many crews. It had become almost impossible to maintain the full establishment of sixteen crews and No 150's contribution was nightly becoming less and less. New crews were not being made ready quick enough to make up for losses.

We flew an easy sortie to bomb Saarbrucken on 28th August. The main force was sent to Nuremberg that night leaving us with the much easier task of attacking a town just inside the German border. It was full moon and we went without the guidance of the Pathfinders. The result was that, despite almost ideal weather, we did not find the target and the bombing was poor. On the way back we had our first brush with a night-fighter. I was flying at about 18,000 feet, weaving and cork-screwing in my usual fashion with the first flush of dawn appearing as we neared the French coast. At the top of a climbing turn to starboard, just before I would have dropped down to port, a grey-mottled Messerschmitt 110 shot out from underneath us and, for a moment, pulled-up to fill the sky directly in front of me. It must have been tracking us on its radar and, confused by my erratic flight, must have misjudged our speed, and overshot us.

I instinctively turned on to the Messerschmitt's tail. I could clearly see the pilot and the other two of the crew. I shouted to Dreschler who was in the front turret, to open fire. He yelled back, 'What is it? Where is it? ' He could not see the enemy right there in front of him, already turning sharply to make an attack. I was not going to be silly enough to tangle with such an adversary and therefore did a wing-over and plunged down into the darker regions below. Slowly, I eased back on the control column and levelled out, by now we were clear of the coast and speeding across the Channel. On the way back to Snaith, we noticed that we were getting low on fuel. When 'Z' for 'Zebra' was given her regular servicing I was told that the starboard wing had been fractured, hence the loss of fuel from the wing tanks. The damage was so bad that the wing had to be replaced.

Jock Brazill was restored to us as navigator and flew with us to Saarbrucken on 1st September and the next night to Karlsruhe. 'Z' for 'Zebra' remained unserviceable so we flew an incendiary bomb-laden standard Mark 3. We got a good photograph at Karlsruhe which had been very accurately marked by the Pathfinders. On the way back, I decided to try something new by flying low. As we were about to coast-out, we got caught in searchlights as we mistakenly flew over Ostend. Bob Frost accurately fired down the searchlight beams and Norman Graham somehow managed to put his foot through the fuselage floor.

We were back in 'Z' for 'Zebra' for the attack on Bremen on 4th September. The Pathfinders had done a good job and we easily found the target. On 7th September it was back to Duisburg and, three nights later, we went to Dusseldorf. That was a big raid and numbers were made up by OTU crews who again, I believe, suffered high losses. There was very heavy flak over the town and I saw quite a few aircraft falling. The target was well marked and, from what I could see, the city and its inhabitants were suffering badly.

Our next operation, flown to Bremen on 14th September, did not go well. On the way back trouble developed in both engines. I could not discover what was wrong, I only knew that we were losing power and became worried that we might not be able to get back to Snaith. As a precautionary measure, I landed rather badly at Ossington, finishing up way off the end of the runway but luckily without damage to the aircraft. The reason for the engine trouble was quickly found during the night while we were sleeping and, the next morning, we flew back to Snaith.

Our next operation was a welcome diversion. On 16th September, we took off just after midnight with a load of two mines and two 250lb bombs, the mines to be planted in the shipping lanes at the mouth of the Elbe, and the bombs to be used on targets of opportunity. The sortie was regarded as an easy one. If all went well, there would be no night-fighters to worry about and the only flak we could meet would come from flak-ships, if we were unfortunate enough to fly near them.

As it happened, the weather was foul and we had to fly through and under thunderstorms all the way to the Frisians. This was at relatively low altitude and I was kept constantly on the alert, not a moment to relax. We got good GEE fixes and found the mouth of the Elbe and, for a while, 'square-searched' to find the best place to lay the mines. They were carefully planted and we ran into no opposition but we did not find a 'target of opportunity', so the bombs stayed on board. We flew back to Snaith through the storms to complete a flight of just over five hours. By nine o'clock that morning, we had been debriefed, eaten our aircrew breakfasts, and were fast asleep in bed.

I had to be forcibly awakened to be told that we were on standby again for operations that evening. We air-tested 'Z' for 'Zebra' mid-afternoon, and took with us Sergeant Dal Mounts, an American in the RCAF, who would be making his first trip with us that night. Most of the crew, including myself, 'cat-napped' until briefing at 18.00 hrs. The target was Essen, a large raid bolstered by many aircraft from the OTUs. A surprising feature of the weather forecast was that there would be what is now called a jet-stream blowing eastwards at 130 mph at above 15,000 feet.

I took off last as usual, following just three other squadron aircraft that represented our maximum effort. I decided to get as high as possible, as quickly as possible, to take advantage of the jet-stream which would cut down considerably the time spent over Germany, getting to the target. We crossed the Dutch coast near Zwolle at just over 21,000 feet making excellent time. All was going well when, without any warning, we were bracketed in flak. There was just one burst and it came very close, I heard it above the noise of the engines.

With the immense tail wind we were soon into Germany and heading into the Ruhr valley. I had, by now, dropped down to about 20,000 feet and ahead I could see a truly extraordinary scene. I had never before seen 'Happy Valley' so lit up with searchlights, dummy fires, marker flares and bursting bombs, all overlaid with a carpet of flak shells sparkling as they exploded. We flew into this barrage, never before had we experienced such a weight of fire. The noise of it developed into a roar and cordite fumes from exploding shells filled the aircraft.

One particular explosion almost caused me to lose control, practically turning us over. I fought with the controls in a state of blind panic, babbling and praying away to myself, as the aircraft was literally tossed in the sky. I managed to regain control after losing a lot of altitude, by which time we were over the target and we dropped our bomb. There was no let-up, we flew in and out of searchlights still within the incredible barrage, and before we could escape the port engine failed and I had to feather it. Our job done, we now had the problem of getting home, heaven knew how badly damaged, heading back into the jet-stream which was cutting our

The only picture I could find which was taken whilst on No. 150 squadron

ground speed down to well below 100 mph.

Then our troubles really began: whatever damage there had been, in addition to the loss of the engine, meant that I could not fly a steady course and, to my alarm, I could only head homewards by sacrificing height to build up speed. I simply wasn't in full control of 'Zebra' and, as we got lower, I found I could only hold the aircraft in a wide descending circle with the high wind pushing us back towards Germany. With a heavy heart I told the crew that I would not be able to fly the aircraft back to England and, as a crew, we decided that it would be best to bale out before we were blown back over the Rhine.

We had time to make an orderly exit because I could hold the aircraft level in its wide turn. Wally Dreschler clipped on my chest-type parachute whilst Jock Brazill told us we were somewhere the right side of the Belgian-Dutch border, maybe over the Ardennes. Bob Frost left his rear turret to rescue the two pigeons we always carried from their cage and came forward with them stuffed inside his flying suit. He baled out from the forward escape hatch, followed by the American, Mounts, then Graham, followed by Dreschler, and finally Brazill.

With the crew out apparently safely it was my turn to go. We were down to about 10,000 feet as I throttled back the starboard engine hoping that 'Zulu' would fly level just long enough for me to jump. As I got down into the nose she began to dive and to turn over, I had to struggle against the 'G' force to get into position to jump from a sitting position on the edge of the escape hatch, facing rearwards. Clutching the parachute 'D'-ring, I was ready to go when the aircraft lurched violently and the 'G' force reversed ejecting me from the aircraft - I didn't have to jump. I don't remember consciously pulling the rip-cord, but I felt a blow on my face as the canopy boiled out of the pack and then deployed above me. All then became wonderfully quiet as I floated down through the clouds.

CHAPTER SEVEN

A large tree cushioned my landing as I slithered down through its branches and finished standing upright underneath it, supported in my harness. I was completely demoralized, it had all been too much for me. I was shaking with exhaustion and scared out of my wits, just releasing my parachute harness and flopping down. For a long time, so it seemed, I did nothing but shake and shiver.

It was a calm, star-lit night and all was quiet. My mind only began to function when I heard a dog barking some distance away. It meant that I was somewhere near habitation but I had no idea where on earth I was. I felt incredibly lost and so very sorry for myself. I must have sat like a fool under the tree for almost an hour until, little by little, I began to think objectively again. As a crew, we had often discussed the unlikely possibility of completing a tour of thirty operations, and what would happen when it was our turn to be shot down. We never thought of death, rather that we might then become prisoners of war. Better still, as we were told at each operational briefing, there was a good chance that we could evade capture and get back to England if we had the good fortune to be picked up by an escape organization. That was why we carried escape kits filled with odds and ends, to help us get on the move and to look for help. Also, there was the constant reminder that it was our duty to return to our squadron.

My chief problem was the unreality of everything around me but I did eventually get to my feet and do something; the air was fresh and the only sounds were the rustling of leaves above me. I checked myself for injury; there was a sharp pain in the cheekbone under my left eye, and I found a small bleeding wound on the back of my right hand, which I wrapped with my handkerchief. I walked around the tree, surveying the parachute canopy which completely covered it, making it appear like a giant mushroom. Looking up at the 'chute, it was clear that it would take an age to get it down and to hide it. No amount of tugging or pulling on the shroud lines would untangle it from the branches, so I had to leave it where it was knowing that it would be an ideal starting point for a search for me to begin. As there was little point in trying to hide my yellow Mae West, I took it off, threw it under the tree. I then set off, with little idea of what I was doing or where I was going.

I travelled quietly and surprisingly easy through uncultivated countryside, dotted with clumps of bushes and brush, copses and small woods. There were no signs of habitation and it took more than an hour before I came upon a road, narrow and badly-maintained, yet lining up with the north-westerly course I had set myself. I had no need to resort to any of the compasses I was carrying as the way ahead could easily be determined by reference to Polaris, standing out clearly in the night sky.

I felt progressively better as I moved on, my mind had cleared and I was working on a plan. I had no idea where I was, reasoning that it could be somewhere in Luxembourg, the Netherlands, Belgium or even France. I prayed that I was not on the wrong side of the Rhine, in Germany. Many briefings by the squadron intelligence officer came back to me; I had not buried my parachute, nor hidden my Mae West, but I was on the move. I had to head away from Germany, walk by night and hide during the day. If all went well, the intelligence systems of the Resistance would, in the end, find me.

A plan of action gradually came together as I walked. Although I did not know where I was, it had to follow that if I kept walking on a north-westerly course, I would eventually reached a point somewhere on the coast, maybe along the Channel or the North Sea. I desperately hoped that I would be picked up long before that but, if not, the craziest ideas crossed my mind. I would have to find some way of crossing the water; would it be by boat, maybe a fishing trawler? Or could I steal something and, perhaps, sail across - or even row or paddle? British ships controlled the seas along the coasts, and they would be sure to see me. Looking back, I know that such ideas were utterly ridiculous but, at the time, at least I had something to work on, something to think about and to keep me on the move.

First light was approaching and I began to search for somewhere to hide. Information passed on at the squadron suggested that the best places were the remote and impenetrable areas. If there was any sort of following search, I had to find a place where even dogs would find it hard to track and to enter. With this in mind, I left the road and headed for a small copse with thick undergrowth between young pine trees. Making sure that I was not leaving any sort of trail behind me I got down on my hands and knees and burrowed my way into the copse, deep into the tangle of brush and brambles. When well inside, I made myself as comfortable as possible, curled up, dozed for a while and then fell asleep.

I awoke in absolute terror, hearing an ever-increasing roar of machinery coming towards me. I shot up, completely bewildered, the brambles tearing at my skin. The noise grew to a crescendo as I looked up to see the huge underbelly of a Junkers 52 passing not more than fifty feet above me. It had flaps down and was obviously about to land, I had found a hiding place very near to the edge of an airfield.

As it grew lighter, I could see through the bushes and trees just how difficult a position I was in. It would be impossible to move from the spot in broad daylight, as it was overlooked by a nearby road that led to the airfield, and my only recourse was to improve my hiding place. Carefully and quietly, I dug down into the leaf mould to make a shallow pit in which I laid on my belly after pulling the branches and tendrils of brambles and bushes over me. As I hoped, no one came near the copse and I could see people and the occasional vehicle on the road coming and going from the airfield. From what I could hear, particularly when aircraft engines were run up, the airfield was only about a quarter of a mile away.

I was kept on the alert for most of the morning, reasonably confident that no one was likely to enter the copse because of its neglected state. I got out of my pit and went further in towards its centre, found a small space between the trees and decided to establish my 'headquarters'. It was now early afternoon on a fine, warm, autumn day. The sky was gloriously blue, fringed at high altitude with cirrus cloud the herald, perhaps, of an approaching warm front. Aircraft had been flying in and out of the airfield continuously, most were Messerschmitt 110s. I concluded from this that I could be somewhere amongst the clutch of night-fighter stations which I knew were strung along the River Maas.

My hand had stopped bleeding, but I still had pain in my cheekbone, and my left eye was swollen. Oddly, I had lost the fear that had been with me throughout the night, but it was difficult to come to terms with my situation; it was still so unreal. Instead of waking in a comfortable bed at Snaith with a cup of tea brought to my side, I had been rudely awakened, Heaven knew where, on the edge of a German airfield, hundreds of miles from home.

I began to take stock of my possessions, laying them out, one by one on the ground. In anticipation of my downfall, I always flew with not one but two escape kits. In the flat tin boxes that held the kits were all the things a would-be evader required to get him up onto his feet and on his way: silk maps of the Netherlands, Belgium, and Northern France; plastic water bottles and Halazone tablets to purify the water; fishing lines and hooks; Dutch, Belgian and French bank notes not many, but enough to be useful; a penknife, sewing needle and thread, Benzedrine pills, Horlick's tablets, and toilet paper. I had also seven compasses hidden in my uniform. There was one as a collar-stud, one each in my cuff-links, two fly-buttons made another, and sewn into the waist band of my battle dress were four small button compasses. There were also two passport-sized photographs of myself in civilian clothes for the Resistance to use on my false passport.

I put the Halazone, Benzedrine, and Horlick's tablets into my top right-hand pocket. In the left-hand one, I placed the maps, money and plastic water bottles. In my trouser pocket I put the penknife and fishing lines. The sewing needle and thread, I pinned into my battle-dress lapel and buried the unwanted duplicates and the two empty escape kit tins. I was not feeling the least bit hungry, but towards the end of the afternoon I began to get thirsty. The first thing I would have to do when on my way again would be to fill the water bottles.

I felt so strangely at ease and unafraid that I actually dozed for an hour or so in the sunshine. I woke in the late afternoon feeling fit and well and anxious to be on my way. I left the copse as soon as dusk fell, first heading away from the airfield for some distance, and then resuming a north-westerly course. I set myself a target of walking hard for six or seven hours which ought to make certain that I was inside the western end of the Netherlands or into Belgium. From the nature of the countryside around me, I was pretty certain that I was north of the Ardennes.

I soon had the airfield well behind me, although I heard the noise of aircraft taking off for quite some time. I walked on paths and lanes whenever possible, reasoning that if anyone from the resistance was looking for shot-down aircrew, they would not be doing so in open country. After an hour of steady walking, during which I had filled both water bottles from a stream, the character of the countryside began to change. I had moved into a cultivated area of small farms, bound by hedges and interspersed with lanes, paths and narrow roads. I also began to feel hungry and ate the eight useless Horlicks tablets. From now on, I would have to keep my eyes open for food, to live off the land, just as I had often practised as a Boy Scout in Devon.

Just after midnight, I lost the benefit of the stars for my navigation, the skies had clouded over and I had to resort to the use of one of the miniature compasses from the escape kit. Not long afterwards I heard the drone of many aircraft flying high overhead on the same course I was taking, no doubt returning to England after a raid on the Ruhr.

It then began to rain, light drizzle at first, increasing as time went by into a steady, drenching, downpour which made me consider stopping to take shelter. However I thought otherwise, remembering rugger and soccer games when body heat alone countered the effects of getting wet. I was warm and moving well, just a bit worried about the possible effects of the wet, fleece lined flying boots, on my feet.

When I came upon a well made road, heading westwards, I pressed on faster. Only once did I have to leave the road to take cover and that was when a small convoy of vehicles drove past, the hooded headlights making it easy for me to spot their approach. At first light, I began a search for somewhere to hide but, by then, the whole countryside was awake and I could see numerous lights in the farm buildings and houses. In the half-light caused by the falling rain, I noticed a gap leading into a field and on to a path which disappeared into the gloom. I splashed through a ditch up onto the path and across the field which was planted with root crops. Before I reached the far side, I had gathered three small turnips and some carrots.

The field was bordered by a narrow lane which I followed for a while until, to my delight, I saw the ruin of a small cottage standing on its own, well back from the lane. I was wet through, the pain in my feet was excruciating, and it soon would be daylight; this had to be my shelter for the day. I went cautiously through a diseased and overgrown garden, up to the open doorway of the cottage and collapsed on the floor, amidst rubbish and dust.

I was in a bad way, feeling sorry for myself, almost to the point of tears. I could have howled in my despair but, from somewhere, I found just enough sense to think of what next should be done. I was soaked to the skin and had to get dry if I was to stay fit for whatever might lie ahead.

I first carefully removed my flying boots and peeled off the sodden socks to reveal badly swollen feet covered with blood and blisters. I stripped off my battle dress blouse and took off my trousers and shirt and spread them on some rubbish to dry. I was left clad in just a damp cotton singlet and shorts but, thankfully, the heat of my body soon began to dry them. Despite the early hour it was, in fact, not the least cold.

I knew how to deal with blisters from my Boy Scout days, using the sewing needle to deal systematically with blister after blister, pricking each one to force out the clear liquid inside, and drying them on toilet paper. I wrapped the paper around those that had burst and bled. As I worked, I began to feel better and decided to stay in the ruin throughout the day, hoping that no one visited; soon after dark I would press on.

The cottage was just a shell, evidence in the form of charred wood suggested that it might have been burnt out. I made a nest of sorts in rubbish stacked in an alcove and there I rested, dozed, and eventually fell asleep. When I awoke, the rain had stopped, the sun was bright overhead, and it was getting decidedly warmer. My spirits rose and I set about making preparations to move on. My battle dress, shirt and boots were by no means dry so, on hands and knees, I crawled through the gap that was once a back door, and spread them out on the grass outside. I considered lighting a smokeless fire to cook the turnips and carrots but decided it was too risky. I was very hungry and carefully peeled a turnip, cutting it into small pieces that I ate slowly along with some of the carrots, washing it down with all the water in one of my two water bottles.

No one came near the place during the day, my only visitor was a stray dog that wandered in looking for food. I just watched it and said nothing, knowing that if I did speak, my unusual language would confuse the animal and might make it bark. Late in the afternoon I went outside again to turn my clothes and found they were dry enough to be worn. The flying boots, however, were still damp. I laboriously cut off the uppers with my little penknife, leaving just a pair of open shoes. I re-doctored the blisters, wrapping some in toilet paper, and carefully pulled on the dry socks. Then, ever so slowly, I eased my tortured feet back into the boots.

As I waited for darkness, I resolved that there would be only one more night of marching. I knew that without proper food, and with my feet in such a poor state, I would be getting close to the end of my tether by the next morning. I had convinced myself that I was inside either the Netherlands or Belgium, and that there would be people looking for me. If they did not find me, I would chance my arm in getting help by asking for it.

It was really dark when I set out again. I made a very painful start with my blistered feet which I stamped down hard in a measured marching rhythm until the pain had gone. I settled down to a walk that I intended should not be across open country, but along lanes and roads where I might be seen. I was not going to push myself, trying to cover ten miles or so, all the time on the lookout for food.

It is surprising how an undisturbed walk can concentrate thought. My mind became disassociated from my body as I swung along, blissfully free from pain or fatigue, yet thinking, reasoning, and coming up with all sorts of ideas. I knew there would be people on the look-out for shot-down aircrew and that there might be local intelligence that enabled the Resistance to find those like myself. If I was not found that night, then at first light, I would take matters into my own hands and ask for help. I had no idea how this could be done, but I remembered briefings back at Snaith. It was, we had been told, always best to approach poor people, the middle-aged and the elderly who could remember the dreadful occupation of their country by the Germans in the Great War. One could try the clergy, but young people should be avoided and, in particular, so should civil servants. How a tired and harassed evader would be able to recognize, at first sight, a foreign civil servant, was beyond me. I also remembered the final piece of advice, to be used in extremis. If all else failed, then someone should be found who was poor, aged, and feeble enough to be knocked down and left, if not disposed to help.

At about two in the morning, I heard Bomber Command on its way back to England. I saw searchlights probing in the far distance, way ahead of me, and once, only once, I heard the exchange of cannon and machine gun fire. I was taking my time, resting at regular intervals and keeping my water bottles filled from pools and ditches, adding Halazone tablets as I went. I was very hungry and finished off the two turnips I had carried from the cottage, deliberately eating slowly and chewing each morsel thoroughly. I had long since lost the feeling that I was being hunted, if a chase had been started from where my parachute had been left, I was far away from there and the trail must surely have been lost. My bravado was such that I believed if I could just find food then I could walk for ever.

At about four o'clock the countryside began to come to life with lights coming on all around me. Walking past a small farm I could see, in the outbuildings, that milking had already begun. I felt certain, in fact, positive, that I was nowhere near a town where Germans would be stationed. It was a neighbourhood where I should be able to chance my arm when the occasion arose.

I was walking slowly along a narrow lane, bordered on both sides by water-filled ditches. It turned in towards a dark stand of small trees and, as I neared the corner, I almost collided with a man riding a bicycle. I couldn't get out of his way and he jammed on his brakes, coming to a stop right in front of me. He dismounted and seemed to come to attention as we stood looking hard at each other. I was flummoxed, not knowing what to do, but took the initiative and spoke first, *'Morgen, Guten Morgen,'* I tried. In the half-light the man must have thought that I was a German in battle dress, I must have looked like a member of the *Luftwaffe*. He then ventured a step closer and peered at my RAF wings, looking up at me, excited, rapidly nodding his head. He whispered, *'RAF? RAF? Ja? Ja?'* I replied in English, 'Yes, I am a British pilot. Can you help me?' Then tried my French, *'Aidez moi?'* Letting the bicycle fall to the ground he grabbed my arm and shook my hand vigorously, finally embracing me and planting kisses on both cheeks. He was excited and made it clear that he wanted me to go with him. Picking up the bicycle, he turned it around and indicated that I should join him by sitting sideways on the crossbar. We cycled off back down the lane, my new-found friend jabbering away all the time in a language which sounded like German, but had to be something else; Dutch was my guess.

We had gone less than half a mile when we came to the outskirts of a village, and then stopped at a large official-looking house, just short of the village centre. I was hustled inside and found myself in a large room next to what, to judge from the wonderful smell of baking bread, must have been a kitchen. Very soon the room began to fill with people who jostled to shake my hand, slap my back, and clearly indicate that they were friendly. They all spoke the same guttural language and, try as I did, I could not make any sense of it.

A smartly dressed middle-aged woman asked, *'Comprenez-vous Français? Comprenez-vous la langue?'* I replied at once in my schoolboy French, 'Yes I do. I speak French, but not well. If you speak slowly, I should be able to understand.' She said she was the village schoolmistress and, for a while, took charge of the proceedings. I told her that I was a British pilot and that I had been shot down two nights before when bombing Essen. I added that I had been walking ever since, trying to reach the coast but hoping that I would be found by an escape organization. She didn't seem to understand and after excusing herself she left the room. I was taken to another room where, to my intense delight, I was given a splendid meal of ham, eggs, and newly-baked bread. Before I had finished, the schoolmistress returned with three men. I rose from my chair but was motioned to sit down again and we all sat grouped around the table.

Her first words were that no one knew anything of escape organizations or where they could be found. Nonetheless, I was amongst friends and would be helped. One of the men was a doctor, he too spoke French, and a little English, asking me if I had any ailments. Using a hand-held mirror, he showed me that the swelling of my eye was going down, but that the bruise was now an odd yellow-greenish colour. He took my temperature and examined my damaged hand, then took me upstairs to a small bathroom leaving me to clean up. I stripped completely, got into a lukewarm bath and scrubbed myself from head to toe with carbolic soap. While I was doing this, someone came into the room and took away most of my clothes: the battle dress, shirt, socks and boots, leaving me just my cotton vest, shorts and a white dressing-gown. I finished the bath as quickly as possible and clad in just my underwear and the dressing gown, went downstairs to the room where the woman and the three men were waiting for me.

I was beginning to feel physically tired but relaxed. The doctor went to work on my feet, deflating some of the blisters, treating them with antiseptic and taping them firmly. He then left us and the woman began to explain things to me. The strange language I had heard was Flemish. She spoke slowly and added that I would only be told what was necessary for me to know. She was a member of the village council, as were the two other men. I asked where I was and the only reply I got was that I was somewhere in Flanders and very near a railway line. I would be safe with them until the afternoon when the Germans would make their daily visit to the village, but by then I should be on my way.

This was not what I had expected to hear and began to feel somewhat confused and apprehensive. It could have been that I had not been able to understand what she had said, but the thought of pressing on in the daylight seemed suicidal to me. I asked if I could be hidden in the village until it became dark. The three of them went into a huddle and after a few moments she looked straight at me and shook her head.

She then told me that what I was doing was wrong, I would surely be captured if I carried on walking through the night towards the coast, in uniform. There was a curfew at night for all Belgian people and, furthermore, the Germans were building coastal defences everywhere following the raid on Dieppe a few months before. I would never be able to get into the coastal areas, let alone find help or a boat. On top of the fact that I was travelling in the wrong direction, I was doing so in the wrong manner. I had to go south, that was where the escape organizations might be, ideally get out of Belgium and into France and on down to Marseilles. The easiest and safest way to get there was by train and I should travel during the day. This was almost too much for me to understand, I was flabbergasted. I no longer had a plan and what was being suggested seemed well beyond my capability. The South of France was hundreds of miles away and train travel was surely dangerous, appearing in daylight with Germans all around seemed ridiculous. At least by night, I could take steps to avoid them. However, the matter was taken right out of my hands when the woman told me that while I was taking my bath, they had taken the precaution of getting rid of all evidence of my arrival. They had burned my belongings: my uniform, shirt, boots, and destroyed all the odds and ends such as my compasses, maps, and water bottles. She was quick to tell me that in any case I would not need them, because I was about to be dressed as a young Belgian boy.

I was stunned, I said nothing until the woman asked me outright to hand over my identity discs which she could see hanging around my neck. I instinctively put my hands over them and declared that they were the only means left whereby anyone would know that I was English. She said I was foolish, explaining that if I was caught wearing them in the clothes I was about to be given, the Germans would not hesitate to execute me as a spy.

It was all too much for me. I handed over the discs which were taken away to be destroyed. I was led back to the bathroom where a pile of clothes had been placed on a chair, a truly motley collection. I put on a dirty, grey, shirt without a collar, and a pair of striped trousers, far too short in the leg and too wide at the waist; tying them with a length of cord. There was also a threadbare jacket, again too big, and a workman's cap. The shoes provided were thin, made of something other than leather, but they fitted well. I looked at myself in a mirror and had to agree that I was well disguised. Sporting a discoloured eye, and needing a shave, I looked like someone down on his luck, some sort of a tramp, unlikely to draw attention.

I went downstairs into the main room to be greeted by a dozen or more villagers who had come to wish me good luck. A woman came shyly forward, mumbled a few words in Flemish and, to my great surprise, handed me a bundle of Belgian banknotes. I was so moved by this generosity that I tried to thank her in French which was translated into Flemish by the schoolmistress.

It was then all hustle and bustle, shaking hands with everyone in the room. I was told that a train was expected within twenty minutes and that I would be escorted to the railway halt. Once outside, there were more villagers waiting to join us and, together, we set off noisily along the road. As we walked, the schoolmistress gave me a ticket to Namur in the

Ardennes, and told me if all went well, I should arrive there late in the afternoon. First though, I would have to change trains at a place called Tirlemont.

There were about ten minutes to wait until the arrival of the train. The villagers packed themselves into the small waiting room. Everyone wanted to wish me farewell and then, to my consternation, an elderly man produced a concertina, and began to pick out a well-known tune, at first softly, then louder, until all joined in the rousing chorus of 'It's a long way to Tipperary.' This bizarre performance was brought to a close when the train was seen to be approaching the small single platform. I was hustled out by the crowd and pushed into an empty compartment. To my relief, there was no delay and I was soon on the move, leaning out of the window for a long time, to wave goodbye to my Flemish friends.

No one entered the compartment after the first three stops of the little train. I was attempting to get to grips with the remarkable turn of events. Nothing I had been told back at Snaith had prepared me for what was happening. It seemed utterly unreal that I could be on my way to the Mediterranean, in an idiot disguise, without papers, and with nothing more than a pocketful of Belgian banknotes. I paid little interest to the passing countryside and wondered about what would happen if things went wrong. It seemed inconceivable that amongst the many people who had seen me off, there could not have been at least one who thought more of the Germans than he did of the British. Such a person could at that moment be telephoning ahead to arrange for the arrest of the strange looking person that I was.

At the fourth stop I was joined by an elderly woman loaded with a basket of farm produce. She made a point of sitting in the far corner from me, and said not a word. Two young men got on at another stop and they too kept quiet, probably wondering how such a disreputable looking person as I could afford to travel by train. When the train stopped at Diest, everyone got out.

Alone in the compartment, I wondered what next would happen. Eventually, the train was shunted to another platform and again began to fill with passengers. After a delay of about ten minutes or so, it pulled slowly away out of the station. This time the compartment was filled with people and I felt ill at ease, sitting jammed into a corner window seat with my eyes fixed on the scene outside. I kept this up until we began to steam into the outskirts of a town that I hoped would be Tirlemont, where I knew I would have to change trains.

As we drew into the station I could see that we had come to a place named Tienen. Everyone got out and once again I was at a loss to know what next to do. I sat tight until, with whistle blowing, the train shunted itself into a siding. We had come to a terminus and I was now alone in the middle of a railway yard. I had to do something, so I got down on to the track, well aware that I would be seen, and walked slowly across to the station platforms, ignoring the shouts of a railway worker. Once there I found that I was indeed in Tirlemont: the name of the station was shown in both French and Flemish, Tienen being the latter. I kept up the pretext of nonchalance and walked slowly through the ticket barrier, holding my ticket in my hand, and mumbling the word, 'Namur'.

I was surprised at how easily I had been able to deal with the problem. As I stood outside in the station forecourt, I felt exhilarated and confident that all else that day would go well. I studied the railway timetable and by reference to the station clock realized that I had two hours to wait for the train to Namur. Alongside the timetable was the first of many German notices I was to see, warning that the penalty for helping *'Terrorflieger'* was death.

With time to waste, I decided to walk around the town, to look at the shops, the people and their houses. I was attracting little attention by my appearance. It was market day and I seemed to fit into the background of this busy market town.

I saw my first Germans while searching for a clock to check how time was passing. As I passed two men dressed in white working smocks, I asked the time of day in French. It was only when one pulled out a fine hunter watch and held it for me to read that I saw on the front of his smock the German eagle and swastika badge. In my surprise, I followed them for a while as they led me into the town square. They entered a building with the swastika flag hanging over the doorway. The remainder of my waiting time was spent sitting on a bench in front of the building which must have been a headquarters of some sort. I thought it was by far the safest place to wait.

Ten minutes before the Namur train was due to leave, I got up and walked across the square into the station. I presented my ticket at the barrier and went on to the platform where the train was waiting. I found a seat in an empty compartment. The train pulled out, exactly on time.

I really enjoyed the trip to Namur, feeling completely relaxed. The only problem was that I was feeling hungry and, like a fool, I had overlooked the possibility of buying food in Tirlemont where I was too preoccupied to think about eating. The train made frequent stops and was twice held up for long periods for no apparent reason, and it was not until early evening that we reached Namur. As I joined the crowd queuing at the exit, I was dismayed to see *Feldgendarmerei* (German Field Police) standing alongside the Belgian ticket collector. As I got nearer, it was a relief that I noticed they were only interested in checking the papers of German soldiers. I kept my place in the queue, handed in my ticket, and left the station as quickly as possible.

I knew that I had to get away from the town before curfew. I walked alongside the riverbank, crossed the bridge, and set off up the valley road that headed south towards Dinant. The weather was fine and warm and everything had gone so well that I decided to press on through the night towards the French frontier, just the other side of Dinant. I had no idea what to expect when once there, but believed that after a good recce I would be able to cross, under cover of darkness, the next night. Then, perhaps, I would be able to get back onto another train.

I was clear of Namur and in open country when dusk fell. I had not discounted the possibility of getting help again, if for nothing more than to ask for a meal. Ahead of me, in the failing light, I saw someone at work in a small plot on the edge of a lane. As I drew nearer, I could see an elderly man in working clothes digging potatoes. Without doubt, this was the text book situation for taking a chance. As I walked up to him he looked up but carried on with his work. I composed my words carefully, and spoke quietly, being ready to run if things went wrong.

'*Monsieur, je suis un aviator Anglais. S'il vous plait, aidez-moi. J'ai faim.*'

He didn't reply, but continued to dig. I stood there like a fool, wondering what to do. Then he looked up at me and pointed to a small bank at the edge of the plot.

'*Restez là, mon ami.*'

He returned to his work as I went over to the bank and sat down. The old man worked until it was dark, then placed the potatoes and shovels in a wheelbarrow and beckoned me to follow. We walked down the lane and turned into a path which led to a farm. Taking me by the arm he led me inside to a kitchen where a family was seated around a table, waiting to start a meal. My arrival caused some alarm, yet I was introduced formally to his wife, his son, and his son's wife. Both women became distressed when he explained who I was and, in the argument that followed, it was clear both thought my presence put the family in danger. The old man restored calm and, with that, his wife grudgingly set a place for me at the table; I was ravenous.

I shared their meal of meat stew, roast potatoes and cabbage, all eating in silence with only glances exchanged between my hosts. I thoroughly enjoyed my meal, clearing every last morsel from my plate with a large chunk of homemade bread. I was then given cheese, a heap of what I was sure was boar paté, and some rough red wine. The meal over, everyone began to ask me questions, few of which I understood because their French was a dialect I found hard to follow. I could understand the son better than the others and, now and then, he wrote down his question to which I was more easily able to write an answer. When he passed on the information that I had been bombing Germany, the news was received rapturously; *'à bas les Boches'* was the cry. From then on, I was in everyone's favour. The cognac was brought out and we toasted each other, our countries, and even the Kings of Belgium and Britain.

The meal over, the son made his excuses and said he had to leave; he had work to do. The farmer's wife arranged for me to wash, and I borrowed her husband's open razor to shave. I was told I would be welcome to spend the night at the farm, but that I should be on my way at first light. I did my best to express my thanks. It had been a wonderful day, all had gone well, and my doubts about travelling across France had almost disappeared.

The farmer led me by lantern to a barn, where I was offered a bed of straw where I lay down and soon fell asleep. The next thing I remember was the creaking of the barn door. A sixth sense warned me to be on my guard, but there was nothing I could do other than lay there, eyes closed. Suddenly, I was grabbed by the shoulders, a bright light was shone in my eyes and I was shaken violently. A harsh voice shouted at me in what I recognised as German; I was absolutely terrified at the thought that the game was up. I blurted out my alarm in English and then, from the darkness, a voice spoke in English, 'It's all right. Calm yourself. We are here to help you.'

A lantern was lit, and in its light, I could see three men, one of them the farmer's son. I got to my feet and followed them outside. I shook hands with the farmer's son who wished me *'bon voyage'*. We left the farm at once, walking in single file, one man leading and the other behind me. It was very dark and we had to go slowly across the fields until we reached a narrow road leading down into Namur, whose dim lights could be seen in the distance. We hurried on and finally stopped at a barred window, set in a long wall skirting the road. A bell was rung, and, after a few minutes, a whispered conversation was held through the window with someone on the other side. I was told to climb over the wall which I did with some help. As I dropped to the ground on the other side, a cowled monk appeared at my side and took me by the hand.

CHAPTER EIGHT

It was the tolling of a bell, almost directly overhead, that brought me out of a deep sleep and it took me a moment or two to realize where I was. The previous night I had been brought to the sanctuary of a monastery and from what I could see, I was in a monk's cell; a small whitewashed room, with a narrow window at one end, and a door, with a grille set in it, at the other. Opposite my hard, wooden bed, placed along a wall, were a wash basin, a mirror, and a shelf with a safety razor, toothbrush, and tooth powder. I could not see my clothes but, on the back of a chair, was a brown robe. The only adornment in the room was a small coloured-glass picture of the Virgin and Child. Underneath it, it read, Notre-Dame de Chevremont.

For the first time since landing in occupied Europe I felt safe. I believed that I had found people who would help me, tell me what to do, and take away the awful responsibility of trying to tackle the task of getting to the South of France. It was absolutely wonderful to be resting in a scrubbed and spotless room, smelling so fresh and clean. Then, not far away, there was the chanting of male voices which had begun when the bell stopped tolling.

I got up and washed and shaved in cold water. I put on the brown robe and sat on the edge of the bed, waiting for what was next to come. Within a minute, the door was opened and a short, tubby, bespectacled monk entered, bearing a tray of food; bread, sliced cheese and ham, and a glass of milk. He spoke to me in English, telling me to eat and that he would be back when I had finished.

I ate slowly, relishing each morsel, unable to believe my good fortune. The monk must have been watching me through the door grille because as soon as I had finished, he came in and sat down. He introduced himself as Father Marcel and said he was the person who had met me at the monastery wall. He must have been in his late forties and spoke English reasonably well. That was why, he said, the Father Abbott had given him the responsibility of looking after me. I asked where I was but Father Marcel was not forthcoming. 'You are in safe hands, my son; the least you know about us and where you are, the better.'

He spent a long time with me that morning. Despite his mild appearance he was a man of integrity and purpose, holding a bitter hatred for the *Boche*, as he called the Germans. His father, mother, and grandfather had been shot in the massacre of hundreds of Belgian civilians during the looting of Dinant in August, 1914. He had grown up with a revulsion of things German. He had joined the Belgian Army in 1935 and had fought during the *Blitzkrieg* when he had been wounded and captured whilst defending the Albert Canal. Although taken to Germany as a prisoner of war, he had been released after a few months to study for Holy Orders. Paradoxically, however, he remained a soldier at heart. He said that he prayed for the day when Belgium would be liberated, adding that he hoped he would be able to fight again. I asked him what was about to happen to me. His answer, surprisingly, was that he did not know; others were apparently making the decisions. He said he was to look after me and left saying that he would find books for me to read, and that if I wanted I could join the brethren at prayers.

He came back just before mid-day looking worried. Apparently, my arrival had been observed by others and the monastery was in ferment. A serious situation had arisen because although most of the monks were Belgian and in favour of helping me, there were also two Dutchmen, a Frenchman, two Spaniards, an Irishman, and even some Germans, who thought otherwise. All were aware that a British pilot was being hidden in the cells. The Father Prior had been petitioned either to have me leave the monastery at once, or to hand me over to the Belgian police which meant that the Germans would get me. All knew the penalties for helping a

British flyer were ruthlessly applied. There was the very real possibility that everyone in the monastery would be put to death if I were discovered.

I immediately asked if I could be given back my clothes so that I could leave. I did not want to risk being handed over to the Belgian police because that would probably have meant that I could be shot as a spy. Sensing my alarm, Father Marcel, tried to assure me that all would be well. 'The good Father Brocard, our Prior, has made the decision for you,' he said. 'He has admonished the reluctant brothers, reminding them that it is their bounden Christian duty to help those in distress. In his wisdom, he has decided to make up their minds for them. There are eleven who are worried more about their safety than yours, and they have been ordered to retire from the monastery for an indefinite period. This afternoon, they will leave for our sister monastery at Chevremont, where the brethren are bound by a vow of complete silence.'

Relieved at this news I happily settled into a routine. The food was spartan but good and I was able to exercise in the monastery gardens, and I actually enjoyed being with the monks at their devotions. The chanting and the overall atmosphere enthralled me. I could get no information from Father Marcel as to when I would be moving on. He said he had nothing to do with the Resistance or the escape *reseaux (organisation)*. They had to guard their security with their lives. The Germans were all too well aware of the widespread assistance given to British flyers, and they were doing their best to smash them. The Gestapo were continually trying to penetrate the escape organizations with their agents and with the help of collaborators. There were even bogus escape routes, managed by Belgians and French in the pay of the Germans who found, collected, hid the flyers for a time while they interrogated them, before handing them over.

In the meantime I was seen by a doctor who came to the monastery. He examined my eye and said that no damage had been done. He found a small broken bone in my right hand and said it would heal itself in time. It was strapped with tape with the instruction that it could come off after a week.

Father Marcel eventually asked me for my identity discs which he said were wanted by those who would later take charge of me. I told him that they had been taken from me and destroyed, somewhere in Flanders. He came back to ask if I could give him any particular information that would positively identify me as a British pilot; something about my squadron, my aircraft, my crew, bomb loads or the like. I was emphatic that I could disclose only my name, rank and serial number, which I wrote down for him. He thought it most unlikely that it would satisfy anyone and asked if I could not, please, be more forthcoming. It was then that thoughts of bogus escape routes came to mind. I said that I could and would not give any more information until I knew that I was in the hands of an escape organization.

This rebuff did not change the happy relationship with my friend. I spent a lot of my time with him either in my cell or helping him in the monastery kitchen garden. I read for the first time, Pilgrim's Progress, the only English book available, and he helped me with the reading of something by Voltaire. The days passed slowly and I began to fret and feel anxious. Father Marcel realized this and went out of his way to reassure me that all would go well. One day, he promised me a surprise and took me to a small room in the belfry tower where he proudly showed me a cache of arms, including a heavy Hotchkiss machine gun, complete with boxes of ammunition clips.

The waiting period ended one warm, sunny, afternoon as I was sitting alone in the orchard at the end of the kitchen garden, dozing after futile attempts to translate a book in French about the life and death of Sir Thomas Moore. Father Marcel woke me with a hand on my shoulder. 'It is time for you to leave us, my son. A friend is here who will take you away.'

I snapped out of my daze and quickly returned to my cell to find a fine suit of civilian clothes laid out on the bed. I noticed by the label that it had been made by Hawkes of Saville Row. Father Marcel stood quietly by as I dressed. He held something in his hand and when I was ready he offered me a small golden crucifix and chain. 'I want you to wear this for your protection, my son. It has been blessed in your name.' I felt very humble and a little peeved that I had nothing to leave him in remembrance. I did find words though. 'One day, when this war is over, and we have won, I will return and try, somehow, to express my heartfelt thanks for all you have done.' We shook hands and said goodbye at the monastery gate. There he introduced me to a thin, well-dressed, middle-aged man. 'This gentleman will be your guide,' he said, 'he doesn't speak English. Just follow him and he will take you to a safe place.'

We set off at a good pace into the town of Namur. There were not many people about. I was feeling in good form, at last being on the move, and decently dressed and not the least bit apprehensive. I happily walked some distance behind the man who never once looked back. After about twenty minutes, he stopped outside a large house, set back from the road, standing in its own grounds. He turned and went in through the front garden and I followed him around to the back of the house. Through the windows I could see that the place was deserted, void of furniture, fittings and coverings. It was most certainly not a safe house and I began to wonder what next surprise awaited me.

We entered the house through the back door which was unlocked. I followed upstairs into a room where, sitting like magistrates behind a single trestle table, were three men. My guide said nothing, only acknowledging them and left. I now faced the men and, after a while, the silence was broken by the one in the centre who spoke good English.

'I am told that you say you are a British flyer, yet you have no means of identity to prove it.'

'No,' I replied. 'My identity discs were taken from me and destroyed some days ago by some gallant people who helped me in Flanders.'

No one seemed impressed. They chatted for a while and I began to wonder what was in store for me. I asked them who they were and this was met with three blank stares, then the leader spoke sharply, 'It does not matter who we are. It is much more important for us to know who you are. We have to know if indeed you are, as you say, a member of the British air force ... you must convince us, or else.'

At this point, any bravado that remained left me. I did not know what would follow but I managed to parrot out what we had been briefed to say, under such circumstances. 'You must know, if you are my friends, that all I can tell you is my name, rank, and serial number. I am 1385872 Sergeant W.S.O.Randle ... and I am Other Denominational; that is the religion printed on my discs.'

'Just so,' came the reply, 'We know what you can say but we must ask you some questions, and you must answer them. If all goes well, you are in safe hands. If not, then ... well.' The man who had spoken placed his hands carefully on the table. I had already decided that I would speak up, no matter what the questions were. Name, rank, and serial number was not going to work. I was very scared.

The first question dumbfounded me. 'Tell us what was the highest score you made playing cricket at school?' Nothing could have sounded more unreal as I stood, mouth agape, staring at them. I had never been any good at playing cricket but there had been a memorable House match when I had carried my bat and, for the first time, made double figures. I will never forget it.

'51, not out,' I blurted out.

What was the rude name you all called your Housemaster?'

'Bullo,' I said. 'But that was not rude. He was a fine man, he won a Military Cross, here in your country.'

'Where was your great grandfather on your mother's side born?' I had no idea. The rumour in the family was that he had been a deserter from the German Navy at about the time of the Franco-Prussian War. He had come ashore at Plymouth and settled down in Devon. I told them this, wondering just how they had found such personal questions.

I felt I was amongst friends and eagerly answered further questions about my squadron and the target we had bombed. They got me to write down descriptions of my crew, which I did. I told them that I knew very little about the sixth member who had flown his first trip ever over Germany with us, virtually as a passenger. I had to tell them that I had forgotten his name.

From their attitudes and expressions, I knew that they were satisfied with my interrogation. I was told I would be taken to a place to be hidden until arrangements could be made to move me out of Namur. They reminded me how to behave while being taken to the place, to walk behind the guide at a given distance or on the other side of the road. From now on, wherever I went, I would be with a guide. If there was any trouble, it would be my duty to keep away from him or her. Guides were valuable people, with important work to do.

Without further ado, I left the deserted house, with one of the men acting as my guide. I followed him into Namur, religiously obeying instructions to keep him in sight. We were soon into the narrow streets leading to the Meuse Bridge, and then walked through the centre of the town. It must have been market day, the place was crowded with people, many of them

German soldiers. Once clear of the market place, we walked on towards the northern suburbs.

In a tree-lined avenue of imposing houses, the guide turned into a short driveway. There, out of sight of the road, I was beckoned forward and, together, we went up to the house. A knock on the front door and I found that I was being welcomed into a family home.

One of the photographs taken in Namur which I still have. The other was used in my laissez-passer

I stayed in the safe house occupied by Madame Davreux and her two daughters for just four days. I did not realize at the time that I was already in the hands of the *Comète* Line, the most successful of all escape routes operating to return shot-down aircrew. The Davreux added the finishing touches so I was ready to travel. I was already well-dressed and was in pretty good physical condition; I just had to be equipped with papers to enable me to pass from safe house to safe house, and to be given some sort of identity. Madelaine, one of the daughters, took me into Namur to have my photograph taken.

It surprised me just how easily the job was done. I was photographed in a chemist's shop by someone who obviously knew why it was being taken. Afterwards, we walked into the town where we sat in a café and ate croissants and drank coffee. Madelaine bought me a copy of the German magazine, *'Der Spiegel'* (The Mirror) which I thumbed through, glancing at the contents. It contained photographs of the slaughter of the Canadians on the Dieppe beaches. I was struggling to hide the distress which must have been showing on my face when I looked up to see a young *Wehrmacht* soldier, who was sitting at the next table, obviously approving my choice of magazine.

My *'laissez-passer'* was ready the next day, complete with photograph and stamped to indicate that it had been issued in Antwerp. I was now a Flemish commercial traveller, Andre de Vougelaar, born in Hasselt, but living in Diest. I was selling agricultural machinery and fertilizers. There was also a work permit which enabled me to travel in the Low Countries and in France. It even had a special visa for me to travel to Biarritz, of all places.

The Davreux family provided me with a small commercial diary and clothing coupons and instructed me how to respond to challenges in both French and German when asked for documents. I was reassured to learn that the Germans seldom spoke or understood French, they apparently just checked one's face against the photograph. The French police also took little notice of any papers but, to be on the safe side, it was best never to speak - just to hold out the document. My table manners were altered in that, although knives and forks were used to eat, it was customary to leave them together, after the meal, diagonally across the plate, and not, north and south, as in England. They didn't like the way I walked, far too upright, they said, as though I was a soldier on the march. And I had to stop whistling and humming tunes, as most were American or British, and unknown on the Continent.

On my last day in Namur, I met a young girl who was to save my life. She was Andrée de Jongh, only a little older than I, yet she was impressive with her firm purpose and ability. She spoke English quite well and briefed me to the letter on a journey to Brussels for which she would be my guide. I was full of questions, most of which she ignored. She emphasized the rules that applied when an evader was being guided and warned me that, if anything went wrong, I would be left on my own. I had to follow her to Namur railway station where I would present the ticket she gave me and then board the train to Brussels, making sure that I got into the same carriage, but to sit nowhere near her. On arrival in Brussels, there would be a change of guide, made in the entrance to the station. Another woman would take me to a large church where I was to sit in the third row of chairs on the right of the aisle. Then, I would be contacted by a man wearing a Belgian red, black and yellow *boutonnière* in his lapel. He would lead me to the next safe house.

She repeated these instructions and tested me with a few questions. She asked me if I knew how to conduct myself in a Roman Catholic Church. I had to say that I had never been inside one. She explained that it was customary to dip one's fingers in the Holy Water on entering and then that I should genuflect in front of the altar before taking my seat. She showed me how properly to make the sign of the Cross and how to bend the knee and lower the body. No trouble was expected during the journey. The train was a fast one, stopping only at Ottignes and Gembloux. 'We have done it many times', she said.' If anyone wants to see your ticket, they will just say, *'billet'*. Make sure you always have it ready for inspection.' She then answered the question that was uppermost in my mind. What should I do if anything went wrong? Where should I go? Her answer was abrupt, I should use my common sense and find my way back to Namur.

My few belongings were packed into a fine leather attaché case and I was given a stylish Homburg hat to wear. I must have looked the part of an earnest commercial traveller. I paid my heartfelt thanks to the Davreux family, all of whom embraced me and wished me *'bon voyage'*. I followed Andrée as briefed, walking briskly about twenty yards or so behind her, down into Namur At the railway station barrier, I presented my ticket to an uninterested collector and went in, carefully watching Andrée as she boarded the train. I followed and took a seat at the end of a third-class compartment from where I could keep her in sight.

The journey to Brussels was uneventful. For the first time, I felt that I was keeping abreast of events, confident I knew what to do, and that I had a good chance of getting back safely to England. On demand I twice presented my ticket to an inspector. No one spoke to me or bothered me and just before mid-day we arrived at Brussels Midi.

I followed Andrée through the crowds leaving the station. In the forecourt, she appeared to meet a friend. They walked for a while together and then parted company at a street corner. I switched my attention to the other guide, another young girl. Taking up a position some distance behind her, she led me on what seemed to be a conducted tour of the city. It was all an enjoyable revelation to me. We stayed for a while in the Place des Princes looking at the flower stalls and mingling with sightseers, many of them German soldiers. We then made off into the old part, stopping just for a moment to stare at the Manikin Pis which was being photographed by a couple of Luftwaffe aircrew. After a while, we came out into a market place, at the top of which stood an imposing church. I watched carefully as my guide went in. I then went to the foot of the steps at the main entrance where I could see from a notice board that the church was Notre Dame du Sablon. I paused for a while, then went in, taking the Holy Water from a sculptured basin set in the place I had been told it would be. I self-consciously crossed myself as I paid my respects. I then went around a heavy wooden screen and walked slowly up the aisle towards the altar, passing my guide who was sitting at prayer, head covered and bowed. I stopped at the base of the altar set under a magnificent window with a large cross hanging overhead; genuflected, and then withdrew to sit in the third row of chairs to the right of the aisle. As I did so, I noticed that the guide was already on her way out of the church.

I sat there waiting for a while and then began to pray, giving thanks for my salvation and for the remarkably successful events of the past few days. I knew that I did not deserve such blessings and hoped that my due deserts as an avenging bomber pilot would be set aside by the Almighty. I prayed earnestly for the safety of my crew.

Almost as an answer from above, a portly, well-dressed man came to sit near me. I noticed that he was wearing the Belgian *boutonnière*. We sat alongside each other in silence for a minute or so, and then he got up and left. I counted off a minute, and followed him outside into the broad daylight, waiting at the top of the entrance steps and watching him cross to the other side of the road. When he got there, he turned and waved his hand in my direction, then walked off slowly to cross a busy main road and enter an ornamental garden shrouded with trees. I followed him into the garden, around a large stone pond in which goldfish were swimming, and up a semi-circular flight of steps at the back of which, in ivy-covered alcoves, stood statues of ancient notables. We left the garden and I followed him along a narrow street which took us past a busy military headquarters, teeming with German soldiers. After about a quarter of a mile or so, we came to the entrance of an apartment block. The lift was not working so we climbed slowly up a staircase to the fifth floor. There the guide knocked on a door which was opened to allow him to speak to someone inside. He beckoned me forward and I was ushered in to meet a lovely, smiling, middle-aged lady. The guide kissed her on both cheeks and left.

My third 'safe house' was a well-furnished apartment, the home of a lady who greeted me as a guest, and spoke excellent English. She reminded me that I was a fugitive about to be hidden in a busy house in the very heart of Brussels. The *Boche* were in and out of the building every day, visiting their friends, mostly women. 'One always has to be on the lookout for them,' she said, 'and for the wretched collaborators who are worse.'

I was shown around the apartment in which my hostess lived alone. We went through the various rooms where I was cautioned not to go near the windows which were overlooked from taller buildings across the street. She explained that if the apartment was raided, I should make my escape through the bathroom window, out down the fire escape or across the roofs of adjacent houses. She showed me how to open the window and then pointed to a trapdoor in the ceiling, a devious smile appearing on her face. She picked up a long bamboo rod, reached up, and rapped three times on the trapdoor. The door was opened and I found myself looking up in amazement at the beaming face of my rear-gunner, Bob Frost. 'Pleased to see you, Bill,' he said, 'you certainly took your time.' He came down followed by a broad-faced, blond-haired man, who looked very Germanic. Then, unbelievably, down came Sergeant Dal Mounts, the American whom we had taken on his first flight over Germany.

The efficiency of the *Comète* Line was only too apparent: both Frost and Mounts had been picked up within hours of our being shot down and they had been held in the apartment for more than a week. The keeper of the 'safe house' was Madame Marechal who was supposed to be living alone. She kept us to a strict timetable and we obeyed her every instruction. Nothing should be done to give any impression that there were others in the apartment. We moved about very quietly and only when it was necessary. We never went near the windows, eating in the kitchen and were forbidden to flush the lavatory more than once a day to avoid any suspicion of overuse. We took it in turns to sleep two to a bedroom, the other two sleeping on mattresses in the attic.

There were regular visitors who were only admitted when we evaders were out of sight and one of these was Andrée de Jongh. As I was the only one with any knowledge of French, I was regarded as an unofficial leader of sorts, and it was to me that she spoke. She said that she was known by the code word 'Dédée', and that was how she preferred to be addressed. It was clear that she was in a prominent position in the escape organization by the way she made decisions and controlled the conversation. She admitted that the *reseaux* were a little concerned over the identity of our Slavic-looking colleague, a Pole. Would I just check his story and background to see how it matched that which he had given to the organization? She was also a little curious over Dal Mounts, the American, who was the first of that nationality they had found.

I took an instant liking to Teddy Frankowski, the Pole, he was by far the most experienced of us, having served in the Polish Air Force as a fighter pilot during the German invasion of Poland. He had been shot down and had somehow managed to get to Odessa where he had smuggled aboard a French ship going to Marseilles. He had joined the French Air Force and flown Potez light bombers until his squadron was wiped out. Again on the run, he got to Bordeaux where he was taken aboard a Royal Navy ship and brought to England. He then joined the RAF as a bomber pilot in the rank of Flight Sergeant and had been serving in No. 301 (Polish) Squadron which was in No.1 Group the same as No. 150 Sqn.

I told Dédée that Frankowski had been shot down during a raid on Wilhelmshaven, the same that I had taken part in as my first sortie to Germany. He had been wounded in the back by a fragment of shrapnel and I confirmed that I had been shown the appalling ragged scar on his back. How he had initially survived without any medical attention, other than his own First Aid, I had no idea. He had been determined to get out of Germany and had stolen a bicycle, clothes and food, and had got as far as the Dutch frontier before managing to get help. The shrapnel had been dug out of the festering wound and he had been stitched up by a doctor. He had carried on, still on his own, across the Netherlands until, somewhere in Flanders, he had been found by an escape cell and eventually taken in charge by *Comète*. Most modestly, he had confided in me that the exiled Polish Government in London had decorated him with the Virtuti Militari, and the British with the Distinguished Flying Medal.

Both Frost and Mounts had been quickly found by *Comète*. Bob had guessed I was alive because he had been asked to think of personal questions about me, those only I could answer. He remembered I had told him about my great-grandfather during a short stay with the Frost family in London. He also knew about my inexperience with the cricket bat, something that had come out when we had been discussing the benefits of a grammar school education. *Comète* knew one of the crew had been taken prisoner, the day after we had been shot down, but they had no news of the other two.

CHAPTER NINE

We stayed just three days in this safe house and were briefed during the last evening to be ready to move the next morning. Dédée was to be our guide and we were to be taken to Paris. Although I was designated the leader, we walked to the railway station in two groups, each following her at a safe distance; I was with Frankowski and Bob Frost with Dal Mounts following us. She presented us with railway tickets at the station and told us that there would be a three-hour delay at Lille where we had to change trains. The only possible complication she could foresee was the unavoidable Customs check at Bassieux on the border with France. She was confident that all would be well but, in the event of trouble, we would be left on our own. Not to worry; *Comète* was an expert network which would find us again if we made our way back into Belgium. In any event, she didn't expect to speak to us again until we arrived in Lille.

Dédée was joined by another good-looking woman just before we boarded the train which was packed. Somehow the four of us managed to keep together in the same carriage as Dédée and her friend. They were able to find room to sit thanks to the courtesy of two German soldiers. We had no alternative but to stand jammed together in the corridor surrounded by all manner of people, many of them German sailors with sea-bags and personal kit. It proved to be a most uncomfortable journey, speaking not a word to each other in the hubbub. Thankfully, the noise level fell considerably when the sailors left us at one of the many stops, and we at last had some elbow room.

There was warning of the approaching frontier check when a conductor forced his way along the corridor repeating loudly in French that we were approaching Bassieux. The train stopped a full length short of the only platform in the little station, making it necessary for passengers to climb down from the carriages onto the gravel border of the track. This was a noisy and confused process, with French police and German soldiers shepherding everyone into a long three-abreast column that stretched the length of the train and headed towards a row of desks where French Customs officials awaited us, with German soldiers standing behind them.

Dédée and her friend were a little ahead of us. Fortuitously, Frankowski and I had helped an old lady to get down from the train, and we had then attached ourselves to her; Frost and Mounts were right behind us. There were hundreds in the column but I could see that the officials way up ahead were dealing with people fairly quickly. As we moved along, the train steamed past us and pulled up at the platform inside the station. Just before it stopped, a commotion broke out ahead of us, near to the inspection tables. A man in a raincoat broke way from the column and ran headlong down the railway embankment and off towards a fringe of trees. There were shouts to stop, and a shot was fired. A French policeman and a German soldier made a half-hearted attempt to follow him but he was well away and disappeared into the trees.

Escorting the old lady forward, I could see Dédée and her friend having their handbags thoroughly inspected, most likely because they were the best-looking females on the train. I fussed and helped the old lady with her belongings, trying to give the impression that I was a relative. We passed inspection with only a cursory glance being given to our papers and it was the same with the other two behind us.

Having regained our places on the train, we had an altogether quiet and relaxed journey on to Lille. I chose to stay standing in the corridor with Bob Frost, even though there were now seats available. At Lille, we followed Dédée and her friend from the train, through the ticket barrier, and out into the station forecourt. There, Dédée's friend left her and, with a cheery wave, sauntered across to greet another group of three, dressed almost the same as we were. They were mirror images of ourselves, one even carrying an attaché case similar to mine and was wearing the same sort of Homburg. They were obviously another group of evaders on the move down the line. They recognized us, and I had to restrain myself from giving a knowing smile and the 'thumbs-up'.

Dédée confirmed that we had three hours to wait for the connection to Paris and that she had arranged for us to eat. She had chosen a restaurant in a narrow street just outside the station within easy walking distance. She told us that we would be left to eat alone in the place that was regularly used by *Comète* and gave me a generous amount of French francs with which to pay. I was to be in charge and we were to finish our luncheon and be ready in time for her to collect us, outside the restaurant, at precisely two o'clock. She left us at the entrance to the restaurant and I passed on the instructions to the others. For the first time we were on our own, and I began to feel some concern both for the group and for myself, not relishing responsibility that had been thrust upon me.

We entered a passageway and climbed the stairs to the restaurant on the first floor to be greeted at the door by a man, probably the manager, who seemed to be expecting us. He seated us at the far end of the room, conveniently close to a fire exit. I noticed that the wall clock was showing 12.45, giving us ample time to eat a leisurely meal. The restaurant was about half-filled and, not far from us, two German soldiers were already well into a meal.

I did the ordering: the others said not a word, just nodding their heads at my suggestions. I ordered a bottle of *vin ordinaire*. The meal was served at a steady pace and without any fuss. We were happily finished with about a quarter of an hour to go, each of us happy and relaxed.

As the coffee was being served, I noticed that Mounts was looking uncomfortable. He leant across to me and desperately whispered. 'I'm bursting for a pee. I can't hold out much longer. Can I go to the men's room?' It all seemed so natural that I quietly said, 'Of course. It's over there, next to the cashier's desk, just behind the curtains. Keep your mouth shut, for heaven's sake.' He was on his feet in a flash and hurried across the room and pushed through the curtains. There was a slamming of a door, followed by a piercing female shriek. The curtains were thrown back and I could see the lavatory Madame struggling with Mounts in the entrance to the ladies toilet. A hush had descended on the restaurant as attention was focused on the embarrassing scene. Luckily it was then that

Mounts did as he had been briefed: drawing back, screwing up his face, and trying to indicate that he didn't understand what was happening. He pointed to his ears and mouth to give the impression that he was deaf and dumb.

We had watched the performance in dismay. People were intrigued, many were laughing, including some German soldiers who had just arrived. We were ready to get up and leave the room by the fire exit, just behind us. I really didn't know what to do but, fortunately, Providence was on our side. I mustered up enough nerve to play my part, walking over I pushed myself past a couple of curious onlookers, and took Mounts by the arm. I quietly said to the woman, *'Mon ami est idiot.'* She nodded her head and babbled back at me in French too fast to understand. I put a franc on her plate and led Mounts into the gent's lavatory.

We were the focus of all eyes as I led the crestfallen American back to our table. There was still time to be wasted before our rendezvous with Dédée but I decided it would be safer to do so downstairs and outside. I asked for *l'addition* and we quietly got up and made our way across to the cashier. The others went ahead and I paid the bill but , just as I was about to leave, a hand fell on my shoulder and someone behind me whispered in English, 'You really must try to do better or you will never get back to England.' I didn't look around just making my way to the door and rejoining the others.

Dédée was waiting across the road when we got outside and was not amused as we tried to apologize. Shamefacedly, we followed her back to the station but she had regained some of her good humour by the time we boarded the train to Paris. This time we found seats together in a third class compartment, and endured a silent and uneventful journey which ended late in the afternoon at the Gare de L'Est. We followed Dédée down into the Metro where she bought us each a book of tickets and explained quietly how they should be used. We travelled quite a distance and then came up to find ourselves in the Oudinot district. We were taken to an apartment house, then upstairs in a lift to a suite of rooms. This was to be our 'safe house' in Paris.

It was there that we met Dédée's father, Frederic de Jongh. He was a headmaster who helped and supported his daughter's efforts and who, from this hideout, arranged the final stages of an evader's journey across

France to the Pyrenees; Paris had become a holding point for *Comète*. There were scores of evaders waiting to move on but they had to wait until guides were available to take them on the long train journey to St Jean de Luz. The right sort of guide was absolutely necessary and was in great demand. The number of evaders in a group was limited to four which meant a fairly slow process overall. Each guide had to make the journey to the mountains and, sometimes, even over into Spain, then return to Paris for another group, and so on.

It was explained to us that we might have to spend a while in Paris. This news was received with mixed feelings by our group but, as it turned out, the delay proved interesting, informative, and even enjoyable. Not confined to our 'safe house', we were actually encouraged to spend the whole day outside and saw the sights of the French capital, in the company of a guide at first, and then on our own. We ate our main meals in the apartment, but otherwise either took sandwiches or bought snacks as we toured around, visiting Notre Dame, Montmartre, the Tuileries, the Bois de Boulogne, and even the Gestapo Headquarters in the Avenue Foch. A truly surreal experience: mingling with the French population and the hundreds of Germans who were sightseeing just as we were.

We tended to get careless and off our guard. I clearly remember an occasion on the Metro when we were returning home to our 'safe house'. I was standing in an overcrowded carriage with Bob Frost, jammed face to face against a German *Leutnant*. The brakes were suddenly applied and the whole mass of humanity shot forward, crammed together Bob involuntarily said 'Sorry' as he was thrust against the German. I could see the instant surprise appear on the German's face and I was sure that he thought we were British. He was carrying a brief case and had a pistol in a holster at his waist, but there was such a crush against him that he could not move his arms and, in any case, he was the only German in the compartment. When the train stopped at the next station, Bob and I fought our way to the exit and got off. As we passed through the door I looked back to see the German still staring incredulously at us.

Another time, we watched the performance of a company of German troops being photographed in front of Napoleon's Tomb. It took them some time to get organized and, when they were arranged in three long rows: sitting on the ground, sitting on chairs, and standing, Bob Frost paraded in front of them, gathered their attention, and then gave them the 'V' for Victory sign in a most derogatory manner.

We also made the mistake of going to the cinema: having settled ourselves in seats near the exits we were set to see a film featuring Jean Gabin about soldiers in the Great War. First, however, there were newsreels and one dealt with the despatch of a French SS unit to the Russian Front. The audience didn't like it and made their feelings all too clear with hoots and whistles. The Germans there naturally reacted and the place dissolved into uproar. We removed ourselves, just in time as the French police arrived.

By then we were all too aware of the dangers of our carelessness and ridiculous bravado, becoming more circumspect and beginning to long for the next move down the Line. Frederic de Jongh was a very busy man and for obvious reasons told us nothing about what was to being planned. We tried to get him to be forthcoming but to no avail, I remember his answer when we asked why he risked his life for us: 'We are soldiers just as you are. This is, for the moment, the only way we can fight. You flyers in the RAF are the way we shall beat the Germans. We want to get you back to England so that you can get another aeroplane, fill it with bombs, and continue with the destruction of the Boche.'

Then, at last, we were warned to get ready to move. One afternoon, just after we had returned from a walk around the neighbourhood, we were briefed on the final stage of our journey on to the Pyrenees. Dédée would be our guide most of the way to Biarritz where we would be handed over. This time we would be travelling overnight by train in first-class comfort. Unfortunately, there were no wagon-lits or couchettes, but we would be able to sleep easily in seats that had been booked for us. Dédée would be in the same carriage, a few compartments from us, keeping an eye on Teddy Frankowski who could not be booked into our compartment. All we had to do was to take our seats, behave as though we were seasoned travellers, settle down, and try to sleep. The train would arrive at Biarritz at about eight o'clock in the morning, when we should be ready to leave it at once.

We stayed in the apartment until early evening, double-checking our documents and practising our responses to what French officials might have to say. We were given our railway tickets to St Jean de Luz, via Biarritz, and I noticed that mine had cost 597 francs. At about nine-thirty we said goodbye to Frederic de Jongh, thanking him as best we could, and travelled by Metro direct to the Gare Austerlitz. The Biarritz train was shunted into its departure platform just before half-past ten and, at a nod from Dédée, we took our places in an empty compartment in carriage 'H'. We had reservations that sat us in a row, with our backs to the engine; Bob Frost at the window, myself nearest the door, and Dal Mounts in-between, facing three seats that were also reserved.

The first to be taken was that facing Frost. A young Frenchman bustled in and hoisted a large expensive looking case onto the luggage rack. He addressed us in a friendly way and directed some words at Bob who, understanding nothing, just nodded and smiled. He tried to give the impression of being engrossed in his copy of the 'Paris Soir'. The Frenchman mumbled something, then switched on the reading light above his head and produced a heavy book. I was astonished to see that it was an English version of George Bernard Shaw's, 'Man and Superman'.

A few minutes later, we were shocked by the arrival of the other two reservations: German officers. They entered quietly, not the least bit officiously, offering polite greetings around the compartment. They took off their top-coats and placed them together with their luggage on the racks then sat facing us. The one opposite me fixed me with a smile on his face and I was terrified that he was about to start a conversation. Dédée had briefed me that as I was supposedly Flemish, my school-boy French might be good enough to fool a German, but I certainly did not want to take the risk. The Germans started muttering between themselves and glancing at the young Frenchman, reading his English book. That was our salvation because they must have asked him why, and, when he replied in German, they opened a friendly and lengthy conversation with him. Long before it was finished, all three of us had switched off our reading lights and were giving the impression that we had gone to sleep, our faces hidden under copies of the 'Paris Soir'.

The train left dead on time at a quarter-of-an-hour before midnight. I feigned sleep under my newspaper all the way to Tours where, thankfully, the two German officers got off the train, then the Frenchman left at Orleans. By then we were able to settle down and sleep which we did until Dédée came along to our compartment to tell us that we were about to arrive in Biarritz. It was a gorgeous morning, warm with blue skies and not a cloud to be seen. We stayed in a group on the platform while Dédée went to the entrance to meet a very good-looking young girl. She brought her back to us and introduced Nadine, who must have been a schoolgirl, saying that she would take us on to St Jean de Luz.

We travelled along the coast in a two-carriage train that stopped at every station and halt. It must have been market day in St Jean when we arrived because the place was thronged with sun-tanned country folk who were buying and selling vegetables, fruit and fish. We followed Nadine around the harbour to a whitewashed house in the Rue Gambetta. That was to be our 'safe house' while we waited our turn to cross the mountains into Spain.

We spent three pleasant days at St Jean de Luz, being allowed out of our hiding place only when we had changed into the local garb of blue denims, rope sandals, and black beret. The weather was surprisingly warm and we were encouraged to spend time in the open in the hope of picking up a tan to make our disguises a little more realistic. We spent much time on the beach and, one afternoon, we were amazed to see the very same group of evaders with whom we had exchanged glances in the railway station at Lille. They were dressed just as we were and it was obvious that they knew who we were. The temptation to speak with them was almost unbearable but, as the person in charge of our group, I thought it best and certainly most prudent to get up and move elsewhere.

It seemed strange that there was no sign of any Germans in the town. The only uniformed personnel we saw were French police whom we were told were as dangerous as the Gestapo, known to be operating all over the area, doing their best to put a stop to the traffic of British aircrew into Spain. At last it was our turn to move on and we were briefed in hard-to-understand English by the owner of the 'safe house'. We gathered that we would leave St Jean by bicycle, under control of a Basque guide. He would take us to where we would meet those who would guide us into Spain. Packing our lounge suits, shoes, shirts and ties in canvas bags that could easily be carried over the shoulder we said farewell to our hostess and cycled away in two groups, around the harbour and out of the town, taking the road to the south.

There was very little traffic and we made good progress. It was now quite warm and we began to sweat, thanking providence for the welcome change of clothes. The ride itself was a pleasure: to our right were the foothills of the Pyrenees, beyond which could be seen the peaks along the frontier with Spain. The road wound for a while alongside a slow-moving river fringed with trees and brush. We eventually turned away from it and left the main road, taking a much smaller one leading up into the hills. It was badly maintained and we often had to dismount and walk. It was a relief when, at last, we stopped near a scattering of poor dwellings and our guide provided us with a drink of rough red wine and a meal of bread and soft cheese.

We rested there for a while and then set off, even slower this time, as we climbed forever uphill, pushing our bicycles. The weather stayed fair with glorious blue skies and a refreshing light wind blowing in from the sea. Our guide was in no hurry, and we were able to take in everything around us, enjoying the sights of the unfamiliar countryside, all in good spirits.

Eventually we came to the end of the road which petered out into a dusty track leading us ever upwards towards the mountains. We made frequent stops and late in the afternoon our guide produced yet more red wine and another snack of bread and cheese. The countryside around us was open and deserted, with no sign of livestock or people. Ahead of us were thickly wooded areas, stretching up to the very tops of the hills, excellent evasion country we agreed. We pressed on slowly and, in the early evening, arrived at a tumble-down farm on the very edge of the tree line and were led to a group of derelict buildings and showed where to leave our bicycles in a roofless outhouse.

We waited patiently as it began to get dark until, without any warning of their approach, we were joined by Dédée and a tough, strong-looking character with a deeply-lined sun-burnt face. It was the legendary Florentino, a Basque smuggler who was now using his skills to lead airmen into Spain. He was suitably dressed in shepherd's clothes, a light sheepskin jacket over greasy denim overalls, rope sandals on his feet, and a wine-sack over his shoulder. Dédée immediately took charge, explaining that she would be with us all the way to a safe house in Spain, because it was vital that we were to be handed over to the right people. Florentino was an expert and he would make sure that we avoided trouble, he had made hundreds of crossings and we were to follow his directions without question. The only real dangers were in the *Zone Interdite*, an area running two kilometres wide all along both sides of the frontier. The French, Spanish, and Germans patrolled this region, shooting on sight, not stopping to ask questions. To be absolutely safe from the Germans we had to get well into Spain where the worst that could happen to us then, if we were captured, would be a rather long holiday in a Spanish concentration camp. If we were caught by the French or the Spaniards during the actual crossing, we would be handed over to the Germans.

She then briefed us on the actual crossing, there would be an hour or so of walking to reach the *Zone Interdite*. The actual frontier was along the River Bidassoa and all the best-known fords were guarded by Spanish police but Florentino, we were told, would find the best for us to use to cross; the river was reasonably low and the actual crossing would not be difficult.

In answer to a question about what we should do if things went wrong, Dédée told us that we should do our best to get well into Spain. She would not tell us where to head for but did warn that before we attempted any contact we should make sure that we were at least twenty kilometres into Spain.

Florentino then checked each one of us to make sure that our slung loads were tight, our rope sandals well-strapped, and our berets well down over our brows. He offered each of us a squirt of red wine from his wine-sack, a messy business as it proved, for none of us could accurately manage the stream of wine into our mouths, but it at least lessened the tension that was mounting. As far as I was concerned, I was as keyed-up as I had formerly been when about to take off on a bombing sortie.

We left the farm and set off at a cracking pace. The weather could not have been better; the visibility was good, the sky was clear and full of stars; Polaris and the Great Bear standing out above us. Our sandals were proving comfortable and the duffel bags did not hinder free movement of arms or legs. Florentino was in the lead with Dédée close behind him, I followed next, then Frost, Mounts and Frankowski. We were soon inside the tree belt and finding it a little harder to see ahead and to keep in touch with each other.

Our first emergency stop was made without a hitch, Florentino had turned and silently raised his hand. Without a sound, the signal was passed along the group and we crouched motionless, hearing sheep bells and the noise of a flock being moved across the path ahead. There were other stops and starts during the first hour as we climbed higher and higher until we were well amongst the trees and shrubs. Just before midnight we stopped to rest, or so I thought. Florentino, however, had gone on ahead and after about twenty minutes came back with news for Dédée. She in turn told us that we were about to enter the *Zone Interdite*.

Moving along narrow paths shrouded by pines and undergrowth we began to walk a little quicker as the way began to go downhill. Then there was an emergency stop, Dédée passed the word that there was a patrol, possibly German, somewhere ahead. We were signalled to get down, ahead of us we heard voices coming our way. Florentino quickly turned our group around and led us back along the path and then off into the scrub where we slowly and quietly picked our way through the undergrowth, continually changing direction, until we rejoined our original path, leaving the noisy patrol behind us. We carried on without further incident down a steep descent until Florentino stopped us at the bank of the Bidassoa.

He went off to reconnoitre, first left upstream along the river bank, returning as silently as a cat and then downstream to the right. We waited, clustered in the riverside willows at the water's edge awaiting his return. When he came back, he had a few words with Dédée and then led us upstream to a place where she told us to get ready to cross. We were at a reasonable ford, a little narrow in places, but one that had been used many times before. Suddenly there was a flash of light to our right, someone had switched on the lights in a building that we could now see in outline about fifty yards from us and on the far bank. Dédée whispered that this was one of the Spanish police guardhouses.

We got ready to cross, placing our bags high on our shoulders and taking the precaution of roping ourselves in line, the loose end at the front being taken up by Dédée. We waited with our eyes glued on the guard-house whilst two figures walked up to it and went inside. A minute or so later, we heard a gramophone playing and people laughing. It was then that Florentino gave the signal for us to begin the crossing, signalling us to get into the cold river and line ourselves up along the river bank under the overhanging willows, waist-deep in the water. Moving into the river with Dédée leading and Florentino close behind, we never once felt the water get above our waists although the ford was obliquely set and leading us towards the blockhouse.

Luckily, there was something of a party developing in the blockhouse and we could hear the voices and laughter of several people, some of them clearly female. Their noise covered the sound of our slow, stumbling passage. Getting to the far side not far from the blockhouse, we slipped quietly out of the river, crawled through the grass at the water's edge, and got up onto the river road. The connecting rope had been undone and we prepared to cross the road, which we did in turns. I was followed by Bob Frost who caused great panic when he disappeared from sight into an excavation by the side of the road from which he could not escape without help. We had to reach down into the hole and feel for him, then pull him out, all within easy sight of the blockhouse. Fortunately, he was uninjured and we soon got clear of the road and made our way into the cover of the woods on the hillside

It was one o'clock in the morning when we began to walk due west with Florentino and Dédée in the lead, moving at a cracking pace. Behind them were the four of us, supposedly fit aircrew, trying their best to keep up but not doing very well. Lagging behind we came into open country just before daybreak, still hurrying westwards along defined tracks. The gap between Florentino, Dédée and us had grown and Florentino was getting furious with us and twice sent Dédée back to urge us to do better. We did our best, but it was by no means good enough and Dédée decided what had to be done with us when we wearily caught up with them on the edge of a well-used road. She first gave vent to her feelings, saying that our tardiness was putting the whole evasion at risk. We were by no means out of trouble not being not far enough into Spain to escape being handed over to the Germans in the event of being captured. We were full of apologies but knew that we could not do any better. She had words with Florentino who left us without even a gesture or a word, heading back the way we had come. Dédée then led us along the road until she reached a place in the roadside ditch in which she ordered us to hide. She covered us with brushwood and pieces of shrub and told us to stay there, ensuring first that someone was always on guard. She then strode away up the road, leaving us in shame.

I was the one on guard at about mid-day, finding it increasingly more difficult to stay awake whilst the others were sleeping. The sun was high overhead and it had become quite warm and I was actually dozing when I heard a car approaching. Pushing the twigs and branches aside and peering out I was surprised to see a Renault taxi coming slowly up the road with Dédée leaning out of the window, looking for our hiding place. As it went past, she saw me crawling from the ditch and reversed, pulling up alongside us. Sheepishly, we aroused ourselves and piled in.

We were taken to a 'safe house' in San Sebastian, a pension near the harbour. From then on we were in the hands of the British Consul. Dédée said goodbye to us and told us that she had to be across the mountains and back into France that night, she had another bunch of evaders to bring across. The Consul told us that, although we were safe from the Germans, it was imperative that we remained hidden until arrangements could be made for us to leave Spain legally. In anticipation of this, we dressed ourselves again in our lounge suits and happily put on shirts and wore ties again.

That evening we had a meal with the Consul at his house and the next morning we were taken by car to Burgos where we lodged with a British family. Two days later we were driven to Madrid, hidden in a closed-up Bentley. I still felt the oppressive excitement of being hunted, heightened, no doubt, by the evidence we saw of the Fascist victory in the Spanish Civil War. We motored past scenes of fighting and destruction, and twice saw what must have been prison camps, one of which had been built into the face of a mountain.

Our 'safe house' in Madrid was none other than the palatial British Embassy. There we met the Ambassador, Sir Samuel Hoare, and soon realized that we were just four in a long procession of returned aircrew who had to be 'processed' by him. We bathed luxuriously in the old Roman baths under the Embassy building and saw scores of names of those who had been there before us, scratched into the stone pillars and walls. Sir Samuel told us that we would not be kept long in Madrid; it would only be a matter of days before arrangements would be made with the Spanish authorities for us to leave the country at Gibraltar. He told us that the Spanish upheld the Geneva Convention which meant that we had to be treated as escaped prisoners of war, and not as evaders. The former could, by law, be returned from a neutral country quickly but evaders were considered as unmilitary persons who could be held for as long as it took properly to establish their identity and status. In the case of Spain that meant incarceration in a concentration camp for anything up to six months or more. Sir Samuel had devised a scheme to avoid the wastage by detention of the much-needed aircrew. A list of supposed escapers from Germany had been concocted of those who had made their way to the sanctuary of the British Embassy. I was given the false identity of a Second Lieutenant John Hoskins of the Northamptonshire Regiment who had supposedly escaped from Fallingbostel.

We left Madrid quite openly in a plush Embassy Bentley with our escort, a junior Secretary. We motored to Seville where we spent a night during which I believe there was discussion as to whether we might finish our journey by sailing down the Guadalamara to Gibraltar in one of the small steamers that plied between Seville and Algeciras. Fortunately, that was not to be and, after a splendid breakfast the next morning, we carried on by road. We stopped at the Williams and Humbert distillery at Jerez de la Frontera to be given a guided tour and a glass of sherry from a special keg from which we were told King Edward VII had tasted the excellent wine. We arrived in Algeciras late in the afternoon of 31st October, 1942, and I touched British soil again at the guardroom on the causeway leading into Gibraltar. Unbelievably, the corporal of the guard was none other than Eric Shuttleworth of the Devons with whom I had been educated at the Church School in Exmouth.

It was hard to realize that I had been on the run for no more than fifty-five days. It had seemed like an age to me, spent in an entirely different world; a fascinating, absorbing experience that had placed very few demands on me. The fact that I was there in Gibraltar, in one piece and a free man, was due solely to the efforts of some remarkable people. They had put their lives at risk for me while operating a most wonderful rescue organization. How could I ever thank them enough?

I gave all the information I had to a Major of the Intelligence Corps, the MI9 representative in Gibraltar. He arranged for us to be kitted out in tropical dress: khaki shorts, shirts, stockings, and shoes. I was able to send a telegram to my mother to say that I was safe and to wish her a happy 46th birthday. I was grouped with quite a number of evaders, including

those we had seen at Lille and at St Jean de Luz. There was only one officer amongst them, a Flight Lieutenant Pipkin, the rest of us were all sergeants.

*Gibraltar - almost home, back row left. Next to me is Bob Frost
my rear gunner. Front row Teddy Frankowski and Dal Mounts*

I was interrogated again on the second day. The Major was surprised
at how little I remembered of names and places, probably putting it down
to ignorance on my part rather than, as I told him, my deliberate intention
to commit as little information as possible to memory in case I had been
picked up and interrogated by the Gestapo. He checked my story against
those of Frost and Mounts and seemed to dwell on the assumption that I
was holding something back. I began to find him overbearing and incon-
siderate.

I went in to see him again the next day, this time to ask when we could
hope to return to our squadron. He abruptly told me that I would be
informed in due course and dismissed me; I hated the waiting. The only
distraction we enjoyed was the nightly attempts of the Italian Air Force to
drop bombs on the Rock. We watched them as they unloaded their cargo

into the sea, not once did they drop a bomb on Gibraltar while we were there. I returned again on the fourth day to ask if any progress had been made with our transportation home. This time I was soundly berated as a bloody nuisance and told that, when he was ready, he would tell me all that I needed to know. He added that perhaps I was scared of the Italian bombing. I had the greatest difficulty in not telling him just how out of touch he was with the world outside, with Bomber Command and, for that matter, with the Royal Air Force.

The unsatisfactory situation was resolved the next night when the four of us were told to get ready to leave. We were taken to the aerodrome where, to our great surprise, we were put aboard an American C47 Dakota. Dal Mounts told us he already knew the pilot with whom he had been swapping experiences during the past two days; they were both Californians. To this day, I do not know who arranged our flight home, whether it was MI9 or, more likely, Dal Mounts.

It was a long, devious and uncomfortable flight back to England. The flight plan involved us staying well away from the French coast and beyond the range of the predatory Junkers 88 night-fighters that had already downed many aircraft over the Bay of Biscay. We sat in the dark on bucket seats amidst a full load of goods and equipment for eight hours and twenty minutes, until we landed in Cornwall, at Portreath, early on a cold, clear morning, still wearing our tropical kit.

CHAPTER TEN

No surprise was shown at our arrival. We met the Station Commander who congratulated us and then set in motion our reintroduction to the RAF. His attempted contact with No 150 Squadron at Snaith revealed the surprising news that it no longer existed; it had been disbanded and was in the process of being reformed somewhere overseas. As there was no way of returning to my unit, I was told not to worry but to enjoy some leave of absence. I handed in my khaki drill and was fitted out with a new serge uniform, wings and stripes. I was given much of my back pay and a railway warrant to Exmouth and told to say at home until I received new orders. I said goodbye to Bob Frost, Dal Mounts, and Teddy Frankowski, and set off on the relatively short train journey to East Devon.

I got to Exmouth late in the afternoon and decided to walk from the town to a new house that my mother had rented way up on the edge of Woodbury Common. Most things were still a bit unreal to me, a feeling that stayed with me throughout the four mile-long stroll. Happily, I met my sister Zon in the lane just a few hundred yards from the house. Then I had the joy of greeting my mother who was inside preparing the evening meal.

The feeling of unreality stayed with me for some time. My mother did everything to make me feel at home; she had never once doubted that I was alive and well. On the night I was shot down, almost at the precise moment I had taken to my parachute, her step-brother had experienced a startling nightmare. It was so vivid and particular to me that he cycled at once from Colaton Raleigh to Exmouth to tell my mother that something dreadful had happened to me, but that I was all right. As he was explaining details of his dream, the postman arrived with the telegram from the Air Ministry stating that I was missing in action. She had also received a German Prisoner-of-War postcard from Norman Graham, my wireless-operator, which tersely said that he was well in Stalag VIIIb and asking where I was?

In the time I had been away, my father had been swept up in the preparations for Operation 'Torch', the landings in North Africa and my brother Peter had joined the Royal Navy and was under training and my younger sister had graduated as a State Registered Nurse and was on duty in Exeter. I stayed at home for just three days doing nothing more than roaming around the nearby countryside, wondering at just how lucky I had been.

I was chopping logs in the backyard when I was puzzled to see a red-capped Army policeman walking up the drive towards the house. I went to meet him, he asked if I was Sergeant Randle and explained that he had been ordered to take me to London, to the War Office and that I had to go with him at once. I tried to reassure my mother that I had not committed some heinous crime, whereupon she upbraided the policeman in the roundest terms. While I was changing into uniform, he did say that perhaps my arrest was something to do with entering the country illegally.

I travelled up to London with him by train but he was not particularly good company, although we were of the same rank. I told him I had not a clue about why my leave had been so abruptly ended. All that I had done was to manage to get back to England after being shot down whilst dropping bombs on Germany. He had little sense of humour and left me alone to read.

At the War Office I was interviewed first by an MI9 officer and then by a clerk. I could add nothing more to that which I had divulged to the MI9 major in Gibraltar. I was then admonished for not obeying instructions: apparently, there had been some confusion over how I and the others had left Gibraltar. I asked if there was any news of Brazill and Dreschler but there was none. They knew that my mother had received a POW postcard from my wireless-operator and opined that it was most likely Graham had been encouraged to send it as the Germans would be looking for the rest of the crew. I was again warned to say nothing about my evasion and, in any case, I was bound by some sort of Secrets Act. Nor could I commit a word to paper or make any contact with anyone remotely connected with my escapade.

I was relieved to be sent next to the Air Ministry, there they set about my re-establishment in the Service. I was pleased to know that while I had been away I had been promoted to Flight Sergeant. They gave me my back pay together with the extra five shillings a day that went with the promotion. In answer to my question about what had happened to my belongings at Snaith, in particular, my diary, I was told that my father had visited the station the morning after I had been shot down to find that most of what I owned had disappeared. An immediate search was made and most of it, including the diary, had been recovered from a corporal's lodgings just outside the camp. This led to the arrest of two corporal policemen who had been operating the Snaith 'Ghoul Squad', stealing the belongings of dead and missing personnel before a Committee of Adjustment could take control. I was delighted to learn that both of these wretched criminals were serving two years' hard labour.

I returned to the Air Ministry two days later to be presented with most of my personal belongings, together with the diary. My log book had been made up and closed with the details of my last operation noted. There was also an endorsement signed by the Squadron Commander to the effect that I was an Above-the-Average medium bomber pilot. My nineteen operational sorties were accounted as completion of a first tour which meant that I would be sent to a bomber OTU as a screened pilot for at least the next six months.

I met Dal Mounts while I was at the Air Ministry, he had been dealt with at Canada House where he had exercised his rights as an American and resigned from the RCAF. He said that his one trip with me was more than enough excitement for a lifetime. He had joined the United States Navy and was on his way back to the America.

I also learned what had happened to Bob Frost. He too had been visited by a policeman at his home in East London and taken to RAF Uxbridge. On his first morning there, he had been ordered out on parade before breakfast together with a bunch of senior NCOs who were fiercely drilled by the Station Warrant Officer. He stood the treatment for just a minute or two and then, in sheer disgust, walked off the parade ground, despite the shouts of the furious SWO. He went straight to the Adjutant, forced his way into the office, and demanded to know what on earth was going on. The Adjutant was astounded to learn that Bob had just returned to England after a successful evasion and then went out of his way to try to apologize. Apparently Bob was being drilled with a squad of NCO aircrew who had been thrown out of their squadrons for LMF (having Lack of Moral Fibre). They were awaiting demotion and punishment at Uxbridge, the place where malcontents were sent.

I continued my leave of absence in Exmouth where my posting came through to go to No 23 OTU at Pershore in Worcestershire. I arrived there on 14th December, 1942, and was quickly put through a short refresher course on the Wellington Mark 3. I had no difficulties at all and easily took to flying the aircraft from the collapsible right-hand seat. While there, I was wonderfully pleased to greet my erstwhile navigator, Jock Brazill, just returned from Gibraltar. He was also now a Flight Sergeant and likewise had been posted to the instructional staff at Pershore. He had not been as lucky as I had been, injuring his leg during the parachute descent. Despite this, he had walked to Namur where he too had been 'collected' by the *Comète Line* and passed down the same route that I had travelled. He had lingered a little longer in Spain than me, having first been taken to Madrid and from there to Seville where he finished his evasion in a cargo boat sailing to Gibraltar. I told him that I knew Norman Graham was a prisoner, but that I had no idea of the whereabouts of Wally Dreschler; nor did he.

I stayed at Pershore until 11th January, 1943, when I was sent to the No 23 OTU satellite station at Atherstone, just outside Stratford-on-Avon. There I joined a hard-working group of pilots engaged mainly in training Canadians. Most of the pilot instructors were New Zealanders, my commanding officer was Wing Commander 'Chips' Mansfield and my flight commander was Flight Lieutenant Pat Brecon. I was the only non-commissioned screened pilot on the station.

A few weeks later, I was informed that I had been awarded the Distinguished Flying Medal, reading the citation in a copy of the 'Aeroplane' magazine. It referred to my having taken part 'in many operational sorties' and finished with the usual 'having displayed courage and fortitude'. I simply could not understand why I had received the honour after only 19 trips and having achieved little of merit. I honestly counted myself as being just one of the lucky ones in the draw.

Myself and brother Peter immediately after my visit to Buckingham Palace to receive the DFM

I went to Buckingham Palace to receive the medal in March 1943, accompanied by my mother and her sister, the relative with whom I had lodged at Tulse Hill in London. What I remember most of this unnerving event was my brief conversation with King George. I had taken my place in the long line of those about to be decorated with the DFM, and was shuffling along awaiting my turn, not knowing that I must have been one of those numbered-off to be spoken to by the Monarch. I noticed that those ahead of me stopped abreast of him, executed a smart left turn so they were face to face, bowed and stepped forward to have the medal hooked on. Then there was a handshake, one pace to the rear, right turn and march away.

I was extremely nervous when my turn came. I made my turn to face the King, bowed and stepped forward, expecting nothing more than the medal to be affixed. Instead, His Majesty looked at me and, after a second or so, asked me in a hesitant voice how many operations I had completed.

My flustered reply was, 'Only nineteen, Sir.' The words must have puzzled him, probably because he expected a number of thirty or more. He looked at me with a puzzled frown on his face, standing there with the medal held in his hand. I had the dreadful feeling that he was about to change his mind. Then he moved forward and, with a smile, said, 'Well done,' pinned it on my chest, and shook my hand.

I liked being an instructor, it was a decided step up in the world and every day there was something new to learn. On 5th February, I was detached to take an instructor's course at No 3 Flying Instructor's School, a Central Flying School satellite, at Babdown Farm in Gloucestershire. There I got down to learning the fundamentals of the art, flying Airspeed 'Oxfords'. After the Wellington, the Oxford was something of a 'kiddy-car' but it served as an ideal training platform. We dealt solely with the theory and techniques of instructing, flying every day throughout a 35 day-long course, and I returned to Stratford early in March with a Flying Instructor Average assessment.

Not long after my return, and to my complete surprise, I was asked by Wing Commander Mansfield why had I never applied for a commission. I was completely baffled, I did not know that commissions had to be applied for, and the thought of promotion of any sort had never seriously entered my head. 'You stick out like a sore thumb here, Randle,' he said. 'You are the only NCO pilot we have. Unless you are going to trot out some dreadful reason why you don't want to become an officer, I intend to make an application for you at once.'

I certainly had no argument, I remembered that I had been recommended for a commission after my interviews at the Recruiting Centre, but there was my disastrous interview with Squadron Leader Kermode back at No 3 BFTS. It was then that I had given up all thoughts of grandeur, just making it a business of trying to do my best, and staying alive.

My application was made there and then, and dealt with swiftly. I was interviewed by Air Vice-Marshal 'Dolly' Gray, my Group Commander, and was commissioned as a Pilot Officer in the Royal Air Force Volunteer Reserve on 23rd March, 1943. Happily, 'Chips' Mansfield did not allow this elevation to lead to the usual posting on commissioning. 'It's not going to make one iota of difference to you, losing your stripes,' he told me, 'Just get on with doing your job.' He also had something to say about my past which had been revealed to him in the commissioning process. Apparently, when I was at Chipping Warden, where I had refused to take part in the third 1,000 bomber raid on Bremen that led to my distressing few days under open arrest, my records had been scored across with the terse missive: 'This NCO should never be considered for commissioning.'

I found the switch to commissioned rank remarkably easy. I kept the same room I had occupied as a Flight Sergeant, but now enjoyed the services of a bat-woman. I preferred the ambience of the Officers' Mess but, best of all, I now felt an integral part of the instructing staff. With promotion came the responsibility of managing the Airmanship Section where the emergency drills of parachuting, crash landing, and ditching were done. I was also given the task of organizing the station's sporting fixtures, including the soccer arrangements, the Wednesday afternoon physical activities, and, strangely enough for a bunch of pleasure-seeking characters, compulsory walks and marches around Atherstone.

Our flying duties were paramount: the Canadian students were generally a fine bunch and good learners. They took easily to the Wellington, studied hard, and always wanted to be away from Stratford as soon as possible and on to the Heavy Conversion Units where, as they said, they could fly real aeroplanes. We did our best to hurry them along in aircraft whose standard had dramatically improved. No longer were the OTUs receiving the cast-offs from the operational squadrons. Most of our Wellingtons were coming straight from the shadow factories and bits and pieces no longer fell off, but there was still a serious fault to be dealt with. When heavily laden, the Wellington could burst a tyre on take-off, usually with most expensive and sometimes fatal results. Every possible precaution was taken to stop this happening; tyre-creep was measured on every sortie by checking the white markings on the tyre and the wheel-rim and the inspection of tyres for cuts and undue wear became a vital action before each flight. Lastly, the runways were swept clear of gravel and sharp particles every day. Nonetheless, I added two more badly damaged Wellingtons to my score of machines bent or destroyed, both incurring tyre bursts during the take-off run. With each incident, the undercarriage collapsed, fuel tanks ruptured, and fire was started. Our crash landing drills were so well done that, in both cases, everyone on board was out of the aircraft quickly, and well away from danger, long before the fire-engine appeared on the scene.

The accident rate was markedly down on that which had formerly applied at Chipping Warden where I had converted. Generally, if there was trouble, it was as a result of 'finger-trouble' on the part of the trainee pilot. Our instruction was good and thorough, flying orders were specific. Yet I had an NCO student who flew extremely well, maybe a little over-confidently but I had him practice single-engined flying, making two circuits of the airfield while I watched from the ground. He made the circuits perfectly, but when he came to unfeather, to my complete disbelief, he feathered the good engine by mistake. I watched him make a dramatic crash landing in a field just a mile or so from the airfield.

We flew in all kinds of weather and most every night. Our Drem-lit circuit almost interlocked with that of Wellesbourne Mountford to the east, and with Long Marston to the west. We used the Drem lighting for flying around the circuit whenever the visibility dropped low, usually just moving from one light to the next around the airfield. It was easy to get lost and to pick up the wrong Drem pattern. Quite frequently, we had our aircraft landing by mistake at Long Marston, the nearer of the two adjacent airfields.

Instruction was carried on at a very high tempo; often I would finish an exercise on a machine, then get out and send the pilot off solo, dash over to another aircraft ready with engines running, and deal with another student. One night, in incredibly bad weather, I made the switch to a second aircraft, strapped myself in, and told the student, a French Canadian, to carry on. He was on his first-ever session of night flying and taxied to the runway, lined-up, and I let him start the take-off. At about what I expected would be the unstick point, I saw to my horror that there was no airspeed registering on the ASI. The student panicked and froze on the controls and I had to struggle to take over the control column by which time we had left the ground; I actually had to hit him in the face to get his rigid arms away from the control column. I then took over and climbed away with no idea at all of what speed we were flying. I flew around the circuit in wretched visibility, just being able to see from one Drem light to another and having to guess my speed by reference to the altitude and engine settings. We landed safely and I taxied to dispersal where I got out to remove the pitot-head cover that my student had missed in his pre-flight checks.

For relaxation and entertainment we had the nearby town of Stratford-on-Avon at our disposal. The Shakespeare Memorial Theatre provided splendid productions and we were blessed with two good cinemas. The RAF had taken over the principal hostelry, the Swan or the 'Dirty Duck' as we called it. It became the centre of most of our nightly activities when we were not flying. It replaced the Officers' Mess and, under the leadership of two extroverted Flight Lieutenants, Johnny Gilbert and Rastus Henderson, it became notorious as the place where the wild aviators enjoyed themselves. We drank and sang, and often took our meals there. It was a place to find girlfriends and we kept it open and active until closing time. A party piece after many a hectic night would be an attempt to walk through the water across the Avon, at a place very near the road bridge. No one was ever successful but many got as far as the middle before they were forced to surface for want of air.

This devil-may-care attitude was also often expressed in the craze of low-flying and I was as guilty as the next one in this flaunting of flying instructions. My particular forte was to fly low up the eastern slope of the Bredon Hill and, at the top, push the control column hard forward, and plunge down the other side. We were certainly not blessed by the farmers and land-owners for disturbing fruit blossom, scaring cattle and sheep, and often people themselves. These ridiculous performances came to an abrupt stop when, after a very boozy mid-day party in the Officers' Mess, Johnny Gilbert and Rastus Henderson took the Vickers representative and his secretary on a low-level flight which finished with everyone being killed when the aircraft flew into trees near Warwick Castle.

This lack of discipline was further illustrated when one of our 'old boys', an American formerly in the RCAF, returned to Atherstone to show us what he was flying in the United States Army Air Corps. He landed in a beautiful silver P38, the Allison twin-engined Lightning and we all inspected a machine that was technically years ahead of our venerable Wellingtons. After lunch, he said that he would demonstrate his aircraft's great power by completing a loop directly from his take-off run. We watched with interest as he held the aircraft at full power on the brakes and then tore away. He held the machine down as he disappeared towards Stratford and then went up into his loop, climbing up and over the top but, sadly, misjudged the height at the apex of the loop for him to clear the ground on his way down. He had almost pulled the Lightning level when he smashed into the end of the runway, disintegrating as he careered along it, finally bursting into flames. There was little left of the machine or its pilot when the wreckage came to a smoking halt.

One day I was called to Station Headquarters to meet a uniformed Canadian nurse, it was Barbara Dreschler, my former bomb-aimer's sister. She had the wonderful news that Wally had returned to England just two weeks before and had immediately been sent back to Canada. She had been told little about what he had been doing for most of the past year but she had gleaned the information that he had made his way back virtually unaided. Apparently, he had been picked up by an escape organization soon after we had been shot down but they were in two minds about him. They didn't like his name, nor his blue eyes and blond hair - he looked too German and they spurned him. Not dismayed, he made his way into France where again the Resistance picked him up and, once more, they rejected him, worried that he could be a German implant. He pressed on, this time into Vichy France, then through Andorra into Spain where he declared himself to the Guardia Civila. He was roughly handled and thrown into the concentration camp at Miranda el Ebro until, five months later, he was released into the hands of the British Embassy. I tried to get more information from MI9 and the Air Ministry but all they would admit was that my crew had been the first almost complete crew to get back, five out of six.

Right out of the blue, I was informed that I had been Mentioned in Despatches. I was given no idea why I had been so favoured except that the award had been made by Bomber Command Headquarters. The mystery was no clearer when, a year later, I received the Mention parchment signed by Archibald Sinclair, Secretary of State for Air, dated 8th June, 1944.

My confidence in the Wellington and my ability to fly it had grown immeasurably. The Mark 3s were being supplemented by the new Mark 10s. Serviceability was good and we maintained a high work rate. We still had our quota of crashes, most of them avoidable, but the burst-tyre syndrome had all but gone. Most of our students were still Canadian, and just a few resented the way we taught them. For my part, I found them receptive and easy to get on with only having one who was a problem. He was a French Canadian and constantly goaded me into speaking to him in my inadequate French. He was often critical of what I was saying, perhaps he thought this redressed the balance of my criticism of him as the poor pilot he was. I rather dramatically discovered the root cause of this wretched behaviour one night when I had just told him to taxi out for yet another bout of circuits and landings. He had been muttering to himself and had been obviously unsettled when, suddenly, he deliberately put his left hand through the bars of the cockpit window and had two fingers and part of his hand chopped away by the propeller. Without any shame and rather with a sense of relief, his crew admitted that they were pleased, they had heartily disliked him. They said he was LMF and had been threatening to do something to stop their posting to an operational squadron ever since he had been appointed as their Skipper.

By the end of the year I was well past the allotted time of six months as a screened pilot and should have been back on a squadron flying a second tour. Furthermore, I now had more than 1,000 hours in my log book, more than the requisite amount of experience for conversion to the Mosquito, the aircraft that most bomber pilots wanted to fly. I applied for a conversion course but, instead, was posted to No 20 OTU at Lossiemouth on the Moray coast of Scotland. At the same time I was told that as my successful evasion was made possible by an escape route, I would not be allowed to operate over Occupied Europe again. If I were to be shot down a second time, MI9 were of the opinion that I would not be able to withstand expert Gestapo interrogation, and would, most likely, disclose vital information about the function of the escape routes.

It was like going overseas again, to be sent to the north of Scotland, it was such an alien environment. I arrived at Lossiemouth on 18th February, 1944, it was bitterly cold, the countryside was snow-covered, and I was depressed after a very long and uncomfortable railway journey from Stratford. However, the station was well established, the quarters were good, and, strangely enough, the weather factor was better than that at most other OTUs further south. The only snag, so I was told, was the dreaded sea mist, the haar, that formed within minutes and came in like a flash to blanket the airfields along the Moray coast.

Number 20 OTU operated from its main base at Lossiemouth, and from two satellites; one a grass airfield situated in the appropriately named Bogs o' Main, just outside Elgin, and the other, a newly-built station with runways at Milltown, a few miles along the coast towards Banff. My first appointment was as a supernumerary pilot in the Gunnery Flight where I flew Wellingtons and the lively single-engine Miles Martinet. We trained the gunners to give instructions to their pilot when to take avoiding action and taught the pilots how best to avoid fighter attacks. I was pleased to hog as much of the Martinet flying as I could, both by day and at night.

Lossiemouth 1944. I am sitting in the middle row,
sixth from the left

After six weeks, I was sent to Milltown to join 'D' Flight and get back to the real job of teaching pilots how to fly the Wellington. In late March, I was switched to the job of training very experienced French pilots and their crews who had been flying Farman 224s in Algeria with the Vichy France Armée de L'Air. I played a main part in this work simply because I was the only instructor with a workable knowledge of French. It was very rudimentary but with a few choice French cuss words added, I was accepted as something of a linguist.

The French pilots were good and very experienced at flying heavy machines. Most of my flying with them was done in Wellingtons with just one set of controls. After I had first shown them how it should be done from the left-hand seat, I had to sit beside my student in the collapsible jump-seat, usually with my fingers crossed. My greatest problem was to teach the power-on approach, goodness only knew how they must have handled their Farmans. With the Wellington, I had to break the habit most of them had of making their landings from a glide approach with both engines throttled fully back. As they were all destined to move on to a Halifax Conversion Unit, I considered this aspect of their retraining to be vital.

Spring came early that year and I swam in the Moray Forth from the Lossiemouth beach on 20th April, and thoroughly enjoyed it. The French completed their conversion and left to fly the four-engined Halifax. They had done well and had suffered just one accident. On a night cross-country a French crew had simply disappeared, no one knew where but it had to be somewhere into the sea most likely on the other side of the Hebrides.

We worked hard at Milltown, I was logging at least 60 hours a month. In addition, I had again inherited the Airmanship Section and I was the Flight Safety Officer. We lived in the fine Innes House, one of the homes of the Tennant family, and it was there we established our Mess. Social distractions were some distance away, so we made our own amusements on the station. I took up golf and gave it up when I found I was not good enough even to get a handicap. I went fishing and shot for the pot, mostly rabbits, although once I did the unforgivable and shot a salmon which I found floundering in the shallow water of the Spey.

Thankfully, my propensity to aircraft accidents had left me, or so I thought. One morning, in late June, I had been detailed to conduct an air test on an old Mark 3 that had been given a new engine. I decided that I would take it well up and see how the aircraft coped on one engine. My only companion was an engine mechanic who had worked on the engine replacement. It was a fine day, the wind coming from the west, and just a layer of stratus covering the Moray Forth at about 5,000 feet.

I climbed to 16,000 feet where I feathered the starboard engine and opened up the new one. We flew along over the Forth for about ten minutes, steadily losing height and increasing power now and then on the port engine. I was flying at the required safety speed of 105 knots when, suddenly, there was a loud bang, an explosion, in the engine. It lost power and quickly stopped. My instinctive reactions were to push the control column forward to avoid a stall, and to begin to un-feather the starboard engine. To my utter dismay, this couldn't be done. I tried all I knew but I could not get the propeller to un-feather. There I was, in a heavy medium bomber that now could only be flown as a glider.

We began to descend at a terrific rate, the Wellington had the gliding qualities of a brick. Neither of us had a parachute so my only options were a crash landing or a ditching in the sea as close as possible to the shore. The airman with me was splendid, he showed no signs of alarm, only asking me what he should do. I had him standing by to use the Verey pistol and to help in getting any flap I might need down by pumping.

As we passed through the layer of stratus on the way down, I could not believe my good luck at finding myself directly above Kinloss, our sister OTU. I immediately thought of a landing on the airfield, and decided to have a go at trying to land with my wheels down; if things went wrong I could always quickly retract them. The airman began firing red Verey cartridges which had their effect on the Whitleys circling below us. They began to scatter while the airman then pumped hard at bringing down the undercarriage which came into lock much quicker than I expected. At 2,000 feet, I realised I did not have enough height to make any sort of a circuit to land. I got lined up with the Kinloss main runway but, unfortunately, not into wind. The runway was clear and my guardian angel must have been sitting beside me, because I floated straight in to make a good downwind flapless landing. The aircraft came to a halt on the verge of the taxiway at the far end of the runway, a very close run thing.

At the end of August, I was given the War Substantive rank of Flight Lieutenant and sent to the other Lossiemouth satellite as a deputy flight commander. The Bogs o' Main grass airfield at Elgin was somewhat on the small side for Wellingtons, but it had metal-mesh runway coverings set out over very firm ground. Its great drawback was its nearness to the town and the lovely church that perched on a rise underneath the final turning point in to land on the east-west runway. There was a tendency with most of us when using this runway, particularly at night, for the final turn to be made earlier and steeper. This was dramatically demonstrated one night by one of our experienced instructors, Freddy Last, who allowed his student to tighten the turn until the aircraft stalled and control was lost. All aboard were killed.

If anything, we flew even more hours at Elgin than at Milltown. Bomber Command losses over Germany had reached their zenith and we were kept under constant pressure to produce the crews for the Halifax and Lancaster Conversion Units. The length of the courses was reduced, but few corners were cut. I personally liked the increased tempo which was made all the easier by working with fine colleagues. There was no strain imposed by those in charge. We were left alone to get on with a very important job.

We were comfortably set up in an old house in Elgin, right alongside the river. This served as an Officers' Mess but to me it seemed more like an hotel. I had a bedroom overlooking the river and from its window, I was able to fish in my spare time. Elgin was certainly not a night spot and our social occasions were held either in the Mess or away from town.

While at Elgin, I taught myself to drive. I had mentioned to my flight commander that although I had been flying for more than two years, I still did not know how to drive a car. He made a small 15cwt lorry available with which to practise, and someone to tell me how the gears had to be shifted and double-declutched. I then taught myself out on the airfield and, the next day, was allowed to drive the Flight's Hillman runabout and the BSA motor cycle.

CHAPTER ELEVEN

On a dismal non-flying day in early autumn, I was made victim of a truly amazing prank. I was summoned to Lossiemouth to see the Station Commander, an Australian, noted for his sense of humour. In his office he congratulated me on my work with the French and my not breaking anything when making my glide landing at Kinloss. He did add that it seemed somewhat out of character with my expensive habit of damaging His Majesty's aircraft. I was then told to follow him to the briefing room where a small number of instructors were assembled. He had me stand beside him on the stage while he produced a scroll of white paper from which he began to read aloud. I could not believe what I was hearing. He went over my history of bending and breaking Wellingtons; seven in all. Then, with a stern look on his face, he mentioned my great value to the German war effort. I had a score of English aircraft to my credit better than that of many Luftwaffe night-fighter pilots and I should be suitably rewarded. Then, amidst the general laughter, he presented me a black and white-ribboned World War I Iron Cross, saying that it was only Second Class, but urging me not try to earn the First Class award.

I thought the whole thing a little unkind because my record at Lossiemouth had been accident free, but I entered into the spirit of it and made a short speech of thanks. It surprised me that someone should have researched my record so thoroughly, but the reason only became clear a few months later. Nonetheless, it brought me down to size which was, in a most dramatic fashion, rather confirmed some days later when I added an eighth Wellington to my total.

As a deputy Flight Commander, I took it upon myself to undertake air tests after any major servicing. Unless there was any special equipment to be tested, such as navigational aids, wireless sets, or guns, I usually made the tests on my own. One morning, I went to Lossiemouth to air test a Mark 10 which had been fitted with a new engine. I took off and flew a wide circuit before returning to put the aircraft unserviceable simply because it didn't feel right. I had no idea what could be the cause but suggested the automatic trimming device might be out of kilter. I stayed with the aircraft and, an hour later, was told that the trim had been thoroughly checked and I could carry on with the test

I taxied out again, lined up on the runway, and took off. No sooner had I retracted the undercarriage than something inside me urged, 'get down, get down!' I was brought almost to the verge of panic, the aircraft felt completely out of trim. I called control to say that I was making an emergency landing, made a very tight circuit, landed, and taxied to a dispersal near the end of the runway. I switched off and shut down the engines, got down through the forward hatch, and had just begun to walk away, when there was a huge explosion as the Wellington went up in a mass of flames. I did not begin to understand what had happened until I began to come out of a daze in the ambulance taking me to sick quarters.

The Board of Inquiry could only guess at the reason for the explosion. Someone had seen a blue flash before the fire had started that had caused the fuel tanks to explode. The consensus was that the oxygen system may have been at fault and that the supply could have been feeding a flame that had probably been burning throughout the first flight and the maintenance check. I was not amused when questioned as to whether I had been smoking. I was more than a little shaken up and had a broken collar bone, two cracked ribs, multiple bruising, and something that did not come to light until many years later at the Remedial Hospital at Headley Court. An X-ray showed that I had fractured my neck. It is now arthritic and a constant reminder of another lucky escape whenever I try to turn my head fully to the left.

I was out of action for just five weeks. During that time I made the long journey to Devon and back to visit my mother. I remember it well because of a frustrating incident that took place on the sea front at Exmouth, nor far from the dock pier. I had been talking to a young second lieutenant who was making his daily inspection of one of the Bofors guns set around the Exe estuary to combat 'hit and run' raiders. I happened to look out to sea towards Torbay and there I saw two Focke-Wulf 190s heading straight towards us, low down, just above the waves. I pointed towards them and instinctively shouted, 'Focke-Wulfs - open fire!' No one moved, the gun crew just stood and stared as the German fighter-bombers swung left into the estuary, opened fire on a train at Starcross and roared away towards Exeter. I could hear more firing away behind us, but no noise of bombs exploding. A few minutes later they swept down the river, still at very low level, firing again at Starcross and, job done, flew away out to sea. Not a single shot had been fired from the Bofors. I turned on the second lieutenant who shamefacedly gave me the sorry excuse that he could not give orders to open fire until the target had been absolutely identified.

Mother, taken on a trip
on leave to Devon

Zon and Peter 1944

Being on a training unit in the north of Scotland kept me away from news of how Bomber Command was doing from its bases in Lincolnshire and Yorkshire. Coastal Command Liberators were now operating from Milltown and Mosquitoes were attacking targets in the Norwegian area from Banff and other airfields along the Moray coast. I was again hard at work tackling the unending job of supplying crews to meet the demanding needs of Bomber Command and was flying at least 50 hours a month, as well as coping with the additional duties of a Deputy Flight Commander.

When British troops liberated Brussels in September, 1944, I wondered whether I could learn something of how those wonderful people who had hidden me in Belgium and then taken me across France into Spain had fared. I had said nothing to my superiors either at Stratford or Lossiemouth about my escape but now thought, with the war on its way to being won, there would be no harm in telling my Station Commander. I told him that I wanted some news and he made enquiries. The upshot was, he told me, that answers could only be found in London, at MI9. So that I might pursue my enquires he gave me permission to take a short leave and to travel to London.

I went first to the Air Ministry where, happily, I met a Squadron Leader Harrison, the MI9 contact dealing with RAF evaders. A less sympathetic man would have sent me away, reminding me of the pledge I had given to remain silent about my adventures and not to interfere with those having the responsibilities of dealing with the escape routes. 'There are scores of you asking the same questions, and it is far too soon for anyone to give the answers' he said. Nonetheless, I spent some time with him and he took me to lunch at his Club. There he told me that the *Comète* Line still functioned despite having been infiltrated by the Gestapo in late 1942, not long after I had been passed down it. Its operations had been brought to a halt and most of the operatives had been taken prisoner, including Dédée de Jongh, her father, and Florentino. *Comète* had rebuilt itself and had functioned right up to the liberation of Belgium. Little was known of those who had been captured, many of whom must surely have been executed. In parting, he did say that the bar against a successful evader operating again over Europe had, of course, been lifted.

Returning with this knowledge I again applied for conversion to the Mosquito. I now had nearly 1,600 flying hours to my credit and felt that I had earned the right for a change. Instead, I stayed at Lossiemouth throughout the winter of 1944/45, still flying at the same satisfying rate, enjoying the excitements of instructing and, thankfully, avoiding incidents and crashes. I liked my first experience of Hogmanay and 'first footing' in a snow-bound Elgin, and began to appreciate haggis, mashed swede, and malt whisky. On 15th February, 1945 I flew with Squadron Leader Green

DSO DFC of the Examining Squadron of Central Flying School and was given a 'B' Instructor's Category. A few days later I was told that I had been awarded the Air Force Cross.

To my delight, I was examined by the Medical Officer at RAF Kinloss and underwent decompression tests that placed me fit for Photographic Reconnaissance, Pathfinder, and Mosquito Light Bomber Squadrons. I was then posted to No 16 OTU at Upper Heyford for conversion to the Mosquito. I had never flown anything so wonderful in my life. It was like starting all over again in a machine that had few betters. True, it had to be watched on take-off and landing when the heavy torque from its powerful Merlins could make it swing with a vengeance but once in the air, it was perfect. I loved the manoeuvrability and speed; the incredible performance on one engine; the compact fighter-style cockpit and, most of all, that I was dramatically improving my status as a pilot. I quickly went solo and was then crewed with the navigator I would take to my operational squadron. He was very good, Flying Officer Jack Swallow, a Yorkshire man from Heckmondwike, and some years older than myself. Together, we moved on to operational training on Marks 20 and 25. We practised bombing from high altitude, flew simulated cross-country attacks at 25,000 feet or higher around Britain and often way down into France.

We were a very happy bunch at Upper Heyford. Most were well-experienced. Many had been decorated with the DFC or DFM. Six of us made up a group which, whenever we were free, went off in a battered MG Magnete to enjoy ourselves in Oxford. This was made all the easier when we moved to the 16 OTU satellite at Barford St John, to complete our advanced training.

It was in Oxford that I met the girl I was to marry. To this day I can still still picture the moment when I first saw her. It was at a dance in the Town Hall, she was standing alone 'across a crowded room', clad in an ensemble of a tartan bolero jacket, pink barathea skirt and low-heeled shoes. She was looking directly at me and I held her gaze. I knew at once that I had to meet her so walked across and asked for a dance. From that moment on, I knew that I was to love her for the rest of my life.

The war in Europe ended before our operational postings came through. There was a sense of disappointment in being posted to No 692 Squadron at Gransden Lodge in Cambridgeshire which was known to be under threat of disbandment. It had been engaged, right up to the end, in the night-bombing of Berlin using Mark 16s with 4,000lb 'blockbusters'. However, there was a rumour that many of us had been earmarked to be part of 'Tiger Force', the British contribution to the proposed all-out bombing of Japan. This seemed to be confirmed when we began to study the Far Eastern operational area and discussing what a Mosquito bomber squadron might do. Already the Japanese had experienced the most devastating fire raid of the war when large parts of Tokyo has been burned to the ground and more than 100,000 people had been killed. We would be working with the 15th American Army Air Force, and taking part in the invasion of Japan. The importance of our work seemed immense. Thoughts of hundreds of thousands of US, British, Australian, and New Zealanders, having to fight their way ashore in the face of the fanatical Kamikaze defenders, could only mean dreadful casualties to both sides.

All our preparations and flying came to a dead stop on 15th August when the second atom bomb was dropped on Nagasaki, overnight came the order for flying to be stopped. Very soon we could be expected to be returned to civilian life. With nothing to do, we found our own ways of filling in the time. In early September, I flew in a Lancaster to Berlin with Air Vice-Marshal John Whitley, another evader helped by *Comète*. On the way, we passed over the Ruhr and took a close look at what remained of Essen, Dusseldorf, and Dortmund. Bomber Command had turned the whole area into ruin and rubble. In Berlin, if anything it was worse. I was appalled by what I saw. The Russians were everywhere, stripping the ruins of anything of value. I went to what remained of the Chancellery where I obtained a small piece of marble from a table supposedly used by Hitler, while all the time Russian troops were stripping the linoleum from the floors. I was allowed by Russian guards to peep down into the bunker where Hitler committed suicide, but could see little. I do remember however the putrid stink of the place. I took pity on the long lines of German women, many with children, who were bartering their *'Mutterkreuz'* (Mother's Cross – German political award introduced in December 1938), and often themselves, for cigarettes and food. Amidst the appalling devastation, I actually began to feel sorry for the Germans.

Another trip I made was to Brussels, this time hitch-hiking in a Dakota to Evère airfield. I wanted to find out what had happened to my friends in the *Comète* Line. I met the redoubtable Airey Neave for the first time in a fleeting interview at British Army Headquarters. He had been commanding an off-shoot of MI9, investigating the work of the Belgian escape routes and the punitive measures taken by the Germans against them. At that time, he was working on briefs to be used in the Nuremberg Trials to come.

I was in Brussels for just two days and the only helpers I was able to meet were the two priests who had hidden me in the monastery at Namur. They had moved to another monastery in the very centre of Brussels, on the Avenue de la Toison D'Or. Both had managed to escape the German purge that followed the collapse of the *Comète* Line. I learned from Airey Neave that Dédée de Jongh and others were in medical care after their rescue from various concentration camps, including Ravensbruck, Dachau, Belsen and Malthausen. Dédée's father, Paul, had been brutally tortured almost to the point of death. He had then been shot while strapped unconscious to a stretcher in the execution yard at Mont St Marzin, Paris. Many others had been killed and I simply could not grasp the extent of the price the Belgians had paid in their efforts to help the RAF. I hitch-hiked back to England by air and went to the Air Ministry to tell Squadron Leader Harrison what I had learned. He already knew, of course, and did his best to reassure me that steps were already being taken to do something about helping all those who had suffered while operating the escape routes.

I was brought smartly down to earth when I got back to Gransden Lodge. There was a letter for me from the Manager of Lloyds Bank, St James's Street. He had assumed that I would soon be released from the Service and had written to say that, as a permanent member of his staff, I could expect to catch up quickly with my banking career. My advancement was already under consideration and I could expect to start again as a clerk in the Loans Department at a salary of £365 a year. Would I give him the earliest possible information of the date of my return?

The letter certainly focused my thoughts, the war had given me the golden opportunity of learning to fly and I was sure that I wanted to continue flying; so much excitement and romance went with it. I wrote a carefully considered noncommittal reply to my bank manager and immediately took steps to stay in the Service. There was a scheme, a temporary one, called the Extended Service Commission for which I applied, hoping I would be successful. If not, I was prepared to stay on in a non-commissioned rank, provided that I could continue to fly.

Whenever possible, I spent time in Oxford and I proposed marriage to Wendy Doreen Howes one night on Magdalen Bridge. We both agreed there was no reason to wait and we were married in the lovely old fourteenth century church of Ottery St Mary on 19th November. On the second day of our honeymoon in a hotel at Churston Ferrers, near Brixham, I was recalled to the squadron to find that it had been disbanded.

Wedding day at Ottery St Mary, 19th November 1945

The problems of dealing with thousands of unwanted aircrew must have been enormous. Most of course, only wanted to get back to civilian life as quickly as possible, although I found myself amongst many who had experienced a war that had given them the heaven-sent chance of doing what they really wanted to do, to fly. Like me, they were waiting to see what the future could hold for them, once the dust had settled.

I thought myself fortunate to get a posting, together with my navigator, Jack Swallow, to No 1552 Blind Approach Beam Systems Flight on a wartime constructed airfield at Melbourne, just outside York. The place was in a state of turmoil; there was a transport squadron in the process of disbanding, and many of its Dakota aircraft were parked around the air-field awaiting disposal; the aircrew had already departed. Training pilots, most of whom would soon be out of the Service, seemed pointless and wasteful. But I was more than happy to fly with either Avro Ansons or Airspeed Oxfords, and a tight training programme that had us in the air almost every day.

The station commander was Group Captain Abrahams, 'Honest Abe' as he had been called when a prisoner in *Stalag Luft 3*. There he had con-trolled the incredible organization that supplied escapers with suitable clothing and disguise, including that used by the 200 who attempted to get out in the Great Escape. He now had the difficult, perhaps almost impos-sible, task of commanding a station with no operational aim and keeping happy hundreds who would rather be up and away from the Service.

The majority of us in the BABS Flight had applied, like I had, for an Extended Service Commission in the Royal Air Force Volunteer Reserve. We were, at least in spirit, apart from the others with enough flying to do to keep us fully occupied. I began instructing in the Anson with Jack Swallow acting as some sort of general dogsbody. On 26th November 1945, I set up home with Wendy in a small two-roomed flat in Gillygate, York, not too far from the York City football ground and we tried to settle down to enjoy what we knew would be an uncertain few months or so.

To my utter amazement, and to the surprise of many of my colleagues, I was granted a permanent commission in the Royal Air Force on 1st January, 1946. This was the first peacetime list of such appointments and I simply could not understand why I had been chosen, but realised I now had something that would shape the rest of my life. Wendy had been expecting me to leave the Service and to return and take up my career as a bank clerk, I had not bothered to tell her of my application for an Extended Service Commission. She was confused and somewhat dis-mayed when I tried to explain that, if all went well, for the next thirty years or so, we would live lives of great interest and variety, and travel to many different parts of the world.

I wrote to the Bank Manager at St James's Street informing him of my good fortune at being able to stay in the Royal Air Force, and that, there-fore, I would be resigning from the bank. There was nothing congratula-tory with his reply, he considered I had made a bad mistake that I would come to regret. His letter finished with the terse statement, '... if ever you should again seek employment with Lloyds Bank, your application will not even be considered.' I had definitely burned my bridges with Lloyds.

The period immediately after the end of the war has gone down in history as the time when many in the RAF simply 'couldn't care less'. We continued with our BABS instruction but, more and more, became involved in things of little consequence. The station began to settle down; the unwanted Dakotas were taken away, together with most of the surplus personnel and we found easier and cheaper ways of doing our job. Small teams went to airfields where ground BABS equipment had been installed and gave the flying instruction on the spot. In April, I was given command of No 5 Mobile Detachment and left for an uncomfortable three weeks at Membury, an airfield only recently vacated by the Americans. I lived with Jack Swallow in a caravan which also served as the Detachment's Headquarters. There was a small technical backup and students came to Membury by road for their instruction. The only memorable event was the difficult removal of some young women who had been living in make-shift huts in a copse on the edge of the airfield. They argued strongly that the Americans had found no fault with them, so why should the RAF be so particular!

I took the Detachment to Snaith in May, a place that was also under threat of closure. There was little left to remind me of the days in 1942 with No 150 squadron. The station had functioned throughout the war as a bomber base, but all that remained was a small care and maintenance party and a rudimentary flying control. We stayed there for a month and then returned to Melbourne.

Wendy, in the meantime, had received her first taste of the rough and tumble of Service life. She had stayed in York while I had been away on detachment and there had been little opportunity for her to make friends because few of the officers were married and none were living on the station. I had to confess to her that I had no idea when we would be able to settle down. I tried to console her with the belief that things would improve once we had left Melbourne.

That day arrived sooner than we expected and in July we were told that the station would be closed in the autumn. Instructional flying stopped at the end of August and the rundown of the station began. The Station

Commander, however, wanted to mark the closure with a grand party, on the lines of parties that were held before the war, so he said, by the 'real' Royal Air Force. We had no idea what he meant but he swung into the task of masterminding the arrangements. The party would be held over a week-end; wives, sweethearts, and relatives would be accommodated on the station in the barrack huts, if they so wished. A top-notch London jazz band was booked, and a concerted effort was made to obtain extra food and drink. We were given permission and funds to find this wherever we could. Aircraft were flown to Denmark and Norway to buy ham, pâté, and sea-food; to Spain and Portugal for wine, spirits, oranges and lemons; and I was the lucky one who flew to Belgium to collect chocolates, truffles, and biscuits.

The party could be nothing but a huge success. My cousin and her boyfriend from Tulse Hill joined us, and for the first time Wendy and I stayed overnight together on the station. We were all on our best behaviour to host the Lord Mayor and Lady Mayoress of York, and some clerical dignitaries from the Minster. The food was absolutely splendid, unbelievable at a time when all food was still rationed. The band was very good and kept us fully occupied until the early hours. My lingering recollection of the night, apart from the mayhem caused by 'high cockaloram' and mess rugby, were the belly-up goldfish that had found a drunken end in an astrodome punchbowl.

In the preparations for this party, it was discovered that there were serious deficiencies in some of the Officers' Mess inventories. A considerable amount of furniture was missing and I was made a member of the Board of Inquiry, set up to find the answer and, if necessary, to apportion blame. No one in authority had noticed that many items had been disappearing, one by one, over a period of time. The matter was aggravated by the fact that there had been three different Presidents of the Mess Committee during the previous six months.

We had to call in the Service police and they soon found the culprit. He had not been very circumspect and had even bragged to his friends about the ease with which he had made off with the furniture. He was a corporal, an Irishman, a steward in the Mess, who had dubious business contacts in Ireland to whom he posted the furniture, piece by piece, carefully wrapped in cardboard containers that he obtained from the Supply

Section. It was difficult to keep the investigation secret and, as soon as 'Paddy' knew he had been rumbled, he fled to Ireland, and that was that. However, we had to make a special footnote to the Board's findings to the effect that before he deserted, we had good reason to believe he might have had something to do with the fire that burned the wooden Officers' Mess to the ground.

At the beginning of December, I was dismayed at being sent to a unit at Wheaton Aston and then, thankfully relieved, to be posted, on the 5th, to No 21 (Pilot's) Advanced Flying Unit, equipped with Airspeed Oxfords at Moreton-in-Marsh in the Cotswolds. Wendy followed me a few days later and we rented two rooms in a bleak farmhouse in Aston Magna. Two weeks later we found accommodation a small terraced cottage in the village of Blockley, tucked away in a fold in the hills that overlooked Moreton-in-Marsh.

I spent the month of December in 'D' Flight, commanded by Flight Lieutenant R.L. 'Steve' Carson. He was another evader who had been shot down in a Typhoon while attacking enemy ground troops in the Beisbosch area of the Netherlands. There he had teamed-up with the Dutch Resistance and soon took command of a unit operating in that area of marshlands, swamps and waterways. He led them in attacks on German troops and was very successful. When the advancing British Army eventually liberated the Biesbosch they found Carson in charge of two barges, crammed full with more than a hundred starving Germans, many of them wounded. He was most appropriately awarded the Military Cross.

'B' Flight Moreton-in-Marsh 1947

I was given command of 'B' Flight at the beginning of January, 1947. Our task was to sharpen the skills of mostly experienced pilots who had been away from flying for some time, many of them ex-prisoners-of-war. It was not a difficult job and by no means demanding although, now and then, we found a person who had lost interest in flying and was best out of the Service, for his own good.

Formation flying in the Oxfords

A basically happy group of experienced pilots at Moreton-in-Marsh to sharpen their flying skills

The winter of 1946/47 proved to be the severest on record. I made a short Flight Commander's check on a student on 1st February, and did not get airborne again until 12th April, 1947. The airfield became snow-bound, and then everything froze solid. The station gradually came to a halt as fuel stocks ran out; buildings could not be heated; aircraft engines could not be turned over; and transport could not negotiate the roads. It was decided to close the station and all but essential personnel were sent home. That included me and most of the aircrew.

Tucked away in Blockley we were snowed-in for days on end. For one period of four days, no one nor any thing could get out from or into the village. The cottage we occupied was the centre one of five in a terrace located alongside the road into the village from the south. It was a desperately cold building in which we felt marooned. For some time we were not spoken to by our neighbours most of whom regarded us as intruders. On one side of us was an eccentric old dear who, whenever we were near, averted her eyes, muttered something like an incantation, and often crossed herself. She had an idiot son of about 30 years of age who was perhaps even worse, often shouting obscenities at us. On the other side of us was a widow of about 70, living on her own. We never saw her because she never left the house. Luckily, there was a homely couple at the far end, a retired policeman and his wife, the only ones with whom we spoke.

Just before the big freeze, I bought my first motor car. It was a rather badly used 1933 Morris Minor for which I paid an excessive price of £125. It had two seats and a canvas hood, very hard springing, was painted British racing green and appropriately labelled on the bonnet, 'Lulu'. It never went above 50 mph, even when going downhill, made a lot of noise, and suffered regularly from burst tyres.

'Lulu'

We decided to ease our boredom in early March with a drive down to Devon. The roads were compacted with frozen snow, but the road up the hill out of the village was negotiable. We packed a shovel, a bucket and a bag of sand in the boot, and rugged ourselves up like Eskimos. It was an altogether silly idea but it worked. We actually tobogganed down Fish Hill into Broadway, but once clear of the Cotswolds were able to motor along easily, apart from twice bursting a tyre. We stayed in Devon for fourteen days until it looked like the big freeze was abating.

'Lulu' having burst yet another tyre

The Royal Air Force's Escaping Society was formed while we were stood down and almost 3,000 successful evaders were canvassed to join. The aim was to set up a charitable organization that could do something about trying to repay the enormous debt we owed to the people who had saved our lives. The Patron and prime mover was the Chief of the Air Staff, Lord Portal of Hungerford and it received Royal approval. I needed no urging to join, as did just 800 others. I believe that this disappointingly low total was partly due to the fact that it was not made clear at the outset the Society would be a working charitable organization, not an 'old boys' occasional get-together. A fortnight or so later, I received a letter from its Chairman, Air Vice-Marshal Sir Basil Embry, inviting me to join the Society's Committee and, needless to say, I accepted at once.

We got back to work again in April. I flew and instructed steadily throughout the summer and into the early autumn; our students were still what we called 'retreads'. In November, we began to re-equip with Wellington Mark 10s and it was a delight to get back into a big aircraft again. Then, at the end of December, we moved, lock, stock and barrel, to Finningley, just outside Doncaster. At last, so it seemed, the Air Force was sorting itself out and the 'I couldn't care less' period came to an end.

Wendy and I moved our few belongings to Finningley by road, stuffed into Lulu. I had the fanciful idea of making the journey to Yorkshire along the Fosse Way that stretched in a dead straight line, or so I thought, from Moreton-in-Marsh to Lincoln - leaving us with just a left turn and a few more miles to travel to our new station. We set off at a cruising speed of little more than 30 mph and followed the main road until it became secondary at Halford. As we pushed on past Leamington Spa and Coventry, the Fosse Way became narrower and narrower, and then became nothing more than a track. We actually opened gates to motor across fields in the hope that the way ahead would revert into a road. In the end, we came to a dead stop in a farm where we were laughingly told that there was no more Fosse Way that we could use. With difficulty, we found our way on to the Great North Road.

No 1 (Pilots) Refresher Flying Unit at Finningley was organized into two main Flights: 'A' Flight, equipped with Harvards and Spitfires was commanded by Flight Lieutenant Bill Bedford AFC, with Flight Lieutenant Steve Carson MC, as deputy and 'B' Flight with Oxfords and Wellingtons under Flight Lieutenant Leonard Clarke with myself as deputy. The station had been built before the war and was well-equipped with good hangars and excellent runways. Its main drawback was the poor weather factor caused by the Yorkshire industrial smog; in winter an almost daily occurrence. Our students were still those whose flying ability had to be brought up to standard, most had elected to stay in the Service and many had taken a drop in rank. There were former Wing Commanders now being refreshed as Flight Lieutenants and many former RAFVR officers, wearing the DFC ribbon, who were now NCOs with the newfangled ranks of Pilot 1 or Pilot 2.

There were married quarters at Finningley, but we had no chance at all of getting one; they were all occupied by the station's senior staff. Hardly any of the married flying personnel lived on the station. For the fourth time in just over two years we went looking for accommodation and found rooms with a very friendly middle-aged couple in Bessecarr, a suburb of Doncaster, and then began to search for a place of our own. It took us six weeks to find Ivy Cottage, recently a shell but now with two makeshift rooms. There was a downstairs room partitioned as a living room and kitchen. Upstairs, which had to be reached by a wide slatted ladder, was a large bedroom that looked out over a tangled orchard of apple trees and brambles, and the end of the main runway of RAF Lindholme. We had a home, and it was a wonderful challenge: Wendy established order in the house while I tackled the chaos in the orchard and it soon began to take shape as a small kitchen garden. The landlord was so impressed with our industry that he reduced the weekly rent to twenty-five shillings.

We maintained high flying standards at Finningley and, as instructors, found few problems. In both flights, one could honestly say that the instructors knew their aircraft inside out. We were able to instil the utmost confidence in our students by flying regularly, and in all kinds of weather. With the Wellington, we emphasized single-engine flying, teaching instrument approaches on one engine, followed by an overshoot and climb away. Our particular party piece was a three-aircraft demonstration, of which I was the right-hand man. We held a very tight formation throughout a range of manoeuvres, finishing with a fly-past in which we simultaneously each feathered the starboard engine, made a circuit and approach to landing, and then overshot and climbed away.

The Flights worked well together. On 23rd March, 1948, I gave Bill Bedford his initial dual in the Wellington and he checked me out in a Harvard and then let me fly a Spitfire Mark 9. I also flew the Miles Magister and the Dominie, the Service version of the De Havilland Rapide Dragon, and I talked my way into a conversion course at Lindholme where I went solo on the Lancaster.

Bit by bit, I found myself learning about duties other than flying. I was appointed Flight Safety Officer which in those days included a responsibility for the fire engines and safety measures, in addition to probing into bad flying habits and evaluating the flying ability of others. I did a stint as Mess Secretary where I found my experience as a former bank clerk of value. Then, one weekend, when acting as Station Duty Officer, I actually found myself having to read the Riot Act.

It happened on a Sunday when the only flying on the station was being done by Mosquitoes of an Auxiliary Squadron. An experienced pilot, a former evader called Cairns, with a DFC and DFM, had been practising take-offs and landings with his navigator on board. There had been an engine failure in the circuit and he had flown around with his propeller feathered while we made arrangements for him to make an emergency landing. On his final turn into land, he let his speed get too low, stalled, turned over, crashed, and burst into flames just inside the airfield, alongside the road into Doncaster.

I was quickly on the scene but had to fight my way past civilians who had been watching the flying and had now invaded the station, some had even driven their cars up to the burning wreckage. The fire was got under control and the two charred bodies could be seen alongside what remained of the aircraft. All the while, the civilians were milling around, gawking at the corpses, and picking up pieces of the Mosquito as souvenirs.

I was the senior officer on the spot and was soon joined by a couple of service policeman and some off-duty personnel. We tried our best to drive the civilians away but fought a losing battle as more and more of them entered the station. Nothing worked until an enterprising sergeant policemen found a portable loudspeaker and a copy of a manual that contained the words of the Riot Act. I got onto a car and read the Act - and it worked, we drove the ghouls away like sheep.

Although I was learning fast, I had yet to understand the responsibilities and nature of exercising command. Those above me seemed remote and unapproachable and here was little corporate activity or Mess life at Finningley. We did not dine-in, nor did the wives 'call' on the Station Commander's wife, as far as I was concerned nothing much had changed since the war. As one of the few regular officers at Finningley, I was doing little to improve myself for a career but matters were taken out of my hands one day when I did not turn up in time to chair a meeting of the Flight Safety Committee. I had been enjoying some unofficial Lancaster flying at Lindholme and didn't get back until the meeting was well under way with Wing Commander Burnett DSO DFC, the Chief Instructor and OC Flying, having taken over my responsibilities.

Quite rightly, after the meeting, the Wing Commander had me in his office where he lectured me on what he said were continued acts of irresponsibility and lack of attention to duty. I was well aware of much of what he said and didn't dare to offer excuses. He added that he had been watching me and was not at all happy with my general attitude to Service life. In his opinion, it was time I came down to earth and buckled into learning more about the Royal Air Force. His words thoroughly chastened me, but the interview had not ended, he took up the telephone and called someone in the Air Ministry. Covering the mouthpiece of the telephone he said to me, 'I'm speaking to the person who took over my job when I left to come here. He's going to find you something much better than flying to focus your thoughts on things that matter.'

'Type hogging' was to be my downfall. I was away flying a Lancaster at Lindholme when I should have been attending a Flight Safety meeting at Finningley

My first Tempest Mk. V

Ready to start up and depart

The Auster with its incredible STOL (short take off and landing) performance was worth adding to the log book

CHAPTER TWELVE

The next day I was on my way to London, absolutely down in the dumps. I arrived early at the Air Ministry and reported to a Squadron Leader Lowe in the Air Secretary's Department. He greeted me with a laugh, 'You're another one sent here to learn! Hard luck, old man.' He then shocked me with the news that I was joining him as his assistant and that I would help with the appointments and careers of all substantive Flight Lieutenants in the Royal Air Force.

I was then shown the mechanics of how this would be done. Each Flight Lieutenant had a card on which all his personal and Service details had been typed and the cards were punched with various holes according to the information on them. I was shown a Hollerith machine which, to put it bluntly, looked like a Chinese calculating device. To obtain particular information, one had to select a pattern which allowed rods to be passed through appropriate holes and, hey presto, the cards with the required information could be pulled out. I was utterly dismayed and asked Lowe if there was anything else I could do. 'No,' he said, 'You have apparently been asking for something like this for some time, so my old boss tells me.'

I spent an hour or so playing with the Hollerith and responding to requests for information. Lowe went to lunch, leaving me in charge, saying that he ought to be back by two o'clock, when I could go. 'If there is anything you can't deal with, write it down for me to handle,' were his parting words.

I was left alone in deep depression. There were a few callers who wanted Lowe, and would call back. Then I answered a call that made me sit up, an authoritative voice asked who I was.

'Flight Lieutenant Randle,' I replied. 'I've just arrived.'

'Indeed, where's Lowe?'

'At lunch; is there anything I can do?' I ventured.

'I doubt it,' said the voice. 'Just tell your squadron leader that Cochrane is still being hounded for someone to take over the Air Intelligence staff post - AI9. Have him call me when he gets back.'

I was sitting on the edge of my seat. I knew I had been speaking to Sir Ralph Cochrane who had commanded No 1 Bomber Group when I was at Snaith. I carefully wrote down the message.

Lowe was late getting back and I had visions of an Air Marshal annoyed beyond belief while he waited. Lowe was concerned when I told him of the call, muttering to himself about the impossibility of pleasing everybody and hurriedly pulled out a few files. 'Have a look through the Squadron Leaders to see if any of them match these qualifications,' he said, handing me a letter taken from another file. I began to set up the Hollerith to trawl through the Squadron Leader cards looking for those who, amongst other things, were regular officers; Bomber Command veterans; able to work comfortably with the other Services, and had either escaping or evasion experience.

Turning to Lowe, I mentioned that if I had been a Squadron Leader, I could easily meet each of the requirements set down by the Air Member for Personnel. His reaction was electric, he sat me down and began to fire questions at me. 'It's simply unbelievable,' he said, 'We've been looking for someone to fill this damned intelligence job for more than a week and along you come ready-made to fill the bill.' He then called AMP's Department to tell them that the search was over and sent me to an office in Monck Street, not far from Westminster Abbey, where I was interviewed by a Group Captain. That evening, I travelled back to Finningley as an acting Squadron Leader with orders to report for work at Monck Street in ten days.

I simply could not believe my incredible good luck. I cleared myself from the station the next day, too embarrassed to tell anyone except the

Station Commander of my unexpected promotion, and very relieved that I did not have to face Wing Commander Burnett who was away from his duties at Finningley that day. It did not take long to vacate our little home at Hatfield Woodhouse, and I managed to sell 'Lulu' for £46. With just a few possessions that we could handle between us, we travelled to London by train, spent a night in a hotel, and then went searching for accommodation. We found it first in what only could be called a communal boarding house at St. Margaret's in Twickenham. Sharing the place with six other couples was quite unsuitable and, before I was due to report for work at the Air Ministry, we found a flat in a house occupied by two spinster sisters, in Manville Road, Balham.

I reported to the Air Intelligence Department feeling like a lost sheep and was heartily welcomed by the AI 1 Wing Commander, and then interviewed by Air Marshal Sir Lawrence Pendred, the Assistant Chief of Air Staff (Intelligence) - ACAS (I). He told me that I had been chosen to set up a joint-Service staff to determine the Forces' requirements concerning escape and evasion in the event of another war. It would be a follow-on from the work that had formerly been the responsibility of MI9. The Air Ministry had taken the initiative because of the likelihood that the Royal Air Force would be the most involved of the Services, as indeed it had been when the War Office had managed MI9.

For some time everything was a mystery to me. I had a 'hand-over' of sorts from Squadron Leader 'Conk' Canton who had been the staff officer who had drawn up the requirement for the AI9 post. He had been a prominent member of the escape committee in *Stalag Luft 3* at Sagan in Poland, from where the 'Great Escape' had been made. Otherwise, it was a question of listening and learning while I began to find my way around the various corridors and offices of the War Office and Admiralty in Whitehall.

The composition of AI9 had already been decided and approved by the Joint Intelligence Committee - the JIC and I had been designated as Chairman and Head of Branch within the Air Ministry. Major John Fillingham MBE was the Army representative, a former member of MI9 with valuable experience of clandestine operations in Italy, and the Royal Navy was represented by Lieutenant Commander 'Tiny' Gaunt, another intelligence veteran. A mysterious addition to the team was a Guardsman who had been awarded a Military Cross for a remarkable escape he had made from a prisoner-of-war camp in Saxony. He was the MI6 man with a watching brief on what we might suggest could be done, and to make sure that we did not transgress into activities which were none of our business.

I must admit that for a while I thought that I had taken on too complex and difficult a task. I was naive as a staff officer and surrounded by those who were experts at the intelligence business. Fortunately, the Wing Commander came to my assistance guiding me in proper Service writing and presentation by personally checking all my written work. From him, I began naturally to understand how to accumulate and impart information, and he showed me how to run an office. Most importantly, he helped me considerably with the drafting of my very first staff paper.

I had been put under remit to report to ACAS (I), within the next three months, with a plan of action in the form of a paper to be placed before the JIC. The platform on which our requirements would be based was our visualization of how the next war would be fought. The policy of deterrence, that was to dominate military planning for the next three decades, had still to emerge. The Americans were the only ones with a nuclear bomb and the only conceivable enemy was Russia. Successful escapes from prisoner-of-war camps in the last war had been relatively few, while evasions of capture and returns to England had been made in their thousands. Most of these had involved airmen in the RAF and, later, the USAF. Almost to a man, they had been due entirely to the operations of escape routes manned by the Resistance. The MI9 interest had been in fostering these routes with money and equipment, not with personnel. However, there had been some clandestine operations involving MI9 in Italy, northern France (after 'D Day'), and at Arnhem.

It was our belief that if war came it would not become global because the Americans could threaten to use, or even actually use the nuclear bomb. In that event, it was difficult to see how territory could become overrun and occupied, and so give rise to the classic formation of escape routes. Our MI6 contact was quick to inform us that any planning of future escape routes was their responsibility. The mists began to clear and the paper took shape. By the very nature of any possible war, we agreed that we were concerned chiefly with RAF requirements. When an airman was shot down, he had lost the weapon in which he fought. His duty was clear-cut: to return to his unit and prepare to fight again. With the Army, any evading soldier would be tantamount to becoming a deserter. He could not desert his comrades and his post; his duty was to fight on to the last; and so it was with the Navy.

We deduced that our first priority was training, followed a close second by the necessary equipment to help evade capture. Without the benefit of escape routes, evasion would be much more a problem of survival than hitherto, until means could be found for either overt or covert rescue. The escape kits used in the last war would now be no more than a token than a real survival aid and would have to be dramatically improved. There was a need to furnish squadron intelligence officers with the best possible information of survival in possible combat areas and to help them with evasion and survival training. Last, and by no means least, might well be the need for the selection and training of personnel to operate in the field just as some elements of MI9 had done in the past.

CHAPTER THIRTEEN

The work load in our office was increasing fast. We added two more officers to the staff. Captain John Young of the Border Regiment was to
become invaluable in trawling through the M19 records and writing evasion and survival briefs on the countries surrounding Russia. Flight
Lieutenant Leslie Pearman MM, who had evaded capture into Vichy
France and then escaped from a French detention camp after being captured in the South of France, joined us on the training side. I picked up
additional work from the Americans who asked me to draft a syllabus for
a survival course and to help with a textbook on how to survive
off-the-land in Europe.

Wendy and I were now well settled into our accommodation in Balham.
With nothing to occupy her time, Wendy took a job with the sales staff of
Smythsons in Bond Street. Despite a very active life, I was already beginning to put on weight. Formerly, the excitement and tension of regular flying had no doubt burned off the excess calories. Now, with a ground job
with its penalties of eating and drinking excesses meant that I was getting
heavier and it had to stop. I found the ideal solution by creating a routine
of getting up at six o'clock each morning to make a 3-mile run around
Tooting Bec Common. Whenever possible, I also cut back on lunchtime
feasting by swimming in the Marshall Street Baths in Westminster.

I did not neglect my flying practice. I was allowed to fly the Proctors
of the Metropolitan Communications Squadron at Hendon and, now and

then, to fly ACAS(I) in an Anson when he made official visits. I kept up my 'type-hogging'. Both Leonard Clarke and Bill Bedford of my Finningley days were still in flying jobs. Clarke, now a squadron leader, was commanding No 1689 Ferry Flight at Babdown Farm in Gloucestershire. Bedford was on the staff of the Empire Test Pilots' School at Farnborough, together with Bill Sheehan who had been trained by the same instructor as myself in the States. It says much for the free and easy control of Service flying in those days, and for the confidence placed by others in my flying ability that, whenever I could spare the time, I enjoyed myself flying one of their aircraft. At Babdown Farm it was the Lancaster, Lincoln, Mosquito, Harvard, Tempest, and Tiger Moth, all solo. At Farnborough, which was not quite so free and easy, I flew with Bedford and Sheehan in the Firefly, Balliol, Athena, and Valetta. My developing contacts with the 3rd USAF, and probably due to a series of lectures I was giving, meant that I was checked out on the Dakota.

The next problem for us to tackle was absolutely unknown territory to me. There had been no change in the general guidance that we had been given about the nature of a future war. We had to assume therefore that there was still a need for the recruitment and training of special units to operate, if needs be, in enemy occupied territory, just as MI9 had done in the last war.

We made a start by asking certain MI9 veterans if they would like to help us build the necessary expertise. Very soon, with the help of MI1, we had a nucleus happy to serve in the Intelligence Corps, Territorial Army. I felt that, this time, there should be a much stronger interest shown by the Royal Air Force and got permission to form an intelligence unit in the Royal Air Force Volunteer Reserve. Airey Neave, whose interest in escaping matters was unbounded, was the obvious leader of the Army unit and became Lieutenant Colonel to command 1S9(TA). Robert Bicknell, a company director in the Air Rescue equipment field, became Wing Commander of No 1 Air Intelligence Unit. In due course a joint head-quarters was set up in the Duke of York's HQ in Chelsea.

The training of the units was our responsibility in conjunction with MI1 at the War Office. As we were dealing with Reserve Officers most of the work had to be done at the weekends. I was well aware of the fine dividing lines between what we were training for and the responsibilities of

MI5 and MI6. The latter were well aware of what we were doing through their liaison officer with us.

The training we undertook centred on the use of communications; the operation of rescue and supply aircraft, small boats and canoes, and weapons. We dwelt on the theory of living rough and off-the-land, and being able to cover country on foot. Almost all this was done in the form of practical exercises with the three Services. I joined them for an enjoyable summer camp at the Royal Marine Depot at Lympstone in Devon. We had a go at the Commando training circuit on Woodbury Common, sailed dinghies by night and day up and down the Exe, and paddled canoes. It was all very good for morale and much was learned. The camp finished with a rip-roaring Guest Night in which the Army came out the winners.

The training exercises for the two units were never dull. One such, held over a weekend, began with the Royal Navy unloading us from a pinnace into steel canoes off Needs Ore Point just after midnight on a Saturday morning. Airey Neave had been given the task of getting the canoes up the Beaulieu River, past Buckler's Yard and Beaulieu, into the cover afforded by the New Forest, before it became light. At a point about 5 miles south of Lyndhurst, a camp had to be set up and a wireless link made to call in a Halifax to make a supply drop. The 'enemy' were local police units and four Auster light spotting aircraft based at Netheravon.

We made very slow progress up the river. We had six canoes that took some careful handling. Airey Neave was in good form in the leading canoe, continually urging everyone to do better. We must have travelled unobserved until we came to a dead stop facing the rock weir at Beaulieu. It was almost first light and we knew that the Austers would soon be in the air, scouting to find us. Airey Neave was furious at the possible delay and gave orders to get the canoes out of the water and ported up and around the weir. Hurrying as best we could, the canoes were lined up on the river bank and the struggle began to get them around the weir and back into the river. When we reached the top of the weir there was only one way to go, and that was through the grounds of a large house. We went as quietly as possible, being careful not to cause undue damage as the canoes were dragged up the driveway and then across the large lawn that fronted the house. I was with the team dragging the last canoe when the lights came on, the front door was thrown open and there was Lord Montagu of

Beaulieu, clad in a dressing gown, shouting at us to stop.

Airey would brook no interference, he ignored the justifiably alarmed Lord Montagu with shouts to the teams to 'hurry up, for Heaven's sake.' As the perpetrator of the exercise, I was left to face his Lordship. I tried to explain what we were doing and that there was no way he could have been warned of the exercise, which was classified Secret. He demanded that someone should be held to account for the damage that he could clearly see being done to his lawn. He wanted to telephone someone in authority, although I explained the only person who would be on duty at the Air Ministry would be the Duty Staff Officer. That was no good, and he demanded the number of my ultimate superior whom I said was ACAS(I). He began to calm down when I got out my copy of the Operations Order and gave him a number which was not ACAS(I)'s but that of my Army colleague, Major John Fillingham. Early that morning, he made the call and was given an abject apology by John with the assurance that the complaint would be put before ACAS(I) when he returned from abroad in a few days time.

On a 'scheme' in the New Forest

Leading the troops on another 'scheme',
this time in Dorset

Another interesting exercise was held within the Metropolitan Area of London. We gave our reserve units the task of operating three clandestine wireless sets throughout a weekend, with at least two transmissions a day to be made from supposed 'safe houses'. The enemy this time was the Metropolitan Police working in connection with MI5. Robert Bicknell was in charge and he used his flair for the unusual by starting the exercise with transmissions from a 'safe house' in Shepherd's Market, the then posh 'red light' district.

There was considerable upset and consternation amongst the madames and ladies in the Market when the police arrived and cordoned off the Market after fixing the location of the first transmissions. Bicknell had by then moved the three sets to 'safe houses' in Fulham, Holborn and Brixton. Our heroes thoroughly enjoyed the weekend although they had only one set still in operation by the end of exercise on Sunday evening.

I stayed with the police throughout the exercise and was with them when they discovered the set in Fulham. At four o'clock in the Monday morning, after staying awake throughout the weekend, I was being taken back to the Duke of York's HQ in the back of a police car. There was a Superintendent asleep beside me, an Inspector dozing in the front alongside a very tired driver. While driving along King's Road, the speed of the car dramatically increased. The driver must have fallen asleep with his foot hard down on the accelerator. I just had time to throw myself down behind the driver's seat before we crashed into a lamp post with such force that it became doubled over the top of the car. I was the only one uninjured and, after seeing my police friends loaded into an ambulance, I walked the rest of the way back to the Duke Of York's.

The Americans were showing ever more interest in what we were doing. In May, 1949, I was invited to the USAF Psychological Warfare Division in the Pentagon, Washington to discuss matters of evasion planning. I travelled most comfortably to New York in the 'Mauritania' and returned in the 'Queen Elizabeth'. I found the Americans' thoughts quite rightly centred on the survival problems that would face a crew after being shot down. Like us, they saw little prospect of organized escape lines in a future war. If the conflict was not against the Russians then it would hopefully be of a limited nature. In that case, they foresaw possibilities of overt rescue and the use of the rapidly developing helicopter. The outcome of the visit was that there would be a regular exchange of information in the future.

That summer, Wendy and I enjoyed our first overseas holiday. Our former station commander, Group Captain Abrahams, had told us how he had more or less walked all the way to the South of France in 1947. He had stayed with a disreputable character called Francis who owned a *pension* just off the beach at Callanques des Issambres. He had so enjoyed himself that he had gone there again the next year.

We booked two weeks holiday at 'Chez Francis' . We did not walk there but travelled in the uncomfortable hard-seated Blue train, *troisième classe*. The holiday was sheer heaven. The South of France seemed to have been untouched by the war. There was no rationing; food of all sorts was plentiful; the weather was perfect, and there was constant music and laughter at 'Chez Francis' which attracted the local young sparks. I got to like *pastis*, which Francis made himself in a shed at the back of the *pension*. I enjoyed the pleasures of snorkelling and spearing the poor little octopus. Together we fell in love with the place and went there every year until 1951.

I was able to play a full part in the work of the Royal Air Force's Escaping Society. We had an office and secretary in the basement of the Royal Air Force Benevolent Fund building in Great Portland Street. I was re-elected to the Committee and found it easy to attend the monthly meetings. We worked hard on our charitable business. We had long since discovered that the Belgians had played the principal part by far in the escape route activity. Each committee member was given the responsibility of looking at the needs of helpers in a particular country. I felt honoured to be given that of helping the Belgians, while others dealt with the French, Dutch, Danes, Norwegians, Luxembourgoise, and the Italians.

It was because of the Escaping Society that I made my first contact with the film industry. I had struck up a friendship with Eric Williams and Oliver Philpott, both of whom had escaped by using a vaulting horse as cover for the entrance of a tunnel they were building in the open playing area of their prisoner-of-war camp. Eric had written a bestseller, the 'Wooden Horse' and a film was to be made of it. I was given the job of being a technical adviser; another was an Army Officer. The stars were Leo Glen, Anthony Steel, and David Tomlinson.

I was to learn much about the business of make-belief that stood me in good stead, years later, when I became involved in script writing and giving technical advice to television companies. I saw my part simply as making sure that every detail was correct and, whenever it was needed, explaining how a shot could be made more realistic. I soon learned that actors preferred the easy way; they did not like to get dirty or uncomfortable. I was greatly surprised to read in a copy of the contract of one of the principals that under no circumstances would he work in a tunnel. The same gentleman insisted that his long johns, such as were worn in actual escape, had to be lined with silk. I enjoyed sitting on the sidelines and watching the tussle of wills that were manifest in almost every rehearsal, and often in the actual shooting. There was no doubt that actors were a race apart from ordinary people like myself.

My particular favourite was David Tomlinson. His infectious humour permeated the place. I got on well with him but he did not particularly like my Army counterpart, a major, who had little to do in any case, and spent much of his time attempting to seduce the girls in the production team, one of whom had become so thoroughly fed up with his attentions that she had reported him to the producer.

Tomlinson decided to teach the major a lesson. He had two microphones hidden near a bed in one of the rooms near the studio. They were connected to a loudspeaker on the main set. One of the production assistants who had been badgered by my Army friend volunteered to play the part of a willing *'femme fatale'*. We had been warned to be ready on the set one morning when Tomlinson would spring the trap. The loudspeaker was switched on. First we heard some ridiculous opening words, and then mutterings and 'ohs and ahs', as the major warmed to his work. It was so difficult to keep quiet as we listened to his ever-increasingly feverish antics. Then, there was an outburst of laughter when the major gasped, 'Hold on a second, I'm wearing braces.' The noise was so great that he must have heard us because he then brought the house down with, 'What on earth am I trying to do?'

The Premiere of 'The Wooden Horse' at the Rialto Cinema. Left to right:
Mrs & Major Fillingham with Mrs & Squadron Leader Randle

I did feel sorry for the foolish man who at least had enough sense to pack up that day and to leave the studio for good.

CHAPTER FOURTEEN

In October I was invited back to the States to see the progress the Americans were making with their combat survival training and had the pleasure of making my first air crossing of the Atlantic. I flew in a Skymaster R5D of the American Military Air Transport Service from Burtonwood to the Azores, then on to Newfoundland, to Wendover, Massachusetts, and into Washington, DC; a total flying time of 23 hours and 35 minutes.

There were two days of briefings at the Pentagon and then I was flown to the Strategic Air Command Headquarters at Omaha, Nebraska. More briefings, then on to Merced, California, to Boeings at Seattle, and back to Washington, DC. Everywhere I went there was evidence of progress and there was also a dramatic feeling amongst the Americans that any confrontation with the Communists would most likely lead to war. Nowhere else had I encountered this feeling; certainly not in Britain.

All emphasis was being placed on survival in the event of being shot down. Rescue beacons, aircrew combat gear, footwear, survival gear, were all under development, together with combat survival schools which were being created at Boise, Idaho and in the Rocky Mountains at Colorado Springs. The Americans were grateful for the little advice we had to offer and agreed in principle that, once the schools were functioning, members of Bomber Command could attend.

Getting back to England was most frustrating. I left Washington DC on 4th November in a Dakota bound for Westover, Massachusetts. There I boarded the MATS R5D Skymaster and flew on to Stephensville in Newfoundland where we were delayed by bad weather over the Atlantic. On 7th November we actually got as far across as Lagens, in the Azores, but had to return to Argentia in Newfoundland as it was impossible to land on the single Lagens runway because of high cross winds. The next day we tried again and this time landed safely. On 9th November, we set out for Burtonwood in Lancashire only to be diverted to Paris because of fog. After a night in Paris, we tried again and managed to get to Burtonwood late in the afternoon, just in time to catch a fast train to London.

I presented my report to my superiors, making the main point that the Americans were pressing ahead with equipment development and training based, rightly or wrongly, on increasing readiness for war. The deployment of Wings of Strategic Air Command to the United Kingdom and bases in the Far East, not to mention the vast back-up in the States (the Zone of the Interior as they called it) had already established a huge demand for survival material and training. It would be pointless trying to emulate the Americans in their developments but much might be gained if we kept up our happy relationship with them. Already, the purely intelligence aspects of our work in the UK were diminishing. The wartime MI9 influence on our work was growing less. Very soon, Bomber Command would have the atomic bomb which should place it alongside Strategic Air Command. When that happened, the attempted planning for the possibility of escape routes and clandestine evasion operations would no longer be necessary; AI9 and the two reserve units would then have little purpose.

Nonetheless, we kept ourselves fully occupied. In March, 1950, I was sent to the Middle and Far East on a fact-finding tour with the Intelligence and Air Force Staffs. I flew out in a York to Malta and then on to Fayid in Egypt. There I spent a week visiting the headquarters and giving lectures to aircrew at Ismailia, Fayid, and Deversoir. The general atmosphere was relaxed; a stark contrast with that I had experienced in the States. There was something 'old-hat' about our attitudes. The only possible enemies in the area were the terrorists in the newly-formed State of Israel, and those who were beginning to get organized in Cyprus. What I felt was that the Middle East was a good cushy posting, a place where life could be enjoyed. This was highlighted when I crewed with a Squadron Leader

Hennesey to win a 14-foot dinghy race on the Bitter Lake.

I flew on in easy stages to Singapore in a Hastings, spending a night at Habbaniya in Iraq. The next day we flew to Karachi and the following day to Negumbo in Ceylon. We arrived at Changi on 27th March, meeting the Intelligence staffs the next day and giving lectures at both Tengah and Changi. The change in atmosphere when compared with the Middle East was marked; I was now in an operational area. Communist guerillas, mostly Chinese, were at large in the jungle on the mainland, attacking villages, murdering and terrorizing the native Malays, disrupting the railways and, whenever possible, having a go at British forces. The Army had established a comprehensive operational sweeping system of the whole Malaysian State, while the Royal Air Force resupplied the Army with air drops and, now and then, attacked suspected guerrilla areas with rockets and bombs. There was a chance, a slim one, of aircrew coming down in the jungle.

I felt it was a duty to learn something of what they might face if that were to happen. I asked the Army if I could visit one of their units 'up-country'. This was agreed with a little help from HQ FEAF. I flew up to Kuala Lumpur fully expecting the usual coddled treatment given to visitors from the UK but was surprised, and more than a little pleased, when invited to accompany a section of the Royal Ulster Rifles on a routine patrol to a *kampong* that had recently been cleared of the Communists. I was kitted out in jungle denims and canvas footwear and given into the charge of a young second lieutenant. I got the distinct impression that he did not take too kindly to having the responsibility for a very unsoldierly squadron leader. He made it quite clear that I was with him as an observer, just an onlooker; he didn't even allow me to carry a weapon.

The patrol began with a ride in an Army truck along the well-prepared road out of Kuala Lumpur to the east. After about 15 miles, we got down, formed up, and made off into the jungle. Naturally, I was very keyed-up but this began to disappear as we got down to moving, very quietly and quickly, under the towering trees. I was walking behind the second lieutenant; there were two scouts out up ahead, the remainder of the section were on the alert with weapons loaded. We made good progress through what was primary jungle. I was enthralled with everything around me, enchanted by some of the things I saw; the magnificent trees, butterflies, insects, and the occasional snake. Then there were the jungle noises and that never-to-be-forgotten smell of a damp, fertile and over-heated paradise.

I became accepted as something a little better than a nuisance as time wore on. We stopped at mid-day, ate some tinned food and brewed up some tea. Just before it became dark, we stopped again to make camp. It was set up with a guarded perimeter and, after we had eaten the evening meal, we took turns at keeping guard and sleeping. I was given no particular duty except to stay awake in the centre of the camp for a specific period. When that time was finished, I made ready and fell into a deep sleep under a tree. I do not know how long I slept but, in the end, I shot awake because of stabbing pain in many parts of my body. I had been sleeping directly across an ant track and the industrious insects had continued their travels over and through my clothes and under my underwear, many objecting to my instinctive body movements, and so stinging me, time and time again. I came wide awake with a shout. I was hissed at to keep quiet while I desperately stripped myself of my clothes and tried to get the ants off my body and from my hair.

No one else had been so foolish as to sleep on ants. The soldiers thought it all a great joke, and 'God bless the RAF'. I waited for dawn, stark naked and very downcast. As soon as the guards were called in, I was taken down to a stream where I washed and scrubbed myself and my clothes.

We reached the *kampong* late that morning. My clothes had dried on my body as I had marched. I was, however, covered with ant bites and extremely grateful when a soldier medic treated them overall with ointment. We paid our respects to the village elders and were told there were no Communists near at hand. We then retraced our steps and continued back through the jungle without a significant stop until the road was reached from where we had started. We were driven back to Kuala Lumpur. It had all been quite a lesson for me.

On 3rd April, I flew in a Dakota to Saigon on my way to Hong Kong. French Indo-China, as it was then, was already in trouble with the Vietnamese intent on getting rid of their French occupiers. We had to stop overnight in a hotel in the city centre. I resisted the temptation to see the sights with the Dakota crew and to visit the night spots. Instead, I turned in early, just as I heard a burst of gunfire not too far away.

We arrived at Kai Tak, Hong Kong, the next day. The AOC. Hong Kong was a fellow member of the RAF Escaping Society, Air Commodore Denis Crowley-Milling. He personally took me to see the Army units in the Territories and the RAF back at Kai Tak. That evening, I was wonderfully entertained at the Floating Restaurant in the harbour. To my regret, I spent only 24 hours in that fascinating city before having to fly back to Singapore via Saigon. There was just enough time to order and have made-to-measure overnight, a lightweight suit and four silk shirts, before I left in a York for the long journey home, arriving at RAF Lyneham on 15th April.

Just two months later the North Koreans invaded South Korea. Within days, the two battalions I had seen in Hong Kong, were on their way to Korea. The Royal Navy made an immediate contribution as part of a Carrier Air Group, while the Royal Air Force stood by with Sunderlands based at Iwakuni in Japan.

Major Giblo flew over from the States to explain to us what help might be given to USAF aircrew unlucky enough to be shot down. An Air-Sea Rescue squadron was being formed to use airborne lifeboats carried by B29s to rescue those down in the sea, and helicopters with fighter protection to pick up those down on land. He said little about anything of a classified nature. It was early days, he said, but there was an intelligence unit in the Pentagon monitoring the developing operational situation. We asked that we might be informed if things went badly and enemy prisoner-of-war camps were set up, our interest would be in making contact with them if at all possible.

In the meantime nothing could be done but wait for news. We studied the build-up of Commonwealth forces, the United Nations containment of the invasion of South Korea, and General MacArthur's resultant push to the Yalu river. We had already decided that the Korean War would provide little scope of clandestine operations unless, somehow, South Koreans could be impressed into service. The chances of any contact with prisoner of war camps through the International Red Cross seemed very remote, and the thought of evaders or escapers with their Western faces being able to move through such a foreign country as Korea was simply out of the question. Although the War Office believed that in due course there might be a need for a small special unit on the ground in Korea to train person-nel in resistance to interrogation after capture, I could only see the overt rescue of personnel by aircraft.

In August, we set up an exercise in the New Forest to study the use of helicopters in a rescue role. The only machines available were the R4 Hoverfly used by the Army Air Observation Flight at Netheravon. I flew throughout the weekend in them. It was absolutely clear there was nothing to offer and nothing to learn. The R4 had limited range and lifting capac-ity, and we had no means of communicating quickly with the helicopter or the ground.

Exercises in the New Forest with helicopters didn't
really teach us anything new

Our exchange of information with the Americans was good. Major Giblo made regular visits to us at Monck Street. In November, I was invit-ed to visit the recently established Strategic Air Command Combat Survival School at Colorado Springs. This time, I crossed the Atlantic non-stop to Washington D.C. in a BOAC Stratocruiser. There was a day of briefing at the Pentagon then I flew to Chicago in a Constellation, on to Denver in a DC6 and arrived at Colorado Springs on the 12th in a Convair 300. Luckily, I had managed to convince the people in the Pentagon that I would derive most benefit by undertaking the 14 day course as a pupil. I had brought with me the experimental barathea battledress, string-netted underwear, loose clothing, and a pair of a new pattern of RAF flying boots.

The course began with a harangue from a Brigadier General followed by a series of lectures and practical demonstrations: how to make fire and create a smokeless blaze; how best to cook the survival rations and how to skin-out squirrels, rabbits, skunk, raccoon, and deer. Naturally a high priority was on building shelters (bivvies) in which to sleep and this was put to the test when we spent a night fending for ourselves and sleeping rough. Later we operated radio rescue beacons and called in helicopters. One interesting exercise that took my mind back to the war involved us in getting down from high trees in which our parachutes had become entangled. We practised climbing rock faces and abseiling back down and it was then I found that my new leather-soled flying boots did not give a good purchase on rock; I was the only one in that day's class who could not make it to the top of the rock face.

I seemed to fit easily into the course and when it became known that I had successfully evaded capture in the last war, I was asked to address the course. I did so diffidently at first but then, in answer to questions, made the strongest possible point that escape routes would be impossible to find in Korea and, for that matter, in a general war. I was also able to contribute something on 'living-off-the-land' as co-author of a book on the subject about, at that time, to be issued as an American text-book.

The second week of the course was devoted to a six-day survival exercise in the Rocky Mountains. We were to live off our survival rations and anything we could find growing or running around as we walked about thirty miles through the mountains to a specified RVP (rendezvous point). For protection at night, I was given a standard USAF flying suit to wear with an Army issue pullover. We each had a big survival kit that held many useful things; the main food content being pemmican, compressed oatmeal cakes, and chocolate. It had a knife but lacked a razor for shaving or a cloth that could be used for drying and cleaning. There was a coffee extract but I told the instructors that I would prefer to drink tea - and to prepare it in a billy can, as the Australians did without, of course, the dirty socks.

The labourious climb from Colorado Springs
and around Pike's Peak

Camp in the heart of the forest

We were split into teams of five and it was made clear that there was to be no hurry; the exercise was not a race. The aim was to get used to living rough, finding and cooking food, and staying healthy. We were taken away in a column of trucks from Colorado Springs and driven up and around Pike's Peak to be let loose in the densely pine-wooded westward side. Members of the Directing Staff were sprinkled amongst the teams and · suggested daily rendezvous areas in which we could report progress, ask questions, or get help if it was required.

Fortunately the weather was excellent throughout the whole six days, bright sunshine and relatively warm, but cold at night. We found it necessary to build a big fire the first night in order to sleep warm, using a guard system to keep the fire protected and stoked-up. During that day, we had heard evidence that the exercise was being held in the middle of the national hunting season. There had been continual rifle shots presumably at targets all around us and we came upon a couple of hunters dressed in flamboyant red jackets and hats. I was told that all hunters wore red, for their own protection. Hunting could be a dangerous business; it was shoot first at anything that moved if it was not showing something red. A case in point was a corporal under arrest at Fort Meyer for having taken a shot at his colonel. His defence was that the bushes moved and he had fired believing the colonel to be a turkey. Another tale I was told was of a successful kill in our very area. The hunter had draped the deer over the bonnet of his car and decided to call it a day. He was driving along a narrow tree-shaded road when he came under fire. He was shot at more than once and, eventually his car was brought to a stop with bullets in the deer and through the car's engine.

We managed to stay out of trouble. The team was good company with just one exception, a crusty old gunner from California. The rest of the team worked together well, there were no complaints and we agreed easily on shared duties. By the third day, I was the only one clean-shaved, and reasonably clean around the face and hands. My billy can was working well, each time we lit a fire, I had a brew-up but I didn't throw away the tea leaves. In the Australian way, I added more and more fresh tea to the grouts in the bottom of the can, provided an ever more stimulating brew. It wasn't long before the others were asking for a taste of what was now a potent drink.

As far as living off the land was concerned, there was little to be found apart from berries, most of which we were scared to eat, except the wild raspberries that were delicious. When we reached the Platte River, I was astounded to find it teeming with rainbow trout. They were very easy to catch and good to eat when cooked over hot embers.

We were making such good progress that we decided to camp at the river for two days. Other teams had the same idea and soon the place began to take on the appearance of a pleasure ground. Then a dastardly crime was committed of which I was but a witness. A very small young bear was knifed to death by a cheering mob. No notice was taken of warnings that its parents could be near at hand. The poor little thing was hung up and skinned, and then cut into steaks that were distributed around. Back at our campsite, we slowly cooked our portions over hot ashes. I found bear easy to eat; tender with a venison-like taste.

*The unfortunate bear being butchered. Fortunately its
parents did not put in an appearance*

At the top of Chimney Rock

There were no further adventures as we moved on to the final rendezvous. The hunting fraternity was still active around us but never once did we catch sight of a deer. Not wishing to linger we were rounded-up, loaded into trucks, and despatched on the long journey back through the mountains to Colorado Springs. As we were driving down the steep, narrow, winding Pike's Peak road, we saw our first deer. It dashed out of the woods, crashed into our truck, and was killed. We loaded the carcass and took it back with us.

The war in Korea was not going at all well for the United Nations whose forces had been pushed back below the 38th parallel. From the outset, both the United States and Great Britain had agreed that they would, under no circumstances, provoke war with Russia, but now the Chinese Peoples' Volunteers were in action and gaining the upper hand. The purely British effort of two brigades had grown and become combined with Australian, New Zealand, and Canadian units into a Commonwealth Division. The Commonwealth air activity comprised that from Royal Navy carriers, a South African squadron of Mustangs, an Australian squadron of Meteors, two RAF Sunderland squadrons based at Iwakuni in Japan, and an Army Air Observation squadron equipped with Austers, not helicopters. Some RAF and Canadian pilots were attached to USAF fighter and reconnaissance squadrons, and to the Australian Meteor squadron. It seemed most unlikely that this relatively small group of British and Commonwealth aircrew would need extra advice on what to do after being shot down in addition to that which the Americans already given them.

For most of 1951, we concentrated on our RAF training programmes, the development of aids and equipment, and the training of the reserve units, IS9(TA) and No 1 Air Intelligence Unit. We held regular exercises and study periods which kept me fully engaged as the senior regular officer involved. The Royal Air Force's Escaping Society had by now grown into an effective charitable force in Europe. I had been re-elected again to its Executive Committee with particular interest in affairs in Belgium. However, in our dealings with the Army, it had become almost impossible to bridge the gap between the M19 veterans and the over-enthusiastic and younger RAFVR officers. Neither the Royal Navy nor the Army had anything like the RAF Escaping Society which had, without doubt, the best liasion with the former escape routes.

Out of courtesy, we made Airey Neave, our principal soldier, an honorary member of the Society. He took the lead at the first-ever official reunion between British escapers and evaders. The most prolific by far were the RAF and the vast majority of them were evaders, rather than escapers. It was organized by the RAF Escaping Society and the most successful Belgian escape route, the *Comète* Line, and was held in the Martini Building in Brussels. It was a great success, honoured by the presence of Belgian royalty and various British and Belgian diplomats. The following day, a Solemn Requiem Mass was held in the Koelkelberg, an event which has been repeated every year since.

The dominant personality of Airey Neave had for some time made it difficult for me to carry out my duties easily as Chairman of AI9. A successful lawyer, he made no secret of his desire to enter politics. He had commanded intelligence units in the field and had made a name for himself at the Nuremburg Trials. He had every advantage over his RAFVR counterpart, Robert Bicknell, and did little to hide his resentment of the fact that the Royal Air Force had been given the lead in the peacetime escape and evasion role.

My first open brush with Airey Neave arose over the Clayton Hutton affair. This was aggravated because Airey did not get on with the forthright Chairman of the RAF Escaping Society, Sir Basil Embry. As time went on, I had regular arguments with Neave over many matters of policy to which he, as a Reserve officer, had not been made party. The dissension came to a head during the reserve units' summer camp with the Royal Marines at Lympstone in Devon. Every day, we had an argument of some sort about the substance and execution of the agreed training programme. Airey, a Lieutenant Colonel in the Intelligence Corps Reserve, outranked me and, at times, made my position most awkward. He wanted to know why we were forever arguing; apparently he could not accept that I was the person responsible for the camp, nor could I get him to see the aim of much of our work and, consequently, we were never able to conduct our affairs on a friendly basis.

I had no trouble with others. I was very lucky in being able to find time to stay in regular flying practice. There were Proctors and Ansons to be flown at Hendon; Lancasters and Lincolns at Aston Down where Leonard Clarke had moved with the Ferry Unit. I took a short course at the RAF Flying College at Manby where I converted to the Valetta, and was often able to fly Chipmunks at Fairoaks. I still maintained my contact with Farnborough where I went to fly with my friend, Bill Sheehan. During one of his regular visits from the Pentagon, Major Giblo surprised us with the suggestion that the USAF would welcome the attachment of British officers with escape and evasion experience to their training units in the United States. A few weeks later, as a result of an official approach from the Pentagon, Major John Fillingham was spirited away to become an instructor at the SAC (Strategic Air Command) Combat Survival School in Boise, Idaho. Then, to my even greater surprise, I was informed that my next appointment was to be as an exchange officer with the Psychological Warfare Division of the USAF, working in the Pentagon.

My tour as Chairman of AI9 had lasted for more than three years and I had enjoyed it immensely, learning much about the working of the services at the highest levels. From what I could gather about the American appointment, which I understood to be something about actions or propaganda designed to weaken an enemy's morale, I would be away from the

Royal Air Force, and flying, for another three years. Six years of staff work on the trot at my early age was surely not the best for a career in a flying service - or so I thought. I sought the advice of an opposite number in the Air Secretary's Department who told me not to be such a fool as to turn down the opportunity of three years living in a country untouched by war, and at a decidedly higher standard of living.

CHAPTER FIFTEEN

Wendy and I sailed from Southampton in the Mauretania on 5th December, 1951. It proved to be wretched crossing with at least two days caught up in a violent Atlantic storm. Wendy had to keep to the cabin for most of the voyage while I, with memories of both my wartime crossings, spent a lot of time on deck, in the wind and rain, exercising my 'sea legs'. After five miserable days, we docked at New York, had a fine breakfast at the Union Station, and then took the train to Washington with all our possessions in just four cases. We were met by John Fillingham and his wife at Union Station. He had been in Washington for the best part of a month, awaiting orders to move on to Idaho. We piled ourselves and our luggage into a blood-red Ford sedan that he had just bought, to be driven to an apartment that had been found for us by the BJSM (British Joint Services Mission). John was fully in charge. He said that he already knew Washington, inside out, and would take us by the most direct route. He was in good form, delighted with his appointment and, as he drove, talking about all the wonderful advantages of living in America. We turned into the long Connecticut Avenue. 'Your place is about eight blocks up this road, just before we get to Chevy Chase,' he said. 'We shall soon be at the Dupont Circle; after that it is all straight ahead.'

As he was speaking, I could see that he was indeed already committed to driving straight ahead, right into the narrow tunnel under the Dupont Circle that carried the trams along the Avenue. We plunged into darkness before he realised his mistake. There were shrieks of alarm from the ladies. Joan Fillingham screamed hysterically that she would never see her children again. John put his foot down, hoping to get to the other end before a tram entered. We got to the tunnel's bottom when, to our horror, we saw the lights of an approaching tram. On went the brakes. We came to a screeching stop, nose to nose with a loaded tram. Like utter fools, we sat there, way down under Washington, facing a perplexed tramdriver, holding his head in his hands. To his credit John didn't panic, it was clear he couldn't get by the tram and had to reverse. He shouted apologies in his best English accent and went backwards at a slow pace, with the tramdriver almost pushing us back up the slope. John kept his head and only scraped the tunnelside twice. Once outside and back into the daylight, he didn't stop to argue. He ignored a policeman and we quickly drove away, around the Circle this time, and up the Avenue. We had all recovered our spirits by the time we reached the apartment. The first thing that Wendy did when we got inside was to make a strong cup of tea.

The transition from the gloom and restrictions of life in London to the immeasurably higher standard of living and freedom in Washington, took us a little time to understand and appreciate. We were administered by the British Joint Services Mission while, in all other respects, we were part of the USAF. We were grateful for a compensating adjustment to my pay to allow for higher costs, even though the pound was then exchanging at 4.25 dollars. The apartment building, the Wiltshire Crescent, was newly-built and our apartment had three fine rooms on the ground floor, equipped with devices we had never before seen. The rooms were air-conditioned and secure, also, for the first time, we had a television set as part of the furniture. We were living directly above a large garage that occupied the entire basement of the building.

Settling in quickly, Wendy was offered a position with the BJSM the day after we arrived, accepting at once. I reported to the Psychological Warfare Division which was housed in the Brewery Annex of the Pentagon, on the Shirley Highway where I was met with extreme kindness and consideration. My immediate superior was Colonel George Ryan Weinbrenner, a tubby, happy-go-lucky, former member of the American Special Forces in Europe. His second in command was Lieutenant Colonel George Stillson, a senior pilot from Strategic Air Command, who would rather have been flying B29s than keeping a desk warm in Washington. The staff was completed by two majors, Rosentretter and Doyle, together with a Captain Grier.

I began work on 12th December, 1951 and, from the very beginning, I had no particular responsibilities. I was expected to advise on a wide range of topics, some of which were beyond my knowledge. When that happened, I searched for answers in the Intelligence section of BJSM which came under the control of Group Captain Thomas Lang. He held monthly meetings at which I was expected to attend and where I could keep abreast with what was happening back home. It was at such a meeting in early January, 1952, that I was congratulated on having been made an Ordinary Member of the Military Division of the Most Excellent Order of the British Empire (MBE).

We became owners of a brand new Ford Sedan, the same model as John Fillingham's but black, not red, more in keeping with my personality. To my great surprise and delight, I found that I had been allotted the same continuation flying time as that of USAF staff officers. This was way beyond the meagre RAF allowance which, in any case, had to be flown in communication aircraft such as the Proctor or the Anson. Because I was a former bomber pilot, I could now fly up to 300 hours a year on the B25 Mitchell or the Dakota. I needed no urging to avail myself of this pleasure. In January, I got checked-out at Andrews Air Force Base, just a few miles outside Washington, and flew a total of 9 hours. In February, it was 18 hours and 35 minutes which included flights to Texas and Alabama, and a check-out and solo in the C45 Expediter.

The work in the Psychological Warfare Division was, up to a point, a reflection of what I had been doing in London. Just as certain things were left to MI6, so I could sense were similar matters in Washington left to the newly-formed CIA (Central Intelligence Agency), or 'Charlie, Idiot, Able' as my colleagues called it. In practical terms, I had little to deal with of a classified nature. The title, 'Psychological Warfare', was perhaps deliberately misleading as most of our work was concerned with combat survival, living off the land, studies of possible future combat areas and, most important, so I thought, overt rescue of shot-down aircrew. The Korean War was at its height and lessons were coming back thick and fast, particularly as regards that of helicopter rescue. I learned from BJSM that the

JIC (Joint Intelligence Committee) had blessed the sending of a small team from 1S9(TA) to Korea, to be attached to the Commonwealth Division there to brief soldiers and sailors on escape possibilities and resistance to interrogation after capture. Although there was an airman in the unit to brief Fleet Air Arm aircrew, no one had been sent to study helicopter and aircraft rescue; the MI9 thinking seemed to have prevailed. It was at this point that I decided I should do something to repair what I thought to be a mistake, I thought it my duty. First, however, I had to learn something about helicopters.

There was nothing demanding about my work and I found it easy to cope with whatever I was given to do. Three years at the Air Ministry had taught me much about writing reports, drafting papers, and preparing briefs. However, I had to adjust to doing things in the American way. My written work was always screened by my colonel. I had to get used to the splitting of infinitives, the use of longer words and sentences than were required, and to learn the differences in spelling and meaning of certain words. I shall always remember the day when I had been working on a schematic drawing in pencil and had made a mistake which I wanted to correct. I called out to a woman clerk working just two desks away from me, and asked her if she had a rubber. There was a sudden deathly hush in the room, followed by hoots of laughter when she realised my misunderstanding of that American word and blushingly handed me an eraser.

Wendy and I were happy to be drawn into the American social round, becoming members of the Officers' Club at Bolling Air Force Base and soon formed friendships with many American families. Right out of the blue, at an Air Force dinner at Bolling, I was asked if I would like to join the Civil Air Patrol which would give me the opportunity of more flying and introduce me to another aspect of local life. I grabbed at the idea and was appointed an honorary major in the CAP squadron at Hybla Valley, near Arlington in Virginia. I underwent an American Civil Aeronautical flying test in an Aeronca 'Champion' on March 7th, and took part in my first CAP air rescue search for a USAF B26 down somewhere in the Culpepper region of the Blue Ridge Mountains on the 19th, flying a Piper Pacer. I obtained the CAP's Senior Pilot's Rating on 23rd April which cleared me to give flying instruction to cadets. In addition to all this joy, I was asked by Group Captain Lang at the BJSM if I would undertake to fly with him as co-pilot in the Dakota each month when he flew his continuation training.

Wendy and I were enjoying ourselves immensely, appreciating every minute of the pleasure we derived from living in America at that time. There was so much that was new to us while, on the other hand, we were surrounded by a culture and history that was only partly known to us. We took full advantage that summer of travelling to places in New England, Maryland, and Virginia. Our summer holiday was spent in the Blue Ridge Mountains where Wendy allowed me to indulge in my favourite hobby of studying the American Civil War. We followed the route of Stonewall Jackson's progress up the Shenandoah Valley staying overnight in small village hotels.

Back from holiday I contiued to add to my flying hours and experience. I flew B25s and Dakotas to many of the American States; Texas, Florida, Mississippi, New Mexico, California, Colorado, Oregon, and Washington. To me, it was all part of a glorious holiday although, as I knew full well, it was doing very little to help me along with my career. Notwithstanding, what I had been hoping for and, in a way, had been working towards for all that summer, suddenly came to fruition in September. Colonel Weinbrenner had schemed a way for me to be taught something about helicopters and, when that was done, he believed he could arrange for me to go to Korea to examine the combat rescue situation. He was the only person that knew what I wanted to do, I had made no mention of it to BJSM, nor had I confided in Wendy, knowing that she would think me crazy and uncaring. George Weinbrenner had considerable influence behind the scenes in Washington and had managed to arrange for the US Marines at Quantico in Virginia to teach me to fly helicopters during weekends. Wendy accompanied me each time I went there and waited and watched me learning to fly the Bell H-13d, completely unaware that it was my intention to have a look at another war. I made steady progress in coping with the entirely new flying experience of helicopters. I flew the Bell solo on 25th October and then moved on to the bigger Sikorsky H-19 which I soloed on 9th November.

Written orders for me to go to Korea came through on 24th November attaching me to the 3rd Air Rescue Squadron of the 5th USAF. They were a bitter shock to Wendy who behaved wonderfully well. She did not argue nor did she question why. I could not bring myself, of course, to tell her that it had been of my own idea. George Weinbrenner helped tremendously in quelling Wendy's fears. He made it clear to her that I would be away for just a short time, and that there was little chance of my meeting with any danger.

Initial hovering exercises dual on the Bell H-13d

The next day, Wendy saw me off in a MATS DC6 at Washington International. We flew to Travis AFB and transferred to a MATS Skymaster in which we crossed the Pacific to Tokyo via Honolulu and Wake Island. It was uncomfortable in the noisy and crowded transport for the whole of 34 hours and 15 minutes. I reported to Headquarters, 5th Air Force at Tachikawa in Japan on 29th November and was kept there until 5th December when I flew to Komati in a Curtiss Commando to begin my attachment to the 3rd Air Rescue Squadron.

With my instructor on the H-13d

Moving onto the bigger aircraft the Sikorsky H-19

*Before my posting on operations in Korea, Wendy joined me
during my helicopter training with the US Marine Corps*

At Komati, the squadron maintained and operated a small number of
RB29s, modified to carry the airborne lifeboat. It was the standard form of
lifeboat, identical to those carried by Lancasters in Coastal Command, and
big enough to house any crew then operating over Korea that might have
the misfortune to come down into the sea. I was told that I was at liberty
to fly with them and during the night of 5th December I took part in a rescue sortie. This involved hours of orbiting at 15,000 ft over Nan Do, Yo
Do, and Wonsan harbour. We saw nothing but I was allowed to handle the
controls for a couple of hours. It was all a little unreal; difficult indeed to
imagine that there was a war down below. I flew again the next night, this
time to orbit over Wonsan harbour. This time, we saw some bomb bursts
away over to the west where B29s were bombing, together with a little
light flak but, otherwise, all was boringly uneventful.

I told the detachment commander that I had seen enough of this aspect
of air rescue and thanked him for his assistance and hospitality. I crossed

to Korea in a Dakota on 11th December to K16, Seoul, where the tactical part of the Rescue Squadron was based. This comprised three Grumman Albatros amphibians, two Dakotas, and quite a number of Sikorsky H19 and S51 'Dragonfly' helicopters.

The weather was desperately cold and I was housed in a Quonset hut together with half a dozen others; many were sleeping in tents. Everything seemed to be rudimentary; the accomodation, the communal mess, and the food. Even the helicopter servicing was done in the bitter cold just under cover of a tent. Yet I had arrived at a very busy and important airfield that also housed and operated fighters, light bombers,and reconnaissance; aircraft were coming and going at all times. K16 would have been a prime target if the North Koreans or the Chinese had had a bomber force. I was told that there was a regular nocturnal visiter, a P02 biplane, nick-named 'Bedcheck Charlie'.

I reported to Lieutenant Colonel Perry Crossom, the squadron commander, who personally took me under his wing. He had flown helicopters for years with the civil police force in California and had been called up as a reserve officer to organise the air rescue force in Korea. He knew that I was principally interested the helicopter operations but thought it best that I should get to know the area first by sampling other squadron rescue tasks. I flew as co-pilot in a Dakota on 13th December, carrying supplies to the forward helicopter detachment on Ch'o Do, in the Yellow Sea, way north of the 38th Parallel. This volcanic island was in permanent use by the squadron, it was just a few miles from the enemy mainland, protected by aircraft carriers of the Royal Navy. We landed on the hard shell beach in the lee of the central extinct volcano that had formed the island and now shielded the helicopters from shelling from the mainland. The engines were kept running as we quickly unloaded and then took off to return to Seoul.

The next day, my sight-seeing was continued. I flew with Crossom in an H-19 back to Ch'o Do, where he wanted to show me how his detachment was operated. In keeping with operational helicopter policy we flew 'two pilots up', I was therefore able to get some useful flying practice. Crossom explained that when a helicopter was approaching to make a pick-up and got within range of the lying-in-wait enemy, the pilot became the obvious target. A second pilot had become a necessity and, in any case, he was there also there to act as navigator.

We remained on Ch'o Do for a couple of hours. I was shown around and was most impressed with the spirit of the helicopter crews. The Chinese were getting expert at shooting them down, but they were well aware of the vital importance of their jobs. A downed airman ran the risk of imprisonment for years somewhere way outside Korea, and there was the horror of torture and brainwashing.

DC3 and H-19 on the hard-packed beach at Ch'o Do

We flew back down the coast to Paengnyong Do, a larger island than Ch'o Do, on which there were refuelling facilities alongside a short landing strip. Again we shut down the engine and I was shown around. While this was happening, a Fleet Air Arm Firefly landed and taxied over to refuel. I went across to pay my respects to other Britishers only to be taken utterly aback to find, sitting in the rear seat, none other than Squadron Leader Frank Leatherdale, someone who had attended one of the AI9 briefing courses on evasion and escape. We eagerly met as old friends and, in the short time it took to refuel the Firefly, I learned that he was the single RAF member of the IS9 team that had been sent to Korea. He was based in Seoul and he gave me his address where he could be contacted.

*US Marine Corps F4 Corsair down
on the beach, victim of a Mig.15*

Perry Crossom kept to his word about first seeing as much as possible of the non-helicopter side of his squadron. Between 15th and 19th December, I flew as co-pilot on eight sorties in the Albatros amphibian. They were flown in support of fighter sweeps and fighter-bomber attacks in North Korea. Each time we had a fighter escort of piston-engined machines; a Cover Air Patrol of Mustangs or Corsairs. We flew low way up into the Yellow Sea, north of Ch'o Do, or up the east coast around the Wonsan harbour region, there to orbit until called in to make a pick-up. We twice landed on the sea where we taxied around waiting, but we were never called upon to make a rescue.

I flew back to Ch'o Do on 20th December with Perry Crossom where he left me to gain some experience with the helicopter detachment. Two H-19s were brought to instant readiness whenever there was United Nations' air activity over North Korea. The 'aircraft down' alarm would be sounded by 5th Air Force and it was then that engines were started. If a rescue was deemed at all possible, the control became localised, usually taken up by the Cover Air Patrol allotted to the helicopters for their protection. The North Korean coast was just a few miles away, guarded only at key points and the helicopters were easily able to pick their way between these defences and on into the mainland.

I flew on four sorties with the detachment, each time flying into North Korea at very low level and at a good speed. In this way we hid our approach and covered our return. I took photographs of nothing much in particular, as we never flew very far inland.

The third of these flights was exciting as it was the only one in which an actual pick-up was concerned. A pilot had ejected from a Sabre and was down somewhere about 15 miles east of us, reasonably near to the coast. Both helicopters were alerted, as was the custom. The one in which I was to fly, with a Lieutenant Kenrotis, was ordered to be the 'back-up', and to follow about half-a-mile behind the first. Our CAP of four Corsairs took up position above us just as we cleared the island. We crossed the coast at tree-top height with the other helicopter just in sight ahead of us.

I then saw that one of the Corsairs had left the formation and dropped down over the other helicopter; it waggled its wings, obviously to indicate that it should be followed. Within minutes we saw a flare burning on the ground ahead in the distance, no doubt marking the pick-up spot. We began to circle at a good speed, still very close to the ground. It was then that I realised that somewhere, well hidden from us, there were people firing rifles. It was not the crack of weapons that I heard but, surprisingly, a sharp 'thump thump' on the metal fuselage as sound waves hit the outer skin. We were not being hit, it was the other helicopter that was attracting the attention while it was in the hover to take the downed pilot on board. We were quickly away but two of the Corsairs stayed for a while and wasted ammunition by firing their guns at where they thought soldiers were hidden. The other two escorted us back to Ch'o Do without further incident.

I began the final stage of my attachment on 23rd December when, after returning to Seoul, I was switched to another function of the squadron, front-line evacuation of casualties. This task was controlled from Seoul and involved flying right up to the front line, usually to battalion headquarters which controlled the forward medical unit. There, wounded strapped on stretchers were loaded onto the helicopter and flown to a Mobile Army Surgical Hospital (MASH), in our case, No 8063. This work was in support of that part of the line held by the Commonwealth Division, with a US Marine Corps on one side and a Republic of Korea (ROK)

Division on the other. The enemy facing them were Chinese who were constantly probing and attacking.

The Dragonfly was something new to me but I was allowed to fly in it as co-pilot. In three days, we flew seven evacuation sorties. On the way forward, we often carried blood supplies to the landing site that was usually tucked into the lee of the hills that formed the front line. The soldiers we brought back were sedated against the pain of bad wounds. We flew them right into the MASH where they were quickly unloaded and taken straight to the operating theatre. From my log book I see that we flew men from the 12th Regiment, ROK; 38th Regiment, US Army, and from a Canadian Regiment.

I had never before been so close to actual fighting. Once, while waiting at a US Marine battalion HQ while a doctor prepared a soldier to load, the Chinese attacked. I could hear the bugles and shouts of the enemy on the other side of the hill, and the crackle building to a roar of gunfire. Soon prisoners were being brought in, most of them wounded. The Marines were standing no nonsense, in fact they handled them very roughly. Despite this, the Chinese were openly defiant. I saw one, covered in blood, a tourniquet around his arm of which that part below the elbow was missing, actually spit in the face of a Marine officer.

I flew the last two sorties on Christmas Eve and was told that my attachment had come to an end. I was back in Seoul on Christmas Day, so filthy and unkempt that I would have given anything for a bath, something that was not available at K16. I remembered that Frank Leatherdale had given me his address, so I looked him up. He had a comfortable little house right in the centre of town and, crucially, a bath but alas no hot water. Nonetheless, I luxuriated in the only bath I had been able to take in Korea. At the same time, I washed and scrubbed my clothes, including my barathea battle dress.

That evening, Frank arranged for me to dine at the Commonwealth Division Headquarters. Never before or since, have I felt so much out of place; it was in fact a Guest Night. I sat at table in my shabby battledress whilst all around me were officers in patrols, a few even wearing mess kit. There was silver on the table, the food was excellent and well-served. The speeches were short and to the point, and we toasted the King as a small musical ensemble played the National Anthem. I was made to feel at home and stayed until just before midnight when 'Bedcheck Charlie' flew over. We went outside with our glasses to wish him a Happy Christmas.

I left Korea the next day in one of the Squadron's Dakotas and was invited to take the left seat and did most of the flying - at least for a while. We had been given a poor met forecast but I knew we had to fly through a cold front that lay between us and Japan. We were soon in cloud as I climbed through ever-increasing turbulence up to 14,000 feet. Even then we were still in cloud; I shall never forget this flight. Soon there were two pilots struggling with the controls; at times the aircraft was unmanageable as it dropped hundreds of feet in seconds. Almost all the passengers were sick, some were terrified and screamed. The weather only began to settle when we were reached Japan. Even then, we could not land at Komati because of hurricane-like conditions and went on to land at Johnson AFB.

I had expected that I would have been returned to the States almost at once, but that was not to be. Instead, I was very comfortably housed in the Maranuchi Hotel where many of the American Headquarters staff lived. I was told that I would have to wait my turn for a flight - maybe a week or more. I signalled Wendy that I was in Tokyo and hoped to be back in Washington within the next two weeks. That left me with nothing to do but to enjoy myself.

I decided that I should pay my respects to the British Embassy and, whilst there, I was told that Air Vice-Marshal C.E. Bouchier, the representative of the British Chiefs of Staff with the US Commander in Korea, would like to see me. He was surprised that I had been to Korea and had been so active. He was curious to know more about the work of the 3rd Air Rescue Squadron and asked me to write a report of my visit for him before I returned to Washington and was given a desk to work on in the Embassy.

I knew I would be expected to produce a report in any case for Colonel Weinbrenner, something that would be suitable also for submission to BJSM. I therefore began by putting down all my thoughts and opinions, with the intention, in the end, of extracting the particulars of the 3rd Air Rescue operations for the Air Marshal's report. I knew I had been the first Britisher to be so involved in Korea and that we had everything to learn from the Americans who were years ahead of us with the development, production, and operational use of the helicopter. I had been very impressed with the efficiency, ability, and determination of 3rd Rescue, and with their servicing and maintenance of their machines in the depths of winter. I had learned much about the command and control of such operations. This is what I collated for the Air Marshal, believing, quite rightly, that he must have been aware of most of it already.

In my general drafting, I included many of the vivid impressions I had gained. I found it a useful exercise, knowing that I could always winnow out the unacceptable when it came to making a formal presentation. The wide differences in the way the British and Americans went to war were my chief concerns. I could not forget the words of a US Marine officer during that Chinese attack when I was waiting at his battalion headquarters. 'Thank goodness we have the Commonwealth Division on either flank,' he had said, 'No chance of them 'bugging-out'.' He had been using the newly-found expression for running away.

I had seen quite a lot of these differences. Most of the time I had been in Korea I had spent at K16 on the outskirts of Seoul, living in quite unnecessarily squalid conditions. There were Americans there whose morale was at rock bottom. They resented being drafted and did not want to fight in Korea. Many went around unshaven and unwashed, spending far too much time in the 'sack'. They were undisciplined and discourteous to officers. Overall there was the belief that the South Koreans were a useless, sub-standard, race something reflected in the general use of the word 'gooks' to describe them. Their attitude to the native female absolutely appalled me. I had been ashamed to see Americans, on many occasions, leaning from the backs of trucks being driven through the streets, waving dollar bills and inveigling poor women into joining them in a 'grab-arse' orgy. Maybe I was out of step, too much of a Puritan who had not seen enough of the war, but I could simply not stomach the sight of human beings behaving like barnyard animals.

It took two days to finish and sanitize the report. I handed the expurgated version on combat rescue operations to the Air Marshal who said it would be sent to London. I still had no idea of when I would be flying back to America, so I began to explore Tokyo and the surrounding countryside. I was surprised at how quickly the Japanese were recovering from the effects of World War II. There was bustle everywhere, everyone seemed to be at work. The streets were filled with cars, all using their horns continually to warn others of their whereabouts. The Ginza, the main shopping avenue, was ablaze with neon lights; the shops full of produce, much of it American but a lot made in Japan. I went out into the country and travelled on the railway which ran on time and at high speed. I went to Mount Fujiyama and visited the Royal Palace grounds and various Shinto shrines. I fell in love with the artistry and sublime perfection of the typical Japanese garden. I liked the respect shown by Japanese to each other and obvious foreigners like myself, together with the way they did business.

I had not spent a single dollar in Korea. My pay and allowances had been accumulating and so I decided to spend most of my surplus cash on a belated Christmas present for Wendy. I sought advice and was told that the best bargain in Tokyo for a lady was cultured pearls. I was taken to Mikimoto's by an American friend and there entered into negotiations with Mr. Mikimoto himself. Our first meeting was conducted sitting cross-legged on mats in a room where tea was ceremoniously served. I mentioned that I was interested in purchasing a three-string set of pearls. An assistant glided into the room with samples from which I was able to indicate what I wanted. The next day I returned to drink tea again in the same elaborate fashion and was given a final costs for the pearls and I placed my order. I returned two days later, once more going through the tea ceremony. The pearls were brought into the room and I accepted them with pleasure; the sordid business of paying for them was conducted in a general office.

The Japanese certainly kept to their rituals and maintained standards. Towards the end of my stay at the Maranuchi, a most extraordinary event occurred. An American colonel had been indulging in an amorous liaison with a well-bred Japanese lady who had been led to believe that he was single and would one day marry her. He was in fact married and had just learned that his wealthy wife was on her way to visit him in Tokyo. The colonel told the Japanese lady in a matter-of-fact way that he was a married man and that their love affair had to end. He had completely misunderstood that his 'shacking-up' with her had become her very existence and hope for a happy future. He unfeelingly suggested a final last fling, a few days before the expected arrival of his wife.

The Japanese lady made traditional preparations for a last farewell. She prepared a ceremonial meal and served it clad in national costume. The

American completely missed the poignancy of the occasion; his thoughts focussed on the expected pleasures of his last act of fornication with her. The meal finished, he was led to the bed where, slowly and seductively, she removed his clothes. When he was thoroughly aroused, she produced a Han Kin knife and cut off his penis at the root.

Thankfully, I missed the sordid scene of the naked colonel staggering down into the foyer of the hotel, pleading for help, with his hands trying to stem the blood pouring from between his legs. Meanwhile, the Japanese lady had washed the ceremonial knife and had quietly packed her belongings and left the hotel. The colonel's wife arrived the next day to be told that her husband was in hospital having been 'wounded in action'. She soon learned the truth of what had happened and returned to the States on the next available aircraft. There she divorced him for loss of conjugal rights.

I left Tokyo in a MATS Skymaster on 13th January after sending a telegram to Wendy that I hoped to be in Washington within the next four days. That day, we made a refuelling stop at Wake Island and flew on to Honolulu. As all the passengers were technically re-entering the United States, all on board had to pass through Immigration and Customs. To my amazement, I was separated from the others and told I could proceed no further, no reason was given. My arguments that I was serving with the United States Air Force and was returning under written orders to my place of work in Washington DC, were brushed aside; I was a foreigner. The national panic engendered by Senator McCarthy meant that I could well be a red-hot Communist about to endanger the people and the Government of the United States.

I protested as best I could but was met by a wall of stupid indifference. No one had any idea of my position with the USAF. Being British added to their confusion; in fact, one official believed that my squadron leader's badges of rank had something to do with the Salvation Army. I had to submit to detailed examination of my person and the contents of my B4 bag and an attache case I had bought in Tokyo to carry my classified report and the pearls I had bought Wendy. In desperation, I asked to be taken to the British Consul but instead I was led away and given into the charge of a Lieutenant Colonel, someone involved with the USAF unit on the airfield. He took pity on me, saying that he was just as mystified as I was.

I was able to see the British Consul and was allowed to leave the airport although I was under some sort of arrest. My colonel friend stayed with me and took me to see the sights. It was a truly lovely day, warm with brilliant sunshine. We visited an Hawaiian village, a pineapple farm, and went to Diamond Head where I spent a few hours on the beach. The next day I had to undergo the humiliation of making declarations before witnesses that I was not or never had been a Communist; that I had no subversive intentions towards the United States; that I had never lived on the proceeds of prostitution and had no sexual disease; nor that I was homosexual. It was difficult to keep my temper and to keep a straight face at this cleansing process. In the end, I was allowed to proceed on my way with just enough time to send another telegram to Wendy giving her a revised ETA for my arrival in Washington.

In another MATS Skymaster, I flew to Seattle on the 16th. There I was left at the mercy of the 'space-available' people of MATS. I was prepared to take anything with wings that had an empty space and managed to get aboard a Stratocruiser going south to San Bernadino, hoping there to find something heading eastwards. I was lucky to find a seat in the cockpit area of a Fairchild Packet freighter flying non-stop to Hartford, Connecticut. This flight took more than ten hours and I was allowed to have an hour or two at the controls but, after a time, I fell asleep and did not awake until we were coming in to land, early that evening. I decided that I had had enough of the 'space available' game and would finish my journey by train. I telephoned Wendy and asked her to meet me at the Union Station at about half an hour before midnight.

CHAPTER SIXTEEN

It was simply wonderful to see her again. We hugged and kissed in the station concourse. She told me that transport was parked outside. Carrying my B4 bag and attache case, I followed her out of the station, across the road, to the dimly-lit other side where a few cars were parked. I saw no signs of any transport or a driver. We stopped alongside a sparkling black and white Ford Victoria. 'That's your new car,' she said. 'It's my present for coming back in one piece.' I was absolutely overwhelmed. I put my bags down and walked around the brand-new car. 'And where's the driver,' I asked. 'Don't worry about that; just get in and relax,' she replied, 'I'm the driver.' It was all too much for me to take in, as far as I knew she'd never before driven a car. Without the slightest fuss, she drove away down Massachusetts Avenue, explaining as she went that she had been working in the the evenings at Brentanos and had earned enough extra cash to pay for the new car, after trading in the old one. She had also taught herself to drive with a little help from a BJSM driver.

My thoughts turned to the present I had bought for her; the pearls that were locked in the attache case together with copies of my classified report of what I had seen and been doing in Korea. I reached behind me for the case but it was not there. I flew into a panic remembering that I had carried the case from the station and, when last seen, I was on the pavement where I had put it down while admiring the new car. In a flash, Wendy made a U-turn on the Avenue and drove at high speed back to where she had parked earlier. Unbelievably, as we drove up, there was the case, standing on its end, on the edge of the pavement.

Satisfied that I had made it as full a report as possible and completely objective, I handed in copies to both the Psychological Warfare Division and BJSM. A week's leave of absence was then made available which we spent motoring around New England in our new car, a marvellous time.

After the excitement in Korea, work seemed very dull in Washington. I did increase the scope of my Civil Air Patrol activities by training cadets in the small 'Airdale' and the larger C-45 Expediter. Then, in early April, I was called back to London; no reason was given. Flying in a MATS aircraft to Northolt via the Azores and Paris on the 7th and 8th, I reported to ACAS(I) in my old haunt at Monck Street to learn that my report on combat rescue had helped to confirm thoughts about the future of the RAF's interest in escape and evasion matters. AI9 was still in business under Wing Commander Jim Marshall but much had changed. The policy of deterrence was emerging now that the Russians had nuclear weapons; the theory being that the possibility of mutual annihilation should put an end to the possibility of another world war and, with that, the need for escape route planning and evasion training. All that remained would be the training for combat survival and the development of the suitable equipment to be carried; both certainly not Intelligence functions.

Jim Marshall had already begun the closing down of AI9. The Army influence had all but disappeared apart from the small unit that was serving with the Commonwealth Division in Korea. The two reserve units were to be disbanded and its officers invited to join the embryonic 23 SAS(TA) in the Duke of York's Headquarters. Airey Neave and Robert Bicknell, the two former commanders, had left to concentrate on their careers and a beginning had been made on RAF combat survival training with the opening of a unit in the West Country.

I gave a few briefings and met departmental heads that had interests in possible helicopter operations. In discussion with ACAS(I) it seemed possible that my exchange tour with the USAF would soon end. I had to admit to the logic of such a decision but asked, if it did come to be, could my next appointment be away from Intelligence and back on flying.

I returned to Washington on 20th April and told the Americans of the intended closing-down of AI9. From that point onwards, it was noticeable how my duties in the Pentagon lessened and I was able to spend more time in the air. I began to give conversion rides on the B25 to officers in BJSM, including Group Captain (later Marshal of the Royal Air Force) Denis Spotswood, and Wing Commander (later Air Vice Marshal) Bird.

In May came the great news that Wendy was pregnant and, a month later, I was told that I had been preselected as a student on No 12 Course at the RAF Staff College, Andover. This was indeed an unexpected feather in my cap. I had not made application for Staff College training for the simple reason that I never held hopes for much of a career in the Service. Now, I could look forward to both the joy of parenthood and the challenge of doing my best at Andover. From then on, I read everything I could about military history, flying, and politics. I religiously went through the New York Times each weekend, forcing myself to take in and absorb the international news. I began to compile scrap books on many subjects as aides memoir, and I sought out and attended lectures on military and political subjects. In the midst of all this endeavour, I found a kindred spirit in a Lieutenant Colonel Rafferty, another Pentagon inmate, who had also been nominated to go to Andover, in his case as a preliminary to an exchange tour at Bomber Command Headquarters.

William Stuart Randle was born at the Walter Read Hospital on 21st October, 1953. We were both absolutely delighted, our son fitted easily into our life in Wiltshire Crescent. We were greatly helped by our American friends all of whom, with the exception of George Weinbrenner, were married and had children. The arrival of Stuart, as we preferred to call him, bound us closely together as a family. Flying around the States lost much of its charm and I spent far less time in the air, not much more than a single trip a month, usually with as co-pilot with Group Captain Lang. I resigned my position in the Civil Air Patrol after completing one last significant job; the organising of an Air Display at Hybla Valley in which I functioned also as commentator.

We began to make preparations to leave Washington in March, 1954. We had accumulated the beginnings of a home, and hoped to get much of it back to England. There was a suite of good modern furniture and, of course, the car. Unfortunately, BJSM were unable to help with transportation, their advice being not to bother but to sell everything before we left the States. Luckily, Colonel Rafferty came to our rescue, he undertook to include our furniture with his, to be delivered to Andover by the USAF. BJSM were able to help me with the car. All I had to do was to drive it to the dockside in New Orleans where it would be loaded aboard a freighter as deck cargo and taken to a port in England. I would have nothing to pay; there was no point in taking out insurance; the only documents involved were those pertaining to the importation of a used car into the United Kingdom.

I drove the car from Washington to New Orleans in two days, heeding the warnings of the many stringent speed traps operated in most of the small towns along the route. I kept religiously to 55 mph on the highways and never went above 35 mph as I trundled through the restricted zones. I ignored the upraised thumb of numerous hitch-hikers, and had no trouble. The car was hoisted aboard within the hour after arriving at the docks and I spent a night in New Orleans enjoying the atmosphere, the food and the music. The next day, I flew back to Washington in a B25 provided by my American colleagues.

We sailed back to England in the Queen Elizabeth. The weather was fine all the way across, and we enjoyed the voyage. We docked at Southampton and went straight to Andover. There we lodged on the out-skirts of town for a few days until we found a small unfurnished bungalow to rent. We were settled in before the Staff College course began.

There were two RAF Staff Colleges at that time, the one at Bracknell being by far the senior. At Andover there was no accommodation for the students and the few married quarters were occupied by the Directing Staff or clergy undergoing instruction at the nearby RAF Chaplains School. There was a temporary feeling about everything; instruction and lectures were given in hutted accommodation and there were already rumours that we would probably be the last course to pass through Andover. Nonetheless, there was something to be said for the more direct and personal tuition that was given to our relatively small numbers. Added to that, we were on the edge of a grass airfield and the pilots among us could fly the Chipmunks of the resident Communication Squadron.

Of the fifty on No 12 Course, a small number were foreigners. There were two Americans, an Indian, and two Pakistan officers, all of equivalent Wing Commander rank. The British were all squadron leaders, each holding a permanent commission. We soon settled down as a very happy bunch and went out of our way to make our overseas friends feel at home. In some cases, a working liaison was struck with a foreigner who really needed help in coping with the language and the British way of doing things; the Indian officer came under my wing very early in the course. We often worked together on written exercises and homework. Sometimes, almost in despair, he even copied my work, word by word.

The course began with a 'knocking off of the edges' period. We were grouped into syndicates of seven or eight, each with a Wing Commander, Director of Syndicate(DS). Very soon, I was taken to task for long-windedness, the overuse of cliches and slang, and, best of all, for offering opinions before fully weighing the facts and properly constructing a reply. We next moved on to a regime of lectures and exercises. As the course advanced, we regularly changed DS, deriving benefit from their different experiences as they represented most of the Branches of the RAF.

We were given up to three lectures a week, rendered by the best people available. They covered a very wide range of topics most, however, directly associated with the Services. It was expected that each of us would come up with a telling question after the lecture; in fact, the question time usually lasted longer than the lecture itself, and was usually more productive. The problem for most of us was to find a suitable question; sometimes it was quite a struggle for me to concoct something meaningful. I cannot forget a particular lecture given by Air Marshal Sir George Beamish, the well-known rugby player. He was then Director of Organization and had given us a dull account of a boring and uninteresting subject. The question period was not much better and most of us had to struggle to find something sensible to say. In my case, my turn to stand up was long overdue. I had found it difficult to follow what the Air Marshal had said, and none of my ideas for a question made any sense. My DS was sitting behind me with his notebook open.

The minutes ticked away and the DS were getting up to ask questions in our stead. I knew that I would be marked down if I did not say something. In desperation, I took a wild chance at bringing a little cheer into the room by changing the subject. I stood up and asked the Air Marshal for his opinion on how a young bunch of students, such as we were, with prospects of a career ahead of us for the next twenty years or so, should spend our money. That certainly got the laughs. Sir George's face lit up;

he was pleased. 'Not the slightest doubt about that, young man,' he said. 'Put your money into something that is not going to lose its value as the years go by. Buy a house.'

That advice had an impact on many of us. Three of us, Douggie Lowe, Bill Asheton, and myself even set up an exercise to determine where and when we should buy. We agreed that it was most likely we would be spending increasing periods of time at the Air Ministry in the London area. Therefore, we ought to look at places around the capital within easy travelling distance; the areas that recommended themselves were the Chilterns and the North Downs. We decided on the latter because of better roads and train services and, after the course, each of us bought a house along the Downs; Douggie Lowe at West Byfleet; Bill Asheton at Chobham; and myself at Tadworth. The Air Marshal's advice certainly turned out to be prophetic.

The visits we made were the icing on the cake; a variety of Service and other establishments were on the agenda. Factories making aircraft, steel, and food were first, then we went to sea, up in a tethered balloon, and slogged across Army exercise areas at Imber and Warminster. We visited the Americans at Lakenheath and Woodbridge, and rode in tanks and fired their guns at targets on the edge of Lulworth Cove. The visit that had the most profound effect on me, however, was to a colliery at Ashington in Northumberland. We toured the buildings and met the management; then we were taken down to the coal face. There I saw the unbelievable toil of the miners cutting out the coal. We spoke to men who were working on a low two-foot high seam dripping with water. From what I could gather, they were content; their only gripes being that there should be better equipment for them to use at the coal face, and better pay for hard and dangerous work. I marvelled that anyone could possibly object to such concessions.

We kept our hands in by flying the enjoyable Chipmunks of the Communication Squadron but were only allowed between three and four hours a month, and most of that in the local area. I found, as usual, that I was not very good at aerobatics.

In January 1954, I went with Wendy to Buckingham Palace to receive the insignia of the MBE from Queen Elizabeth that I had been awarded almost three years previously. Some months later, we went to the

American Embassy in London where I was presented with the United States Air Medal. This was indeed a unmerited surprise made the all the more embarrassing for me when the Air Attache, a Brigadier, read a citation signed by President Eisenhower, to the effect that, 'Squadron Leader Randle had distinguished himself by meritorious achievement while participating in aerial flight on SB29, SA16, and H19 aircraft in air rescue operations consisting of behind-the-line pickup, orbit and search missions.' Later, when cocktails were served, the Brigadier while paying far too much attention to Wendy, managed to empty his glass down the front of the dress she had bought especially for the occasion.

American Embassy October 11th 1954

As we neared the end of the ten-month long course we each had to go through the formality of attending the Commandant's Dinner Party. Until then, Air Commodore D Lane had only been seen at a distance. The Dinner Party was his opportunity for him and his wife to get to know a little more about how we and our wives conducted ourselves. When my turn came, I was pleased to find that Wendy and I would be joined by Douggie and Betty Lowe, and an irrepressible Irishman, Micky Flynn, and his wife.

We were on tenterhooks as we sat down to eat. The dinner was very formal and more of an exercise than a pleasure. The Air Commodore and his wife drew each pair of us into conversation as the meal progressed but the atmosphere remained tense and starchy. When it came Mickey's turn to hold the court, the conversation had been diverted to the current plague of myxomatosis that was sweeping the countryside clear of rabbits. Mickey answered a question from the Air Commodore that turned the conversation to cooking. He warmed to the subject and, over his refilled wine glass, he smilingly propounded how some people were such good cooks that they could serve rabbits disguised as chicken. A dead silence followed as the main course was brought to the table; sliced chicken breast smothered in a cheese sauce.

The other judgement made by the Commandant was his evaluation of the thesis which rounded off our work on the course. We were allowed to chose the nature of the thesis; the only stipulation being that it should have some bearing on military or aviation matters. For some time, in syndicate discussion, I had found myself a lone voice on the use of air power. Air Commodore Spaight's book, 'Air Power Can Disarm' had been a sort of bible to most, backed with the wartime results of Bomber Command and the emergence of the nuclear bomb. What I had seen for myself in Korea had reinforced my belief that the Air Commodore's book was out of date; it had been overtaken by events. I believed that there would always be limitations in the use of air power in future wars, if the deterrence policy held. I had seen how the Chinese and North Koreans had kept their lines of communication open and had been able to resupply troops in the front line in the face of overwhelming air power. The countryside had been laid waste with high explosive bombs and napalm. Villages and towns had been swept away; thousands had been killed; yet air power, in the end, had been powerless. I proposed the thesis, quite perversely I suppose, that 'Air

Power Can No Longer Disarm.'

My Directing Staff in this the final stage of the course was a Wing Commander in the Equipment Branch. It was not often that we agreed on anything of importance and I found him at a loss when we spoke about the military use of aircraft. When I submitted my thesis he was surprised at the title and then very critical of the argument. He marked it down as unproven and went as far as to write, in comment to the Commandant who would have the final say, that he thought I had deliberately gone out of my way to be controversial; in any case, he did not understand the argument. When it was returned to me, the Commandant had written - I am inclined to agree with your DS. I find your thesis unproven; but do not be discouraged. Seldom in reading through 10,000 words have I found not a single spelling mistake or punctuation error.

I do not know whether this trenchant comment had anything to do with my next appointment. I had effectively been out of the front line of the Royal Air Force for almost seven years, dealing with intelligence matters. I had every reason to expect a return to productive flying duties, hopefully as a squadron commander. I had made my wishes abundantly clear in the final interviews, hoping that I would be posted to Bomber Command or maybe to the emerging helicopter force. I was utterly dismayed when told I was to be a military secretary at the Ministry of Defence in Storey's Gate, Whitehall, dealing with scientific matters. That meant another three years away from the Royal Air Force and I had been given an appointment about which I knew absolutely nothing.

Wendy was not unpleased at the news. I had long since realized how much she worried when I was flying. We both saw the opportunity now to put down our roots and, mindful of the advice given me by Air Marshal Beamish, the first thing we did was to find a house to buy. We had already decided on a location somewhere in the North Downs and it took us less than a week to find the place we have lived in ever since. It was a small two-bedroom house, just a year old, situated along an unmade road at Tadworth, not far from the Epsom racecourse. We took out a mortgage for £1,800 of the £3,500 we had to pay for the building and a half an acre of land that went with it. It proved to be an excellent investment and in our time the we have added substantially to the original two bedroom specification, as well as laying out gardens in the ground which came with the house. The area itself has remained pleasant and our once unmade road has now matured into a typical English tree-lined avenue. Given today's prices we have also acheived something of a return on our initial investment.

CHAPTER SEVENTEEN

The Ministry of Defence in those days was a relatively small organization that co-ordinated the work of the Civil Service, Admiralty, War Office, and Air Ministry. My appointment was one of the three major-equivalent posts that rotated with incumbents from the three services. It was the RAF's turn and I found myself joining Squadron Leader Freddie Sowrey, responsible for operational secretarial matters, and Squadron Leader Cartwright Terry dealing with the administrative. I was to be the junior Secretary of the Defence Research Policy Committee (DRPC) and the Secretary of the Commonwealth Advisory Committee on Defence Science (CACDS). My chief was Sir Frederick Brundrett, the Defence Scientist, and my immediate superior, Willy Wright, an Assistant Secretary.

For weeks I worked in a daze, slowly beginning to understand the business of defence scientific matters. I was pitchforked into a meeting of the DRPC the day after I arrived, luckily with Willy Wright telling me just to do my best, to put down what I had heard but not to worry because minute preparation was his responsibility. The great men around the table, all of Deputy Chief of Staff status or better, dealt quickly with the agenda under the spirited chairmanship of Sir Frederick Brundrett. My early efforts at minute-taking were pitiful, I didn't have the experience to determine what was substance and what was waffle. Nor could I get down on paper quickly enough what I was listening to, and I didn't have sufficient scientific knowledge to understand what was being said. I knew very little about the technical background of many of the items that ranged over problems of the three Services. Luckily I was working with a brilliant Assistant Secretary who was, of course, the person that made the DRPC function. He was sympathetic to my ignorance. Apparently, all my predecessors had experienced the same problems at first; the Army ones coped the best; the Naval, the worst.

Gradually, I settled down, beginning to enjoy the work as the veil of mystery slowly lifted. I studied the papers to be taken in detail and did my best to anticipate what the great men had been briefed to say. I took the short cut of asking the briefing staffs what they had in mind for their masters. Bit by bit, I worked to the point where I felt confident to take the minutes in Willy Wright's absence.

I was on my own in the CACDS meetings which, fortunately, were rare occurrences. Each country in the Commonwealth with a defence policy was represented on the Committee. Sir Frederick was again the Chairman. I had the responsibility of organizing the meeting, preparing the agenda from the many papers that were submitted for discussion, taking the minutes and, whenever called for, reporting on the result of meetings themselves.

Wendy and I settled down happily happily in our little house in Tadworth. We still had the Ford Victoria that I had brought back from America but it could only just be manoeuvered into the tiny garage. I did not use it to travel to London; that was done by train from Kingswood station, just over a mile away, a tedious two-hour round trip. We joined the local church at Kingswood, and I was able to keep my hand in by flying Chipmunks from Kenley.

The fact that the house was newly-built presented something of a challenge. What passed for a garden was nothing more than half an acre of a former cornfield, bounded by metal markers with a long stand of elms at the far end. There was even a right-of-way through the trees up to the house and out on to the road. I began to enclose the property by putting up barbed wire on the far side of the elms. For a while certain people tried to exert their rights by climbing over the wire that now interfered with the right-of-way. I drew up a garden plan which entailed the planting of many trees and began the development of a woodland bordering the elms, by planting it with primroses, bluebells and wood anemones around young birch and evergreen trees. I laid down paths both at the front and rear of the house. I was in my element, almost every time I worked in the garden, I was joined by Stuart, my son. He was developing as a very intelligent child; active, full of questions and promise.

In October, 1955, our world almost fell apart. Stuart was the just two years old when, one night, we noticed a swelling in his side. In great panic, Wendy and I immediately called our doctor and he was rushed away to the Great Ormond Street Hospital for Children where, the next day, he was operated on and a cancerous tumour and a kidney were removed. It was a savage operation that had to be followed by a course of radiotherapy. During the next six weeks, I took him to Great Ormond Street Hospital at regular intervals for this nerve-wracking treatment. He was bright enough to appreciate that it was to be an ordeal. Each time, I helped the radio therapist to prepare him for treatment. I tried to sooth his fears as he was laid on the operating table, held in place by lead-filled bags for receipt of the radiation rays. I can never forget his pitiful cries, 'Daddy, Daddy, help me,' as I had to leave him for the radiation machine to go to work; they are with me to this very day.

At the end of January, 1956, I was sent on a four-week-long visit to Canada to help the Canadians with a conference of the Commonwealth Advisory Committee of Defence Science. Stuart's treatment had finished; all we could do now was to wait to learn whether it had been successful in stopping the spread of the cancer. In a sense, I must have been the lucky one, because I was off and away on a task that would keep me fully occupied and tend to push Stuart's illness to the background.

I flew from London to New York in a BOAC Stratocruiser, via Prestwick in Scotland and Gander in Newfoundland. From New York, I flew on to Montreal and then Ottawa in an American-operated Vickers Viscount. I was settled into the Chateau Laurier where most of the conference was to be held. To my surprise, I was asked by the Canadian secretariat, a major and a captain, if I would take the overall responsibility for managing the daily meetings. This seemed to be a sensible suggestion because at least I knew something about CACDS affairs while they admitted to know nothing. I took over the secretarial duties for the inaugural meeting and then established a routine.

I took minutes while my Canadian counterparts tried to do likewise. I sat alongside the Chairman of the day - this function rotated between eight different nationalities. Many of the Chairmen were uncertain of what to do and I furnished each with a brief at the beginning of the day on how I thought the proceedings might be managed. Often I would slip a note to a Chairman on how a particular point of procedure could be resolved. Some openly turned to me for advice on what to do next. Once the meetings were over, we drafted the minutes which I then checked and had typed for presentation the next morning. It proved to be a task that kept me at work far into the evening and did away with any chance of entertainment.

There were two weeks of daily meetings with just a break at weekends. I made a start on the report which had to be agreed before we departed. There was a welcome break when we flew in a noisy RCAF North Star, a DC4 fitted with Rolls Royce Merlins, to Fort Churchill on Hudson Bay. We landed in a snow storm and were quickly taken to the centrally heated hutted complex of the camp. We stayed there for just two days being briefed on cold-weather problems and taken around the Barrens looking out for polar bears. We examined igloos and were invited to spend a night sleeping in them. I made the valid excuse that I had work to do on the report and the business that remained in Ottawa. I do remember the next morning when those who had decided to spend the night on the Barrens returned to our super-heated quarters. The Indian representative who had refused to have his sandals replaced with fur leggings for the night, avowing that resistance to the cold was all a matter of the mind, was in deep trouble. Two of his toes were so badly frost-bitten that they had to be amputated.

There were just a few more meetings to be held when we returned to Ottawa and, of course, I still had to draft the Conference report, get it approved, and signed by the principal delegates. This business was uncomplicated and soon dealt with. I left Canada from Montreal on 26th February and flew directly to London in a BOAC Stratocruiser, the first time I had crossed the Atlantic non-stop by air. Back at Storey's Gate, I was congratulated by Sir Frederick Brundrett on a job well done.

It was only a few weeks later that Wendy and I were told that our son only had a short time to live. Nothing could be done to arrest the spread of the cancer to most parts of his body. We just had to keep him comfortable, allay his pain, and watch him die. We hired a nurse to be with him during the day, which he spent in a semi-conscious condition. I did my utmost to behave as I thought I should; trying to push the thoughts of his suffering from my mind. I threw myself into my work. In doing so, I knew that I was of little help to Wendy, but I had no idea what to do for the best.

We buried Stuart in the Kingswood churchyard in April; the flowers on the coffin were daffodils. Friends rallied around to comfort us, our vicar and his wife did their best but the words they offered by way of sympathy made no sense at all. I could not accept that Stuart's death was God's will, and that time itself would heal, and that we would be the stronger for what had happened. I rounded on the vicar and suggested that if God's will was involved then maybe we were being punished for my killing of German children in the war. Although I managed to keep a 'stiff upper lip', it was Wendy who did the better, by giving vent to her emotions and crying the dreadful hurt from her. Much went on in my mind that I kept to myself. I had lost my faith; the funeral was the last time I went voluntarily to church.

With the house now empty during the day, Wendy went back to work at Smythsons. I had certainly grown in confidence with my secretarial duties and could be left alone at DRPC meetings to deal with the taking and writing-up of minutes. I had begun to like the rarified atmosphere of the Ministry and felt privileged to be working in company of great men. I had even been drawn in to help with minute-taking at meetings chaired by Duncan Sandys. It was there that I first heard of how the Government was working on a review that would result in the greatest change in a defence system ever made in normal times.

In July, I was able to take three weeks leave of absence. We both need-ed a holiday and decided to make it a good one by using the Ford Victoria to drive to Italy, a country which both of us had never visited. We did not hurry; we kept off the auto routes. Our route took us to Grenoble and then down through the mountains to Antibes. From there we drove into Italy and along the coast to Genoa; then up into Tuscany. After a few days, we decided to return to the coast to finish our holiday in a villa at San Remo. The weather was excellent; we swam each day, lazed on the beach, did some snorkelling and, in the end, realized that we had benefited because we were ready to return to work.

We had read in the Italian newspapers that President Nasser of Egypt, reacting to the building tension in the Middle East, intended to nationalize the Suez Canal in which Britain and France were the major shareholders. When I got back to the office, I found that we had already begun to concentrate naval and air forces in the Mediterranean, and that there was a plan shaping, Operation Musketeer, under which British and French troops could be landed to occupy key points along the Canal.

There was considerable scepticism amongst us in the Ministry of a plan that could well involve us in a war already being fought between Israel and her Arab neighbours. We dearly hoped that the ultimatum delivered to both sides by Britain and France on 30th October, calling on them to end the fighting and stay clear of the Canal Zone, would have effect. When we learned that Musketeer had been put into action, there was an almost universal groan of disbelief at Storey's Gate; certainly at least at my level. We could not see the political justification for an operation against Egypt nor did we like the idea of using our overwhelming bomber force. The early knowledge of Musketeer did, however, result in the sale of my large petrol-guzzling American car. It warned that if fighting was protracted then petrol rationing would be imposed.

Towards the end of the year, I asked for an interview with the Air Secretary's Department just to discover if and when I would ever be returned to flying duties. I was assured that my next appointment would indeed be as such and, because of the long time I had been away from the RAF front line, already eight years, I would undergo both refresher training and jet conversion.

Our daughter, Beverley Jane, was born on 23rd April, 1957. It was simply marvellous to be parents again. Unfortunately, within just three weeks of her birth, she was stricken with whooping cough in its very worst form. The coughing was so bad and continuous that she could not be fed. We were told that she was in dire trouble. We began to despair of ever being able to raise children as the poor little mite seemed to be coughing her life away. Our doctor did everything she could, in desperation I even considered hiring an aeroplane and nurse and climbing to a height of 15,000 feet from where I would put the machine in a dive to earth, hoping that the violent increase in pressure would put paid to the cough. So worried was I that I contacted the Central Medical Establishment of the RAF for help. They were not sure that the flight would achieve anything but believed that a special serum under development in Switzerland might do the trick. This they obtained within thirty-six hours and, to our great relief and joy, Beverley began to get well within hours of its first dose.

During April, Duncan Sandys published the long-awaited White Paper on Defence. It held the shattering view that manned aircraft were becoming out dated and that in due course missiles would take over both the defence of the country and the maintenance of the deterrent. The preparation of the White Paper had been in the background of our work for some time, and its contents were already affecting the work of the DRPC. The idea that missile development would destroy the requirement for a fighter aircraft to follow the Lightning, and also that for a supersonic bomber to replace the V-bombers, was anathema to the RAF members of the Committee. Furthermore, the burgeoning costs of research and development had reached the stage where it had become impossible accurately to establish a fixed-price contract for a major project. The DRPC was faced with muddle and indecision as projects were either set up for cancellation or put into abeyance.

I well remember one meeting in which Barnes Wallis had been invited to present his ideas for a variable swept-wing bomber he had named the Swallow. This could have been considered as a replacement for the Valiants, Victors, and Vulcans, if the White Paper had not just put paid to such a project. Barnes Wallis held the floor for about twenty minutes or so as he demonstrated how the variable-sweep mechanism for the huge wing would work. We were fascinated; all he said made sense. The only real mention I made in the minutes was that the Americans were interested. I concluded that the Committee had simply taken note.

My tour at the Ministry of Defence effectively came to an end on 1st July, 1957 when I was sent to join No 89 Refresher Flying Course of No 3 Flying Training School at Feltwell. I was there for twelve days during which I flew just 19 hours on the piston-engined Percival Provost. I liked the machine and thoroughly enjoyed myself. All the students were staff officers returning to flying duties. We flew together in pairs and were given very much a free rein but my heavy-handed aerobatics and penchant for low flying made it hard for me to find willing partners. I did most of my flying with just two Flight Lieutenants who were as bad pilots as I was.

On 18th September, I went to RAF Debden to fly the Vickers Varsity.

By then my replacement had arrived at the Ministry, a Royal Engineers major, and so I was able to stay at Debden until 1st November and flew just under 60 hours in the Varsity which reminded me so much of its line-al predecessor, the Wellington. Emphasis was placed on instrument flying, blind approach to landings, and single-engined work.

On 7th November, I began the No 110 Jet Conversion course at Worksop airfield, courtesy of Airwork Ltd. Again there was a collection of staff officers hoping to return to flying duties. We converted to the DH Vampire, affectionately called the 'Clockwork Mouse', taking instruction in the two-seater T11 with ejector seats, and flying solo in the delightful single-seater FB5. I was blessed with a very good instructor, a Flight Lieutenant Redding, who had just the right touch for 'old stagers' like myself. He sent me solo after my third trip yet he seemed to take perverse delight in making me apprehensive by flying the Vampire to the very limits of its capabilities. We indulged in aerobatics on every sortie; the climbs were usually high speed; there was a daily flame-out practice, and then, Redding's speciality, a barrel roll all over the sky at 40,000 feet where we flopped about in the rarified atmosphere. The course lasted just 13 days and I flew 13 hours and thirty-five minutes. It had not proved to be to everyone's liking; two 'retreads', one a Group Captain, refused to fly solo.

CHAPTER EIGHTEEN

On 1st December, 1957, I received an appointment as commander of a Vampire NF10 training squadron at No 2 ANS (Air Navigation School), Thorney Island. I had hoped for something better. I would dearly liked to have been posted again to Bomber Command, but then, I could see the sense in not taking a chance with someone like me who had been off productive flying for almost ten years.

No 2 ANS had the job of training navigators, undertaken jointly with No 1 ANS at Swinderby. The student made his first flights in the Varsity, and then moved on to more detailed work with electronic equipment in the Valetta. The final stage was spent in the Vampire squadron where emphasis was placed on rapid decision at altitude and at high speed, while working in the cramped space alongside the pilot. I started flying on 4th December and quickly converted to the NF10. I underwent training in the Valetta T3 and flew a few sorties in the Varsity. This all took place while the Vampires remained in the hands of a squadron leader waiting to leave the Service.

Wendy and I decided to remain in our house at Tadworth until things settled down at Thorney Island. I used a new Standard Vanguard, which I had bought after selling our beloved American car, for the daily trip between home and the station; I cannot remember why I bought such a vehicle. Maybe it was because Lord Tedder, formerly our Chief of Air Staff, was then on the Board at Standard's or, more likely, because hundreds of them were being used in the Services as staff cars. It was, however, something I came to regret. I suffered the embarrassment of a complete electrical failure and was stranded on the Hog's Back on my way to the Farnborough air display. The brakes failed in heavy traffic in Park Lane leaving us jammed into the back of a taxi. Then, to cap it all, one dismal evening, the engine blew up as I laboured up Bury Hill in the South Downs on my way home after night flying. It happened just below the top of the hill. In disgust, I left the wretched machine by the side of the road and trudged miles down the other side of the hill to Watersfield where I managed to arouse the owner of the only garage in the district. He undertook to get the Standard back for repair, and gave me a car, a Renault Dauphin, to get home. On my way back to Thorney Island the next morning, I traded in the Vanguard for the Dauphin and I have driven Renaults ever since.

Thorney Island was a busy place. It was commanded by Group Captain Rex Boxer AFC whom I had seen performing tied-together aerobatics in No 1 Squadron's Hawker Fury team before the war. The Wing Commander Flying was Mike Fleetwood DSO, a well-known former Coastal Command pilot. Eventually, I took command of the Vampire squadron at the beginning of February.

Valetta's of No. 2 A.N.S

The great thing about the new appointment was that I could fly as often as I wished. There was no call for me to be involved in the navigation training; my job was managing the fifteen or so pilots and aircraft. I flew with each of the pilots in turn and did, now and then, take on an instructional flight. The other squadron commanders allowed me to keep my hand in on their Varsities and Valettas. I was more than a little out of place amongst the young Vampire enthusiasts, being the only one who had seen any sort of operational action. I did my very best to inculcate a corporate spirit amongst them, and I think I was reasonably successful. Best of all, I was enjoying myself, every day learning something new about the men and machines. The only drawback was the intentional separation from the family, something I could have rectified if I had hired accommodation in the neighbourhood.

Then, one fine sunny afternoon in early August, my world began to collapse. I was air-testing a NF10, happily cruising along at about 30,000 feet with my mind wandering on thoughts of what might have been had Stuart lived. Suddenly, I burst into tears. It was though a dam had burst; all I had kept pent up since his death seemed to be released. I began to choke in my oxygen mask, panicking as I began to feel I was losing consciousness. I just had enough sense to put out the air brakes and put the aircraft into a steep dive. I unstrapped and threw aside the mask as I passed through 12,000 feet and felt I began to breathe better and, when I reached the circuit, I managed to fly straight in to land. I taxied to dispersal, switched off, and then found that I was too weak to move. I sat in the cockpit for quite a while and had to be helped out to be taken to sick quarters.

I offered no explanation for what had happened; in fact, I was too ashamed to mention the tears and panic. The Medical Officer checked my rapidly fluctuating blood pressure and took a sample of my blood. He found that the blood sugar content was extremely low and thought that was probably the root cause of my problems. Within hours, I was on my way to see the specialists at the RAF Hospital, Halton. There I was thoroughly examined and underwent a series of tests aimed at finding out at what stage I would indeed lose consciousness. Thankfully, I never reached that point. The verdict, however, was that I was hyperglycaemic; that the pancreas had lost control of the supply of blood sugar. I was told that it was a condition if not rectified might result in my becoming grounded. I could see the end of any career I might have had in the Royal Air Force.

I spent two weeks at Halton and was then sent to the Central Medical Establishment for a reassessment of my medical category. Fortunately, I was interviewed by a sympathetic Air Vice-Marshal. He fully understood my fears of a non-flying future. He decided that I could return to my duties at Thorney Island but cautioned that I should pace myself slowly for a while. I should continue with my flying duties but should not fly solo for a while. If ever I felt faint, he instructed, I should take glucose. You cannot imagine the effect of this reprieve. The Air Vice-Marshal must have had an inkling of what I had already judged for myself; that I had gone through something very close to a nervous breakdown.

I was able to take a longish leave before going back to Thorney Island. This I spent at home, working in the house and developing the garden. The wretched panic attacks still came and went but I said nothing at all about them to anyone, not to Wendy. Quite trivial matters could bring them on; usually just thoughts, seldom actions. My blood pressure would rise and I would gasp for breath; I could hear my pulse thudding in my head. There was a terror about them because I did not know what would happen next. I had reasoned that the cause of my troubles was something to do with the loss of my son and that I had to get the self pity out of my system. The remedy was in my hands; the matter was so personal that it could not be shared. I drilled myself whenever an attack came on. I forced my mind to dwell on something radically different. I would take glucose, then sit down, and reason how lucky I was to have got so far with life, and that there was still much to be done.

The attacks continued for a while when I returned to Thorney Island. Happily, I found that the harder I worked the less likely it was that an attack would occur. I was pleased to find that my reactions and judgement had in no way become impaired. Step by step, I mastered the affliction and then, one day, I dealt with a major problem without the slightest vestige of any alarm.

A full flying programme was in being when Thorney Island became enveloped in a thunderous line-squall that had not been accurately forecast before the aircraft had set off. The visibility fell to a few hundred yards in heavy, driving rain. The Varsities and Valettas were diverted to stations to the north of the squall but for some reason the decision to divert the

Vampires had not been made and they were becoming dangerously short of fuel. I was called to the Control Tower where the Station Commander and Wing Commander Flying were already dealing with the problem. The Vampires had but twenty minutes of fuel left and were high above the storm on a final leg from Lands End. I told my superiors that there was not enough time left for a diversion. The decision of what had to be done was left to me.

I could see no other option but to get them into Thorney Island before they ran out of fuel and would be forced to bale out. I took over the Radio Telephone and instructed each pilot to let down through the towering turbulence and break cloud over the Channel. From there, he would be vectored by QDMs (radio directional bearings) to the Nab Light, a few miles south of the airfield. He could then use the ARC7 approach to fly in at low level, with wheels down. The airfield would be cleared for each approach. The runway and approach lights were switched on, and the airfield was put on alert. Without incident, eight Vampires flew in through the storm, one by one, and landed safely. Each had just about five minutes fuel left.

A few weeks later, Mike Fleetwood retired from the Service under the 'Golden Bowler' scheme and, to my utter amazement, I was appointed Wing Commander Flying with acting rank. This released one of the principal married quarters and I was able to move Wendy and Beverley into the large house that stood just behind the Officers' Mess. It was simply wonderful to have the family with me.

Within weeks there was also a change of Station Commander. Group Captain Guy Devas, another Bomber Command veteran, took over. My moving up a step in rank had given me an altogether different perspective on Service life. I welcomed the greater responsibility which was made all the easier because there was no resentment shown by others at my unexpected promotion.

Surrounded by mud flats and the waters of Chichester harbour, protected by hills away to the north, Thorney Island was an ideal airfield from which to fly. With excellent approaches to land coming in from the sea on the south, there were not many days when flying had to be cancelled. We had wing commanders in charge of Administration, Training, Technical and Flying. I firmly believed that my particular responsibilities set the pace for the achievement of the station's aim.

The centre-point of the Flying Wing was a supremely efficient Standardisation Flight of experienced Flight Lieutenants, all qualified instructors. Its leader was Jack Challinor, ably supported by 'Nibby' Fellowes, Mike Currie, and Ted Bates. Between them, they set standards for the whole station and directly helped to maintain flight discipline. The fact that there were no flying accidents of any sort during my time at Thorney Island was largely due to the excellence of this group.

I flew as often as I could and I went up with every pilot on the station on navigation exercises, air tests, continuation flying, and overseas flights. We parted with the Vampires in June 1959 and they were replaced by Meteors T7 and NF14. I underwent a thorough checkup at the Central Medical Establishment and was restored to full flying duties. Unfortunately, my flying category had to be reduced because I had become short-sighted. From then on, I flew wearing spectacles with corrected lenses which neatly tucked in under the first-patterned protective helmets that had just been issued.

I flew all three types of aircraft on the station and much preferred the Meteor in which I first went solo in October. RAF Tangmere was just a few miles away where I was able to fly in the Canberra, courtesy of Group Captain 'Mickey' Martin, the Australian of Dambuster fame. He was replaced by Denis David, a Hurricane ace of the Battle of Britain, with whom I formed a sound friendship which lasted until his death in late 2001. Other aircraft types that I 'hogged' were the Jet Provost, Comanche, the one and only Percival EP9, the Chipmunk and Saro Skeeter helicopter.

I had not forgotten a vow I had made during my illness, that was to work for others. It was at Thorney Island that I began to raise money for charity, something I have been doing steadily ever since. Fund-raising, nowadays such a professional business, was in its infancy in those days. I started very modestly with raffles and sponsored walks. I dragooned reluctant aircrew into taking part, usually when I found them loafing on the Wednesday sports afternoons; another activity for which I had been made responsible. I organized schemes from which a revenue could be extracted, such as go-cart rallies, light aircraft fly-ins, and sporting events.

Inevitably, I came to the conclusion that the most productive could well be a concentration of the station's effort into one big fund-raising event. I got the Station Commander's permission to open the airfield to the public for a whole day which would give us the opportunity of extracting money from every single visitor. I submitted plans which included a five-hour flying display, a go-cart rally, a regional fly-in of light aircraft, some folk-dancing and two brass bands. There were to be more than a hundred stalls selling produce, gadgets, mementoes, garden equipment, souvenirs, and, my own creation, which I hoped would become known as the famous Thorney Cockle.

It proved to be a considerable undertaking and the aim, that we were raising money for charity, always had to be kept in mind. Wherever possible, sponsorship was found for the setting up of events and exhibits. This happened with the go-carting, much of the flying, and all the publicity. I was promised that two of the hangars would be cleared for the day to house the stalls. I charged a heavy rent to commercial traders who had to erect their own stalls and arrange their insurance. The station rallied wonderfully. The Wives' Clubs did well and came up with some good money-making ideas. One, for which I had to allocate the equivalent space of three stalls, was a gigantic cock-shy on which relays of previously thrown away crockery, cups, bottles, and cooking pots could be set up to be smashed at sixpence a throw. Administrative Wing undertook to keep the books, collect the rents and the expected accumulation of money taken by the stalls during the day. Technical Wing had the heavy jobs of moving aircraft and preparing the hangars.

I was able to drive Flying Wing hard, particularly during the sports afternoons. I encouraged them to come up with their own fund-raising ideas. At first, I had difficulty in getting the Standardisation Flight to move and, in the end, penalised them by giving them the task of organizing the sale of the Thorney Cockle. This meant digging the cockles out of the mud, collecting them in buckets for washing, cooking, and bottling in the Airmens' Mess kitchens. Although there must have been hundreds of thousands of the molluscs waiting in the mud-flats, my heroes, at first, went about their duties half-heartedly and with an ill-grace. I did not threaten them but expressed my displeasure, with the result that cockle-collecting improved so well that we reached our target of 250 bottles during the last week before the Fair.

Everything went well on the day, the sun shone throughout; the flying display went without a hitch and the station was absolutely crammed with people. The money began to accumulate fast with a section of the Accounts staff kept hard at it, counting and packaging the cash, most of which seemed to be in the form of sixpences. Prudently, we began the clearing up as the day wore on. Hundred-weights of broken crockery and glassware had to be shovelled into bins. One aspect of planning that went horribly wrong was the lack of provision of toilets for the ladies. The only lavatories in the Fair area were in the hangars and they simply could not cope with the overwhelming need.

The first Thorney Island Air Fair

Our AOC-in-C., Air Marshal Atcherley arrived in his Meteor during the flying display and was spirited away from the fund-raising confusion by the Station Commander. 'Batchy', as he was fondly called, was in his habitually good form; he graciously understood the purpose of it all.

I was thoroughly exhausted by the end of the Fair, in fact too 'whacked' to attend the gala dance that went on into the early hours. The next morning, a Sunday, I was up early to deal with the remaining clearing up; another aspect of the planning that had been underestimated. I had to root people out from all Wings to help with the removal of the stalls from the hangars and the traders from the station. The rubbish, lorry-loads of it, had to be collected; the perimeter tracks had to be swept, and aircraft moved back into the hangars. Nonetheless, the immediate verdict was that the Thorney Fair had been a fund-raising success.

However I was greatly taken aback, five days later, when visited by a police inspector. He told me he was investigating a widespread outbreak of food poisoning that seemed to be caused by something bought at the Thorney Fair. I at once thought of the famous to be Thorney Cockle which as far as I knew was the only item we had sold in quantity. We had a few jars left and the inspector took a couple away for analysis. The next day, he was back to tell me that the cockles were contaminated and that it was likely I could be charged for selling bad food.

I asked the Medical Officer to check our culinary and bottling processes. The news of possible disaster soon got around the station and, within the day, the reason for the contamination was found. My friends in the Standardisation Flight, looking for a way to ease the burden of meeting the collecting norm I placed on them, had found an area in which the cockles were larger, more plentiful, and easier to dig. A great proportion of the cockles we had bottled had, in fact, come from this area, my heroes not realizing that they had been feeding on the effluent of the Emsworth sewers.

I was duly called to account at the Emsworth Magistrates Court, pleading that no one had the slightest idea that the Emsworth sewers were contaminating the Thorney Island mud. I apologised most profusely and that was accepted. I added that we hoped that not too many people had been badly inconvenienced. The chief magistrate asked the policeman who had given evidence if he knew if any serious damage had been done. 'I cannot

say for sure, your honour,' he replied. 'All I know is that these flying people have got them farting sideways all the way from Portsmouth to
Brighton.'

I fell foul with the law again a few weeks later. This time it was as a
result of something I had done in an attempt to improve the station amenities available to the families. I had been asked by the Wives' Club if there
was some better way for the ladies and their children to get to Pilsea
Island, a small outcrop of rock with a decent beach on its south side, situated at the end of the main runway. All else was mud, and Pilsea Island
could only be reached at low tide by their venturesomely picking their way
across a mud-filled channel.

Directing work on the causway which, at least
at first, was undertaken by hand

I came up with the idea of building a causeway between the two islands.
It seemed well within our capabilities because of the hundreds of tons of
rubble that still laid around the southern perimeter, left there after the
German attacks on the station in 1940. I reasoned that I could find a labour
force on Wednesday afternoons from the non-sporting aircrew and at
weekends from volunteers. There was not much enthusiasm at first but as
the summer progressed and the lost opportunities of sunbathing were realized, the Causeway project began to develop. Unfortunately, it was not

easy work moving the heavy rubble on to the mud and as time slipped by, I began to see an enormous 'white elephant' coming to life. It was quite clear that the causeway could not be built before the end of the season. Luckily, a friend in the Aircraft Construction Branch came to my help by laying on a training exercise. In a matter of days the causeway was finished by the experts; the surface levelled and impacted.

*The causway from the air as it progressed
towards Pilsea Island*

The day for the opening of the causeway was hot and sunny. Many families had already decided to spend some time on the Pilsea Island beach and were gathered at the end of our hard-worked monument. As the instigator of the project, I was privileged to be the first to use it and to test its strength. I decided to cross in a jeep and then drive around the island, before the families would be allowed to move.

I set off to the cheers of the crowd finding to my pleasure that the causeway could easily have borne the weight of a ten-ton truck as I drove steadily across and then, at walking pace, on to the narrow shingle strewn beach that circled Pilsea. All went well until I had to make a dead stop on the Chichester harbour side. I could not believe my eyes, there ahead of me, blocking my route, were a couple stark-naked; a large florid fat-bellied man and a very attractive young woman. The man was instantly enraged, sitting up to face me and shouting offensively that I was disturbing him on Admiralty property, and asking what on earth was I doing driving a filthy vehicle along the beach. I said not a word as I drove slowly past them, unable to take my eyes off them. I was still laughing when I got back to the causeway where I delayed the rush of the families on to the island long enough for the sun-bathing couple to pack up and leave. I noted their departure as I saw the top of the mast of a small dinghy moving away into Chichester harbour.

I heard nothing by way of complaint from anyone about the sun-bathing couple. The rumour was that the man was a retired Rear Admiral who had quite a number of young girl friends. Pilsea Island became a favoured place for many of the families who went there to sunbathe and swim.

It was well into autumn when, one day, I was asked to visit the Surveyor of the Chichester Council. Householders on the Wittering side of the Chichester harbour were worried by the gradual erosion of the shoreline that edged their properties. The matter had been investigated, measurements had been taken, and the belief was that the tidal race into the harbour had somehow speeded up and changed direction. At a Council meeting it had been agreed that the reason for this change was my causeway that stopped the incoming tide from taking its former route between the islands.

I attended a meeting of the Harbourmaster, the Chief Magistrate and the Surveyor. I tried to defend my position by avowing that nothing more had been done than to improve Defence property. I pointed out that now, crash and rescue vehicles could get further out into the mud-flat areas. The Chief Magistrate asked if the causeway project had been sanctioned by the Defence authorities and, of course, I had to admit that it had not. I realised that I was in the wrong and did not want the matter to brought out into the open. I therefore agreed to have the causeway dismantled in such a way as to allow the tide to ebb and flow as it must have done for centuries. In late December, my friends in the Airfield Construction Branch blew two large gaps in the causeway.

In January,1960 I was warned that I would be taking the course at the

JSCC (Joint Services Staff College) that would start in May. Again, I was surprised and wondered what sort of career lay ahead for me. After JSCC there would surely be another staff tour, and I would be denied flying duties again. I was not particularly happy at this unexpected news, but Wendy was pleased. The JSSC was at Latimer, just north of London and we could return to our house in Tadworth also allowing me to be able to drive to the College each day.

During my last few months at Thorney Island, I managed to fly almost every day. With 'Nibby' Fellows as pilot and with me in the front seat of the Meteor T7, armed with a cine camera, I put together a coloured film of all manner of aerobatics. I did my own editing and fashioned the film into a progressive story of what was possible, both low down and at high altitude. I got my hand back in on the helicopter by flying the Tangmere air rescue Whirlwind, the Westland copy and development of the Sikorsky H19 that I had flown in Korea, eight years earlier.

A Whirlwind helicopter down on the
Thorney Island mud flats

The only way out of the mud

I was dined out on 20th April and in my farewell speech I referred to the most interesting and rewarding time I had spent at Thorney Island. As I spoke I could not fail to remember the sympathy and many kindnesses that had been shown to me; in particular, the forebearance and understanding of my station commander. I knew that I had been very lucky indeed to have been allowed the time and opportunity to get over my troubles.

CHAPTER NINETEEN

It was not an easy return to our house in Tadworth. While we had been in Thorney Island it had been let on short-term leases through an agent in Kingston-on-Thames. There had been two tenancies, the second being with an American family who must have lived as though they were still on the trail out West. The house was absolutely filthy from top to bottom and parts had actually fallen into disrepair, for instance the garage door was hanging on its hinges. Windows were cracked and broken, the garden had been completely neglected and the grass on the lawn was at knee-height. At the far end of the garden, there were two large scorched areas where someone had been cooking, most likely in Red Indian fashion; naturally, we asked for an account from the agent. They admitted that they had collected only one month's rent and had not checked on the Americans during the two months they were laying waste to our property. We had been taught a sharp lesson.

I had just a week at home with which to deal with the awful mess before I had to start the JSSC course. As I left for Latimer on the first morning I was overtaken, when rounding the Epsom Racecourse, by an RAF officer driving an American Plymouth car. I followed him for a while, intrigued that we were going in the same direction. After crossing Hampton Court bridge, he drew away in his much more powerful machine. I was more than a little surprised when I parked my Renault alongside the Plymouth at Latimer, to find that a Wing Commander Bill

Blair, living just a hundred yards or so from me in Tadworth, was also a student on the course.

Bill Blair and I took it in turns to drive from Tadworth each day and got to know each other quite well. Bill was an excellent pilot, having flown bomber aircraft consistently from early in the war. He had just completed an exchange tour in the USAF Strategic Air Command where he had flown the jet-engined North American Tornado. His career to date, unlike mine, had been absolutely straightforward, just moving from one flying appointment to another.

I enjoyed the course at Latimer, principally because it was the first time I had been in the company of members of the other two services in large numbers. We naturally tended to fall into three distinct service groups, however there was an affinity between the Royal Navy and the Royal Air Force, possibly because JSCC appeared to be used as a stop-gap between sea and flying appointments. Not many of us had been staff-trained; I believe that there was only one other amongst the RAF officers who, like myself, had been to the RAF Staff College. The Army officers were the experts, almost all had been to Camberley. They were way ahead of us with the writing and preparation of papers and had a much more rounded idea of warfare. Best amongst them were the Sappers, the Royal Engineers. There were six of them, all of whom eventually reached the rank of Brigadier or better.

JSCC was good value, being lectured by the best and meeting them under ideal conditions. We did not work in syndicates but mainly on our own, being set problems and tasks to which we found our own solutions. Thankfully, we did not have a thesis to prove to finish the course. There was predictably constant banter between the Services, the RAF very often being the one under attack. Up to a point, the Duncan Sandys' ideas for the replacement of aircraft by missiles had by then been watered down. The Blue Streak ballistic missile that was intended to replace the V-bombers in the deterrent role was getting beyond the capabilities of British design and development. It was also considered to be too vulnerable above ground on its launching sites. The decision had already been made to cancel it and possibly to replace it with an American ballistic rocket that could be carried by the V-bombers. The requirement for a supersonic, multi-purpose, supersonic bomber, the TSR2, was going ahead - together with a wealth of research and development into a possible successor to our front line fighter, the English Electric Lightning.

In discussion, I often found myself straying from the approved light-blue line. I had spent more time than other RAF students working with the other Services and, with the exception of Bill Blair, I was the only one who had served with the Americans. I had experienced a little of what had become known as 'limited war' in Korea. The Air Force line, quite rightly, was centered on the maintenance of the deterrent, almost to the exclusion of all else. Limited wars had been fought in Korea, at Suez, and in Malaysia and there was no way of knowing where the next conflict would break out. However, one thing was sure, there would always be a Royal Air Force role to play. For instance I believed we could make better use of the helicopter. It had been used most successfully for air-sea rescue, and for resupply of the Army in difficult jungle areas. Without being original, I pursued the argument of the concept of the battlefield helicopter, appropriately armed to attack tanks, vehicles, and unprotected troops. I even wrote an article on the scope of possible future helicopter operations for the JSSC magazine, together with a humorous 'tongue-in-the-cheek' account of American-style deer hunting in the Rocky Mountains; only the latter was published.

All too soon the course came to an end, six months of fascinating study had simply flown past. As was to be expected, we all received staff appointments; mine being as Wing Commander (Admin) Plans at Headquarters, RAF Germany. Bill Blair was deeply upset to be given an Org 1 job at a Training Command Group Headquarters. I had to agree with him that it appeared as though a good bomber pilot was about to go to waste, but tried to get him to realise that he had to undertake some staff work before he could expect to make what he hoped would be command of a Bomber Command station. He didn't agree, convinced that his performance on the JSSC course, which he so heartedly disliked, had led towards the curtailment of his flying career. Within the week, he resigned his commission and, a few weeks later, was on his way back to the United States with his family, there to take up a job in the American aviation industry.

I had another of my unexpected surprises at the end of the year. The New Year's Honours List included my advancement in the Most Excellent

Order of the British Empire to that of Ordinary Officer. A few days later, I received a note from the Order's Secretariat stating that, after the investiture with the OBE, I would be expected to return the insignia of the MBE; a strange arrangement, I thought, that seemed to indicate the citation of the lesser honour was to be forgotten.

At the same time, we had the wonderful news that Wendy was carrying our third child. Luckily, we were given ample time to make ready to go abroad. This time, I put the letting of our house in the hands of the Defence Authorities knowing that although the house would be let at a relatively low price, we would be able to return to find it in first-class condition. We sold the Renault Dauphin for a good price, intending to buy a new car in Germany at tax-free rates.

Our introduction to life in Germany was truly miserable. The Headquarters of RAF Germany was included in the Allied Headquarters at Rheindahlen, not far from Munchen Gladbach in Nord-Rhein, Westphalia. We arrived there one desperately cold winter's day to be told that there was no accommodation vacant in the Headquarters' complex and that, for weeks at least, we would have to live in private accommodation, a few miles away. We were taken to view two places before we were accepted at a *Gasthaus*, a gloomy place where we were the only foreigners. For five weeks we lived most uncomfortably out of suitcases. It was very depressing, especially for Wendy, who was left with Beverley during the day in a most inhospitable place. The Germans shunned us, some even made it quite clear that we were not welcomed. It was indeed a great relief to leave for a married quarter in Rheindahlen.

RAF Germany was commanded by Air Marshal Gordon Jones. My immediate superior was the Senior Officer Administration, Air Commodore R.A.C. Carter, a former commanding officer of my old squadron No. 150, who lived just across the road from our house in Dundee Way with his delightful American wife, Sally. As Wing Commander (Admin Plans) I had a direct line with the Air Commodore. Radical changes were being made in the size and shape of RAF Germany. No longer could we afford the ever-rising costs of maintaining bases spread over much of Western Germany, the time had come to retrench. I became involved in the plans to close the RAF Stations at Sylt and Butzweilerhof, and storage depots such as at Duren in the Eiffel. The cold war was at its height and plans had to be reviewed for action in the event of the failure of the deterrent. One, 'Operation Safekeep', was a major concern, a nightmare plan to evacuate all British dependants from Germany in the event of all-out war. I found it difficult to see any sense in trying to move thousands of women and children during what could only be a nuclear exchange. The plan only began to make a little sense when we were told to allow for a week-long warning period before the destruction of our world would begin.

My appointment took with it the Joint-Chairmanship of administrative planning at the Allied Headquarters. We all thought alike on the evacuation plans but, nonetheless, were instructed to prepare them to meet both general war and the possibility of some sort of limited conflict with the Russians.

I had gone to Germany thinking that administrative planning would be a dull job, certainly taking second fiddle to air planning. It was most certainly not the case and I was soon involved in detailed work with the Belgians, Dutch, and Germans in the Allied Headquarters. At home, we settled down as a family in very comfortable surroundings. Beverley started school at the St George's School and began at once to show promise. Caroline Emily, our second daughter, was born at the RAF Hospital, Wegberg, on 5th May, 1961.

Despite the advantages of living in the tax-free cocoon at Rheindahlen, and being kept happily at work, I had to admit that I did not like living in Germany; a feeling shared with Wendy. We had made a bad start with the Germans when we had lived in the *Gasthaus*, and whenever we left the Britishness of Rheindahlen we often found ourselves marked down as unwelcome strangers. We protected ourselves against this by avoiding Germans whenever possible. We were just a few miles from the Dutch border and soon regularly did our weekly shopping at Roermond, just across the Maas. Sometimes we went a little further into the Netherlands to Venlo. I even found it difficult to work with some German officers at the Headquarters and many, like me, were veterans of the last war. They would admit they had been soundly beaten by the Russians and that Hitler's greatest mistake had been to invade that country. Not much else seemed to be of interest, some even argued there had never been a 'Battle of Britain', merely the *Kanalkampf (Channel fight)* to clear British shipping from the Channel in preparation for a suitable peace agreement with an already beaten enemy. The Allied bombing campaigns were judged to have been criminal, especially the area-bombing by the RAF. What I found absolutely baffling was the lack of guilt shown over the persecution of the Jews. Apparently the concentration and extermination camps went about their ghastly business without the knowledge of the German people. Amongst some younger officers I even found a firm belief that the genocide had not taken place; that the stories about the extinction of six million Jews had been wartime Allied propaganda. Whenever it was known that I had been a member of Bomber Command, I was sometimes accused of the wanton murder of women and children. Once, when dressed in uniform, I was even spat upon by an elderly German civilian.

Wendy and I seldom went anywhere within Germany, only occasionally visiting the nearby town of Munchen Gladbach, almost all of our off-duty time was spent in the Netherlands or Belgium. There we made many friends, particularly amongst the survivors of the escape routes that had done so much to help Allied aircrew to get back to England.

I was so pleased with the fact that there was never a dull moment. I had ample time for my hobbies of making models of steam engines and aircraft, and for the business of keeping fit. Without the excitement and tension of flying, I was once again putting on weight. I countered this with regular exercise, some of which was quite demanding. Each day I began with a two-mile run around the athletics track behind the Officers' Mess, often in the company of a German Brigadier who made no bones of the fact that he had served in the SS. I played football regularly, either as left wing or left half and did myself some good one afternoon when playing in a special charity match against the Belgians. I took a swerving-in corner kick to the far post which was neatly headed in for a goal by the tall Air Marshal Gordon Jones. I became President of the RAF Germany Athletics Board, and managed two quite successful championship meetings between the RAF, Belgian Air Force, the Royal Netherlands Air Force and the *Luftwaffe*. My principal sporting preoccupation by far was, however, in developing RAF Germany interest in the Dutch national pastime of *Wandeltochten* (organized marching).

I know of no other country where people enjoy themselves by simply marching in groups over measured distances as they do in the Netherlands.

Almost every Dutch town organises a *Wandeltochten* during the year. It is not a competition but simply a 'wandering group', walking around a given course of about 15 to 20 miles. Teams come together from all over the country, usually setting out early in the day and either march or stroll, according to age, around the chosen course. At the end, refreshments are available and there is a short ceremony at which commemorative medals are given to all those who complete the distance. The *Wandeltochten* 'Cup Final' is the celebrated Nijmegen 4-day event where teams from all over the world daily march 25 miles, carrying loads of 12 kilos or more. It finishes on the fourth day with a grand marchpast where the salute is usually taken by royalty or a senior military chief.

It did not take me long to recruit a team of enthusiasts. The attraction of a carefree day in the Netherlands was so great that I had to restrict numbers and set up a waiting list. We began with practice marches around Rheindahlen and then entered the Dutch marching programme. We were the only foreign team involved and we soon established a reputation for smartness and good nature. We always marched in uniform and became well-known by the various organisers. I was in charge of a fine bunch of airmen with Squadron Leader Larry Osborne, a Supply officer, as my second-in-command. Regularly, during the marching season which stretched from late April until the beginning of October, we took part in a *Wandeltochten* somewhere in the Netherlands.

We went to Nijmegen for the first time in July 1961 and finished the course easily, without a single drop-out. I proudly led the team in the final parade across the finishing line where the salute was taken by Lieutenant General Baron Michel Donnet of the Belgian Air Force, a former Wing Commander in the Royal Air Force, a fellow member of the Royal Air Forces Escaping Society, and then Commander of the Second Allied Tactical Air Force.

I became intrigued by the smooth organization and conduct of the Nijmegen Marches. Many thousands of people, mostly banded together in teams, had to be accommodated and fed in the town. They were of all ages, even people in their seventies came back, year after year, to take part in something they had enjoyed for decades. This huge gathering was then fitted into the march which began very early in the morning and covered a different route each day. Along it were three large rest camps where food and drink could be obtained, and where medical staff were on hand to deal with strained muscles, blisters or even worse. Many national teams took part, most of them striving to make their particular identity known. They carried national flags and emblems and, in many different ways, did their best to entertain the thousands who thronged the route. Outstanding, in terms of popularity, was the Israeli team of alert young soldiers, that always included a number of good-looking women. The Dutch loved them, particularly when, at regular intervals, the Israelis stopped to dance and sing their national songs.

*Marching into Nijmegen at the end of the four day
Wandeltochten. The young Dutch boy on my left joined
the RAF contingent for several years. He eventually
became a pilot with the Dutch Airforce*

Nijmegen 1964 with Lt. Col. Len Thacker
leading the RAF Odiham team

We had a most pleasurable season of marching throughout 1962, taking part in many significant events at Volendam, Utrecht, Rotterdam and Arnhem. We took part in Nijmegen, and did well and, again, the Israelis stole the show and were the most popular group by far. Unfortunately, the event was marred by the death of a young British soldier, a member of a UK-based team. He died of exhaustion on the fourth day; the weather throughout the march had been very hot and humid and for some ridiculous reason the Army team had been trying to race, to establish some sort of unofficial record, most definitely against the rules. The team had not fully prepared itself and its leader had forced many beyond their physical limits.

I decided that during the 1963 Nijmegen march the RAF team would do something for spectators to remember. I discovered that although scores of bands played throughout the four days at particular places around the route, no band had ever played and marched around the 100-mile course. We had a pipe band at RAF Laarbruch, the very instrument for me to use. I must have been a very persuasive person because I managed to coerce the whole band into undertaking what many thought was impossible. They agreed to march the whole course and, whenever I gave the word, to play the pipes and drums. We happily took them under our wing and induced them to practice marching in suitable footwear. They went with us on two token marches around Laarbruch and it quickly became clear to me that I was running a serious risk of creating a noticeable failure that might result in discredit to the Royal Air Force; however I prepared to take the risk.

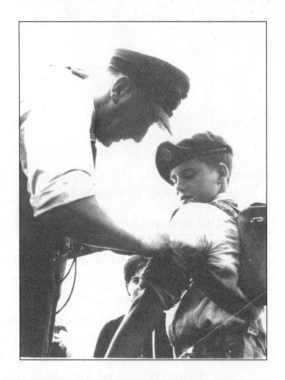

Our young Dutch companion being invested with an RAF armband. As can be seen, he already had an RAF beret & badge which he wore with huge pride, as well as a fair complement of kit webbing

   We were a sensation from the start as we marched out of Nijmegen on the first day behind the kilted band of eight pipers, four side-drummers and a base-drummer, playing the heart-lifting '100 Pipers and all'. We carried on throughout the day with the band responding to my command to play every twenty minutes or so. We finished in good form; the band was exhausted but were pleased to find that they had made the national newspapers.

   On the second day, we noticed that the Israelis had taken up position in the line of march quite close behind us. When the pipes were played, the Israelis kept in step with us and when the pipes took a rest, the Israelis sang. At the rest stops, we joined together in the entertainment; some of us took part in the Israeli dances and the pipe-master taught the Israeli girls how to dance Highland reels and the Gay Gordons.

   By the end of the third day, the Laarbruch band was beginning to falter. Their lack of exercise and practice was all too evident. All were suffering from blisters. The base drummer had come to a dead stop quite a way from the finish and had to be helped along; we took turns in carrying his drum. Our musical renditions had been few and far between; mainly restricted to the rest stops or when we were marching through a village. The Israelis had overtaken and left us and I therefore insisted on no partying that night, and had everyone in bed long before midnight.

   By the fourth day, the band was in serious trouble. Some were so stiff and blistered that they thought they would be unable to start, leave alone trying to play the pipes. It had begun to look as though my great idea was about to fail. I told them that they had done well but could not take a chance with their possible disintegration as a band during the march. Pride of Service came to my rescue. To a man they vowed that they would complete the course while I promised that the team would do everything possible to help them along. After a very hesitant and painful start, we made off and, mile after mile, the feeling grew that all would be well. Towards the end, I have to admit that we were almost carrying the band, yet they kept up the playing of the pipes and the beating of the drums. We took a final rest at the beginning of the long road leading into Nijmegen and up to the finish. Everyone smartened up and we gave each bandsman a tot of Glenfiddick. Troubles were forgotten as we rejoined the line of march and headed into town and marched past the saluting base in great style pipes playing 'Scotland the Brave.'

Later, I had a bill to pay for my indulgence. Apart from the absolute exhaustion of the Laarbruch band which brought me adverse criticism from their station commander, I had to find money for the re-reeding of the pipes and the re-skinning of three of the four drums. I wondered if we had achieved anything but I know that, to this day, no other band has ever managed to complete the 4-Days at Nijmegen.

Just after Nijmegen, I was summoned to an Investiture at Buckingham Palace. It was the second call for me to receive the insignia of the OBE. The first such summons had arrived during the final stages of Wendy's pregnancy and my request for a postponement had been accepted. With the summons were two invitations for relatives to attend. Wendy was unable to accept because of our new baby but suggested that her brother, John Howes, a scientist working at Harwell, should go and that he would be able to look after Beverley who could go in her place It seemed a good idea; Beverley was just five years of age but very assured and well mannered. She had the abilities of girls much older and looked older than her years. I did not see any problem in accepting the responsibility of taking her to England and back.

We travelled by train to the Hook of Holland and then spent a wretched night crossing by ferry in atrocious weather to Harwich. We stayed at the Russell Hotel in Russell Square where we met my brother-in-law. I was pleased that the care of my daughter had gone so easily; she had behaved impeccably. She did her own preparation for going to the Palace and dressed herself in an ensemble of a ballet-style white dress, white stockings, white bonnet, and fine leather light blue shoes. I was proud of her.

It was my third visit to the Palace and I remembered the procedures. John and Beverley took their seats amongst the audience in the Throne Room. I was led off to take my place with those who were to receive the emblems of the Order of the British Empire; the Knights, Commanders, Officers, and Members-to-be. We were lined up in the long corridor that leads into the Throne Room, each awaiting his turn to be called forward and to be presented to Her Majesty.

I suppose I had been in the queue for twenty minutes or so, the Knights and Commanders had been honoured and the longish line of Officers-to-be was getting close to the entrance of the Throne Room. I was way back towards its end. Then, to my utter amazement, I saw my daughter Beverley approaching with a major general in dress uniform holding her by the hand. She must have seen my open-mouthed astonishment as she daintily tripped past us, for she piped in a clear untroubled voice, 'It's all right, Daddy; I'm only going to the lavatory.' The spontaneous laughter around me must have been heard in the Throne Room.

I maintained an active liking for my job throughout the tour in Germany, however, I did not appreciate my total removal from the flying scene. Unlike my earlier periods of staff duty, I did not have means of finding an aircraft to fly, nor was there any requirement for me to do so. Only once did I get airborne and that was in a Belgian Air Force Alouette helicopter, courtesy of General Donnet. I kept my fingers crossed that my next posting would allow me to get back nearer to the active side of the Royal Air Force.

During the last year in Germany, we became much more mobile as a family. Caroline was now walking and had suffered no childish illnesses, not even a cold. Beverley was full of herself. She was doing very well at primary school and considered herself something of a traveller. For a young girl she had a quite extraordinary mind. She was for ever asking searching questions and had the ability to accumulate facts and figures. She could categorize steam, electric, and diesel railway engines in a flash; identify aircraft and motor cars at a distance, and knew a lot about birds, flowers and fauna. We had traded in the Dauphine and bought one of the first six Renault Caravelles for the German market, direct from Paris. We had a second car, a front-loading BMW with a 855cc engine that served us well as a runabout. Our favourite place to visit was still the Netherlands. We went there every week to shop, and further afield to the bulb fields, the polders, the delightful children's pleasure grounds at Amsterdam and just outside Utrecht, and to the Dutch 'Alps', as they were humorously called, around Maastricht.

In early October, we took three weeks leave and drove to the South of France, going through Switzerland where we spent a few days. We had hoped to have stayed at Chez Francis at Callanques des Issambres, but found it in other less carefree hands than before; our old friend Francis had finally drunk himself to death.

News of my next posting awaited me when we returned to Rheindahlen.

It was another mystery to me, I was to go to yet another Staff College, this time to Greenwich, where I would be a student on the Senior Officers War Course.

Happily leaving Germany, the BMW was passed on to another family who wanted cheap motoring. We managed to get the family and our belongings into the Caravelle and motored to the Hook of Holland where we took the ferry. The Defence Authority had been given ample warning of our return so enabling us to drive straight from Harwich to Tadworth and take up residence in our own home. This time, the house was in fine condition and everything was in order.

CHAPTER TWENTY

The Senior Officers War Course had been dubbed the 'Poor Man's IDC' (Imperial Defence College). The course was made up by half and full colonels, commanders and captains RN, and just three airmen, two group captains and myself. Greenwich was a place for reflection, argument, and relaxation. A happy daily event was organized by a Guards Lieutenant Colonel, a tote of estimates of the tonnage of the largest ship that would sail past Greenwich between the hours of 10 am and 4 pm. The pace was indeed leisurely; most work was done in discussion or by attending lectures delivered by very senior people. Lord Mountbatten, then Chief of the Defence Staff, had us engrossed with his review of the defence situation, the uncontrollable rising cost of developing new weapon systems, and how we might maintain our own independent deterrent. I got short shrift from him with my cheeky question as to whether we could expect any dramatic reduction in defence expenditure if the Labour Party was to win the pending General Election.

I travelled to Greenwich each day by train from Kingswood, having slipped most easily back into suburban life. I had ample time to indulge in the development of the garden, and we began work on enlarging the house, first by doubling the size of the garage and then by constructing a small third bedroom in the attic.

As a course, we made a mid-term visit to Berlin and were allowed to enter eastern sector, staying just long enough to pay our respects at the

Russian War Memorial. We returned through Checkpoint 'Charlie' impressed by the drabness and regimentation of what we had seen. The contrast with the bustling western sector was so marked. There could be seen the results of American investment and German productivity; all enterprise, activity, and Coca Cola. We even got a glimpse of Berlin's renowned pre-war nightlife when most of us visited a really decadent cabaret. The cost of the drinks was astronomical and the entertainment weird and mainly homosexual.

I got my answer to the question I had posed to Lord Mountbatten at a Guest Night held in the Painted Room at Greenwich on Trafalgar Day, 21st October, 1963. Although I was the junior of the three airmen on the course, I was privileged to be seated on the top table between Denis Healey, the Shadow Defence Minister, and Mr Roberts, the Shadow Army Minister. It was a most impressive affair held in a setting that hardly could have been bettered. The food was excellent, a Royal Marine band played throughout dinner and the single speech proposing the Nelson toast was made in excellent style by our President, Rear Admiral Morgan Giles.

As the evening mellowed, I was drawn into conversation with both the politicians on my either side. I eventually felt bold enough to ask what would happen to defence expenditure if Labour was returned to power at the pending General Election. I had taken a liberty with our guests but Mr Healey was happy to answer. Defence expenditure was out of hand and the most uncontrollable part of it was research and development of new weapon systems. Immediate steps would be taken to bring it under control and that would mean the cancellation of the TSR2 supersonic bomber and the Saunders Roe SR53 rocket/jet fighter, the stopping of work on the Hawker development of a Hunter replacement and research into a replacement for the Lightning. It seemed a doomsday decision but I knew enough about the extrapotential costs of research and development costs not to enter into argument.

The reason for my attendance at Greenwich became a little clearer when, on 1st January, 1964, I was promoted Group Captain. A few weeks before the end of the course, I was informed that my next appointment would be command of Royal Air Force, Odiham, the principal helicopter base in the country. Naturally, I was overjoyed particularly when told that I would have the task of developing support helicopter operations with the new Wessex.

I underwent a refresher flying course at the Central Flying School, Ternhill on the Whirlwind 10 helicopter, the Westland development of the Sikorsky H19 I had flown in Korea twelve years previously. The main changes were the elimination of the twist-grip throttle on the cyclic control and the installation of a jet turbine to replace the radial piston-engined Wright Cyclone. I took easily to the machine and quickly went solo. In all I completed just over 15 hours flying, most of which was done in the Welsh mountains and on the slopes of Snowdon.

Group Captain Des Sheen, a celebrated Battle of Britain fighter pilot, handed over control of Odiham to me on 26th July 1964. It had been a fighter station throughout the 1950s and had been placed in Care and Maintenance for three years before being reopened to operate helicopters. No. 18 Squadron was already in being and another Wessex squadron, No. 72, was in the process of being formed. A Belvedere conversion unit of six helicopters occupied the single hangar on the southern side of the airfield together with a fixed-wing element of three Twin Pioneers. In addition, pilots and crews were being supplied to Whirlwind squadrons on operational duty in Borneo, confronting the Indonesians. The dependants of both these squadrons were my responsibility, just a few living on the station but the great majority having to accommodated in hirings in the neighborhood. Also located at Odiham was the Headquarters of No. 38 Group commanded by Air Vice-Marshal Tim Piper of Berlin Airlift fame with my friend, Air Commodore Mickey Martin, as SASO (Senior Air Staff Officer).

I made two mistakes in the space of my first three weeks at Odiham which directly involved me with the Air Officer Commanding-in-Chief of Transport Command, the renowned Air Marshal Sir Kenneth Cross or 'Bing' Cross as he was called behind his back. He had taken command of Transport Command as something of a step down after years of dragooning Bomber Command to the highest possible level of efficiency. As I was to discover, he did not allow mistakes nor did he accept excuses.

On my second day at Odiham, I was called to pay my respects to the C-in-C at his headquarters at Upavon. As I had never flown the Wessex I chose to fly there as a second pilot in a No. 18 Squadron machine. Dressed in my best blue, I was kept waiting in the C-in-C's outer office for about twenty minutes before being ushered in. As Sir Kenneth was engaged in signing a pile of letters I saluted and stood rigidly to attention in front of his desk, and that is how I remained for at least three or four minutes without a word being spoken. At last, he put down his pen, looked up and glared at me. 'Was that you in the helicopter?' he barked. 'Yes, sir,' I timidly answered. 'You do not waste fuel coming to see me in that way; in future have the good sense to come by car.' Silence then resumed as he returned to signing letters, I remained standing at attention. When he spoke again, his words were very much to the point. 'All I require of you is to obey orders. I expect you to carry them out to the letter.' With that, he went back to his signing, just indicating with a flick of his hand to me that the interview was over.

Just four days later I was informed by telephone that the C-in-C would be visiting Odiham to meet the crews and ground staff of three Whirlwinds that had been assembled at Odiham for detachment to Guyana on security duties. The initial preparations had been made by my predecessor; all that I had to do was to arrange for the visit of Sir Kenneth. I discussed what I had in mind with Air Vice-Marshal Piper who agreed that the three helicopters with their equipment should be lined up between the hangars and that the air and ground crews should be assembled in the No 18. Squadron crewroom to await an address from the C-in-C.

The C-in-C arrived dead on time personally flying a Pembroke. Air Vice-Marshal Piper and I stood to attention as he shut down the engines and got out of the aircraft to join the AOC in his Jaguar to be driven away. I doubled across to the No. 18 Squadron hangar just in time to meet them after the car had made a circular tour of the hangars and control tour to give me time to get into position alongside the three Whirlwinds. I saluted as the C-in-C and AOC got out of the car.

'Where is everything?' shouted Sir Kenneth. I had no idea what he meant. 'These are the aircraft, sir,' I said, pointing at the Whirlwinds. 'The crews and ground crew are waiting for you in the crewroom.'

Never before had I seen an Air Marshal lose his temper. He turned to Air Vice-Marshal Piper and told him in blistering terms that this was not what he expected. He was absolutely furious with me. 'If this is how you are going to run your station, you won't last long. I'm not staying in this place for another minute!' He turned away, forced his way into the Jaguar, pulling Piper with him. Although I was flabbergasted, I did not lose my head, running as fast as I could back to the Pembroke to get the handling party back into position to be ready to start the engines. Unfortunately, they had been stood down after the arrival and I could not find them.

I do not know whether Sir Kenneth realized there was no one there to help start his aircraft but he got out of the Jaguar and stormed his way into the cockpit. I had by then found the starter trolley and plugged it in. Sir Kenneth made no signals to start engines so I kept the trolley button pressed. The engines were started, I unplugged the trolley and rushed around to take up the starboard wheel chock rope. Tim Piper had already sensed the problem and was holding the port wheel rope. The C-in-C did not wave chocks away, he just opened up both engines not realizing the chocks were still in position. The two of us struggled to pull them clear from the wheels and nothing we could do would make him throttle back. I was first to get my chock clear with the result that the Pembroke, with engines roaring, swung violently around on to Tim Piper who had to throw himself to the ground to avoid being hit. Off went the Pembroke, at very high speed, across the grass and onto the runway. Thankfully, the Control Officer was on his toes and had cleared the airfield and the circuit. With the station now at a standstill, I watched the closing minutes of the appalling visit. All I could say to my AOC when the Pembroke disappeared to the west was, 'When do you want me to pack?'

In the quiet of his office, I told Tim Piper that no one had given me the slightest notion of what the C-in-C's intentions or what he expected. He rang Air Marshal Craven, the SASO at Upavon to tell him to await the return of a furious C-in-C and to ask why I had not been given detailed instructions by written word or by signal on the C-in-C's visit. Later, I was told that a certain Group Captain, also new to his job, was the root cause of the upset. At least this fellow unfortunate had the decency to call me and apologize. He also mentioned that the C-in-C would be told of the mistake when matters returned to something like normal. In any case, I could take it that my head was no longer on the block.

Fortunately for me, the task of re-inspecting the Whirlwinds and their crews fell to Air Marshal Craven. He arrived by car and I had everything polished and scrubbed as though I had a Royal visitor. The air and ground crews were lined up in front of the helicopters and the Air Marshal could find no fault. He acknowledged that a mistake had been made at his end but he confided in me that he was sure I would benefit from the experience. Only too true, I thought. From then on, I would not trust a soul nor would I take anything at face value. Not only would I double-check, but I would treble-check everything that was my responsibility.

I was to learn that Sir Kenneth went out of his way to keep station commanders on their toes. He had fourteen stations under his command, the more important ones were commanded by group captains already earmarked as 'high flyers'. Neil Cameron was at Abingdon, soon to be replaced by Freddie Sowrey; Alisdair Steadman had Lyneham, and Alistair Mackie, Colerne. Transport Command was run as efficiently and ruthlessly as had been Bomber Command. If you made a bad mistake, you seldom had another chance; you were on your way out. Three of the fourteen station Commanders fell by the wayside while I was at Odiham.

There were those who thought that having a Group Headquarters on a station was a drawback and a diminution of responsibility. This was certainly not so. Air Vice-Marshal Piper and his SASO, my friend, Air Commodore 'Micky' Martin, went out of their ways not to interfere with my running of Odiham. Both were soon replaced, respectively, by Air Vice-Marshal 'Duke' Mavor and Air Commodore Ian Macdougall, both of whom became good friends and from whom I was to learn much. The only drawback of the No. 38 Group appendage was the demand on living accommodation. The AOC lived off the station at Hartley Whitney, but all others had to be fitted into the overall station demands. The principal married quarters were already in their hands; mine was the only one occupied by a serving member of station staff.

As soon as I could, I got checked out by day and by night in the Wessex. It was by far the best helicopter I had ever handled. It was easy to fly and it could lift a good load of freight or carry a lot of troops. Servicing was easy too, both on the station and in the field. Added to that, the Wessex force at Odiham was controlled by an excellent Wing Commander Flying in the form of John Parker. The two squadron commanders were good but unfortunately surrounded by many over-age pilots and navigators whose average ages were very close to mine, 43 at that time. Most of them had been converted to helicopters and had been posted to Odiham after their fixed-wing Communication Squadrons had been disbanded. Sedate flying around in Devons and Pembrokes was hardly the background for crews that had to develop and work up tactics for support helicopter operations. One 18 Squadron crew of a former communications pilot and navigator had an aggregate age of 108 years, which was clearly demonstrated in the way they flew; very carefully and without any verve.

I tackled this problem at once. Within the first two months my paper on the selection of pilots for the Support Helicopter Force had been blessed by 38 Group and Transport Command, and action was being taken to reverse Air Board policy that directed the brightest youngsters into the fighter and bomber worlds. Very soon, some of the best graduates from Cranwell and the Advanced Flying Schools were flying helicopters.

I was not so fortunate on the administrative side of things. It took me some months to realize that my Wing Commander Admin. was well below standard and a dipsomaniac. Odiham, the largest community in that part of Hampshire, next to Basingstoke, had been left to rot during the three-year Care and Maintenance period between the end of fighter operations and the arrival of the helicopters. My predecessor had done his best to reverse the rate of inevitable decay but, hampered with limited funds and a lack of a clear operational role for the station, he had been fighting a losing battle. All four hangars needed repair and adaptation for the housing and servicing of helicopters. There was serious abuse in the state of the airmen's living and messing quarters; woodwork was rotting, pipes were rusting, electrical wiring needed renewing, even the drains needed attention. The Airmen's Mess was overrun with legions of cockroaches and the entire kitchen area needed replacing. Last but by no means least, an enormous rat-ridden refuse dump, not far from the end of the 72 Squadron hangar, had to be cleared away. However, overriding all else, were the needs of hundreds of so-called 'headless' families most of whom could not be found accomodation on the station.

I was happy with my Wing Commander Flying but very disappointed with the Wing Commander Admin. It took me a while to discover that he was a secret drinker, but all too soon I realised his lack of initiative and purpose. He could not accept responsibility and all too often I found that I had to undertake any new development myself. Odiham was a relatively small station way down in the financial pecking order of Transport Command. Requests for improvement funds were turned down and the only immediate way ahead I could see was to find ways of doing the jobs ourselves. I tackled the disgraceful state of the Airmen's Mess by carrying out fumigations with the help of a willing team of volunteers and managed to get a specialised firm in from Basingstoke to make sure that everything had been done properly.

To get just a dribble of funds from 38 Group to patch up an airmen's dormitory, I put the whole place out of action by personally tearing out the rotting window frames during an inspection. This forced the Clerk of Works to move, but only after he had reported me unsuccessfully for committing malicious damage. I instituted a series of fund-raising schemes to pay for the building of cubicles in the aged sleeping quarters to give each airman some measure of privacy. Ironically, after our creation of the first ten cubicles, the idea was accepted by 38 Group and general modification began in all sleeping quarters. Best of all, I drew up a plan of what really had to be done at Odiham. This was agreed by Group and, little by little, was put into effect, eventually to be completed long after my time at Odiham.

The most pressing concern, however, was dealing with the needs and activities of the hundreds of dependants of officers and airmen who were serving on one-year unaccompanied tours in Borneo. As many as possible were packed into the station but the great majority of them had to be accomodated in billets around Odiham and as far afield as Basingstoke, Alton, and Farnham and all manner of problems and transgressions arose. Within my first two months on the station there was a suicide of a mother with three children; an assault case when a sergeant returned unexpectantly from Borneo to find his wife in bed with an energetic airman (ironically it was the sergeant was the one taken to hospital).There was also a messy divorce and a rape.

Unfortunately, I often had to deal personally with such problems and, for instance, I got myself very involved in trying to find homes for coloured personnel. Two had been found quarters on the station, another three were living in London with friends or in bedsitting rooms. Colour prejudice in the neighbourhood was rife and it had become impossible to find billets of any sort for these families. In desperation, I composed the following letter and had it published in local newspapers.

'I am a coloured member of Her Majesty's Armed Forces from Barbados, married with three small children, aged five, two, and nine months. Being not eligible yet for service married quarters, I have searched everywhere for rented accommodation in the Basingstoke, Farnham, Alton, Aldershot and Fleet areas without success. Can anyone help me to find a home for my family so that we can be reunited?'

There was an immediate reaction to the letter, not in terms of help but in scathing comment of my raising a nasty problem. In 1964, black faces were seldom seen in rural Hampshire and people kept their likes and dislikes to themselves. Within hours, the national Press had taken up the story. An article appeared in the Sunday Telegraph headed 'Airman Worrell pleads for home.' The tabloids descended on Odiham and I had to allow Worrell to be interviewed. He was educated and well-spoken, better I thought than some of the reporters. As a distant relative of Sir Frank Worrell, the West Indian Test captain, he did very well. The padre spoke for me and confirmed the extent of local colour prejudice.

Unfortunately by now, matters were taken out of my hands. Both Group and Command became involved and told me to say no more. On the credit side, suitable accommodation was found for all three families; on the debit side, I received some disgusting letters, mostly unsigned, accusing me of being a faceless spokesman eager to turn England into a multi-racial muckheap.

It was Wendy who came up with the idea of forming what she called a social flying squad ready to tackle most of the domestic problems that arose. She headed a team that consisted of the padre, medical officer, and a senior member of the Wives' Club. It went to work at once, dealing with problems that should have been the responsibility of our almost defunct Wing Commander Admin.

Thankfully, I was relieved of this gentleman immediately after my first AOC's Inspection which took place soon after the Worrell incident. Air Vice-Marshal Mavor had just assumed command of No. 38 Group and this was his first Inspection. I had no place in the final parade and marchpast for the Wing Commander Admin. but gave him the easy duty - so I thought - of meeting the AOC at the guardroom where he would be in charge of a Guard of Honour. After it had been inspected, he would escort the AOC on to the station. As was now my habit, I checked and rechecked the expected performance and found it to be satisfactory. On the day, however, the

wretched Wing Commander took up his duties in a very drunken condition. He was an utter disgrace and only just managed to stay on his feet.
As expected, after the Inspection, I was called to account in the AOC's
office. Luckily for me, Air Vice-Marshal Mavor accepted the fact that I
was unaware that the Wing Commander was a dipsomaniac. He even
made a joke of the man's attempt to bring his sword to the salute. 'He had
me scared,' he said, 'I didn't know whether he was trying to have my head
off or to run me through.'

The Wing Commander Admin. was on his way the next day.
Arrangements were made for him to go to a 'drying-out' clinic where he
was found to have serious cirrhosis of the liver. A replacement was quickly found. I was so pleased that I could now leave administrative matters in
more capable hands and concentrate more on operations.

At the end of August, most of the station's effort was diverted into
preparations for the SBAC Show at Farnborough, just ten miles away. All
Wessex helicopters were to take part in the flying programme on both public days, contributing to the biggest collection of helicopters yet seen in the
country. The Odiham role was to participate in a low-level mass arrival,
carrying troops and under-slung loads to be quickly unloaded, and then
away. I flew in practice with this force during three rehearsals on 1st, 2nd,
and 3rd September.

Far more demanding of the station's resources was the setting up of an
Instant Airport. In the four non-public days of the Show, during which the
SBAC guests travelled from all over the world to visit Farnborough, some
3,000 people used landing facilities at Odiham. Aircraft movements aver-
aged well over 100 a day, the machines ranging in size from DC6s and
Hercules to Tiger Moths. In a 100 ft-long tent which constituted the 'terminal building' were passenger lounges, customs and immigration offices,
and a restaurant. Aircrews were helped at an operations centre which provided necessary flight-planning functions, from refuelling to airways
clearance and meteorological briefing. A coach shuttle service ran to and
from Farnborough, depositing visitors within the Exhibition and collecting
them again at night.

Everything went like clockwork throughout the SBAC Show week. We
were congratulated on the Instant Airport and also on our flying performances. I flew in the mass 'assault' on 11th September, a most unrealistic

but thoroughly enjoyable event milling around the sky with about 40 to 50 helicopters, including some from the Royal Navy and the Army.

From the very beginning of my stay at Odiham, I concerned myself with maintaining the best possible relationships with the local communities. The focal point from where the station drew most of its civilian support was the town of Basingstoke. I paid an official call on the Mayor and, in return, the Mayor and Mayoress called on the Station. They arrived by car and we flew them back to Basingstoke in a Wessex which landed them in the Memorial Park, a few yards from the Mayor's Parlour.

On Battle of Britain Sunday, we took part in an impressive service at St Michael's Church in Basingstoke. The Standard of No. 72 Squadron, who had played such a vital part in the Battle, was received at the entrance of the chancel and laid on the altar. I read the lesson which included sentences inscribed in the Royal Air Force Memorial at Runnymede. Afterwards, I walked with the Mayor and Aldermen to a saluting base in Church Street where I was proud to watch more than one hundred of our airmen march past in great style.

Very soon we became involved in fund-raising in the Borough. The first event of any note was a very successful Autumn Fair held on the Station from which we were able to donate more than £1,000 to local charities. I was pleased with our progress in community relations because, at the back of my mind, was the hope that, one day, the Station might be honoured with the granting of the Freedom of Basingstoke.

During World War II, Odiham had been used as a briefing centre for SOE agents who were then either flown across the Channel from Tangmere in Lysanders or dropped by parachute in France. This activity was cloaked in secrecy and the briefing done in the oddly-named Snatchanger's Farm, on the south side of the airfield. I was still a Committee Member of the RAF Escaping Society and the Chairman, Oliver Philpott MC, of Wooden Horse fame, asked if I would host a party of some thirty French SOE operators, many of whom had passed through Odiham more than twenty years earlier.

With the full backing of 38 Group, we were able to treat the French veterans right royally; each had a host, many of whom could speak French. The station was toured and then they witnessed a good flying display which included many different types of aircraft, including a Spitfire and

Hurricane. They were taken to the now derelict Snatchanger's Farm, and flown around Hampshire in an Argosy. As they left the Station to return to London, a Wessex flew alongside their coach trailing the French Tricolour. In his 'thank-you' letter to me, the leader of the French party wrote that they would remember the time spent at Odiham to the end of their days.

The squadrons were making good progress with ideas on how support helicopter operations should be conducted. We began to take part in named exercises with the Army; 'Storm King' in Yorkshire, 'Autumn Trot' and 'Wagon Train' on Salisbury Plain. There was nothing spectacular about these events, just the loading and lifting of troops and freight. On our own, we were experimenting with ideas of how best to operate in battlefield conditions, but we had yet to work out with the Army such basic matters as command and control. Thoughts of the vulnerability of the helicopter directed our attention to operating at night. One dark yet very clear night, 72 Squadron flew from Odiham in a loose line astern formation at low level to a small DZ (drop zone) near Warminster on Salisbury Plain. They flew with just formation lights showing and were guided to land by torch-light. These were, of course, the days before the use of night vision goggles and helmets.

Another step forward was made in late November when two of our Wessex made landings on HMS Albion in mid-Channel. There was a slight roll and some pitch as the ship steamed at about 15 knots. We were 'struck-down' (a naval term for securing the aircraft to the lift to prevent it moving) and the helicopters taken down to the hangar deck on the lift. The welcome given was superb with Chinese food for lunch in the Wardroom, followed by a guided tour of the the ship.

Much of our training was done away from the airfield. We had two hel-icopter low-flying areas, one stretching between Alton northwards to the Odiham to Basingstoke road, the other was on Hankley Common, near Farnham. The first was an undulating region of open fields bordered by small woods and copses in which most farmers and land-owners were happy to let us practice vertical descents between the trees, low-level approaches from behind cover, and quick flared-landings. We naturally avoided all livestock, but we were notorious for putting up partridges and pheasants. Hankley Common was very different, being a place of heather, gorse, and low shrub. It was a Defence property used by the Territorial

Army with just one building, a wooden weekend headquarters from where, now and then, a tethered balloon was flown from which parachute jumps were made. It was out of bounds to the public.

I preferred flying at Hankley Common which was absolutely devoid of livestock. I had already made it my practice to fly with every pilot on the station, and I encouraged as many others as possible to get airborne whenever there were spare seats. One brisk, sunlit day, when I was flying some of my Continuation Training, I took our padre along. I had him strapped in and sitting facing the open fuselage door where he had an excellent view of the countryside flashing past. I flew to Hankley Common and indulged in some very low flying and quick stops. As I came over the brow of an undulation near the wooden headquarters building, I was puzzled to see a Mercedes saloon car parked about a hundred yards from it. I made a quick turn and flew over to investigate the mystery. I went into a hover alongside the car and, to my utter amazement saw a naked couple hard at work on the rear seats. The padre was the man of the moment. He unstrapped himself and went to the fuselage door where, with his dog-collar showing his status, he made the Sign of the Cross and blessed the now frantic couple.

In April, 1965, we took part in our first large-scale exercise with the Army, 'Easter Lightning'. The setting was in Ulster and the concept was of initial terrorist activity followed by an outbreak of limited war. This was a few years before the troubles were rekindled and there were no thoughts of the IRA or how they might interfere. We were to concern ourselves with the logistical problems of getting troops to Northern Ireland, setting up bases, moving in equipment and then playing limited war games in the Antrim hills. Transport Command was heavily involved in moving 3 Division, the so-called Spearhead Division and keeping them supplied. Every Wessex at Odiham would fly to Aldergrove, near Belfast, and set up camp with the Army Air Corps and their Scout helicopters. I had been nominated Forward Air Commander of 3 Division and would be based with Divisional Headquarters.

'Easter Lightning' began on 20th April and lasted for ten days. To me it was the beginning of our realization of what British helicopters could and could not do. The exercise operational plan unfolded in such a way that no one could fail to see that the support helicopter was a very different machine to those used for reconnaissance or attack of troops on the ground. Our Wessex were unarmed and were nothing more than thin-skinned flying lorries; used too far forward, their vulnerability to ground fire made them a wasteful liability. As the exercise developed, I often had to argue with Army commanders over the misuse of the Wessex.

Wessex in formation out of Odiham 1966

At that time, I know that few RAF planners would accept that if we were to play a 'tails-up' role with our helicopters in the future, then machines had to be developed, just as the Americans were doing, that were armed and could use machine-guns, cannons, and missiles just as we did with our fixed-wing aircraft. If such machines became available then their control would surely fall to the Army commander on the spot - to the Army Air Corps. I knew that, as an RAF officer, I was 'shouting against the wind'. This, in some way, was emphasized for me when I was told that C-in-C Transport Command would be visiting and would like to fly on an exercise operational sortie.

As had become my habit, I checked with 3 Division and HQ Transport

Command as to the C-in-C's exact requirements. All I could extract from them was that he wanted to get a feeling for the nature of the exercise by flying over the operational area; the details of how best this would be done were left to me. We had been exercising for almost a week, the anti-insurgency phase was over and 3 Division were deployed in the Antrim Hills to meet what was thought to be the beginning of a major ground attack. The Odiham part in the exercise was now confined mainly to the resupply and repositioning of troops by night. I therefore thought that as the C-in-C intended to fly in the daytime he would see the deployment of 3 Division best from an Army Scout helicopter.

Once again I had got it wrong. When Sir Kenneth arrived at Aldergrove, I met him and gave him a quick briefing on how 'Easter Lightning' was progressing and what he would be able to see during his flight. I then took him out to the Scout squadron. Before we got anywhere near the machine, which had a smart Army pilot standing alongside, I could see that tell-tale glare beginning to cloud his face. 'You don't expect me to fly in that,' he growled. 'I came here to see the RAF, and I will do so in one of my own aircraft.' I knew enough not to argue that he would see the exercise best in a Scout. I had to leave him there while I rushed away to find a helicopter as quickly as possible. A half an hour later he was airborne as a passenger in a Wessex; another black mark for me.

I believe that we learned a lot from 'Easter Lightning'. I was not at all happy with the command and control of the supply helicopters. Some Army commanders could not appreciate the problems of keeping a complicated machine like the Wessex serviceable in the field and, for that matter, we still had much to learn about that ourselves. There was also the belief that the Wessex was little more than a lorry that could be flown, and that the taking forward of men and supplies was no more difficult than driving them along a road. The realization that there were now ground-to-air missiles that could be fired by a single soldier had escaped many. These weapons were obviously so much more effective than the rifle and machine-gun fire of the Chinese in Korea who had, effectively, driven the helicopter from daytime skies. Furthermore, although I was the Forward Air Commander, I had little say in how the support helicopters could be used. Often, I found myself faced with an exercise fait accompli, too late to be changed to anything making sense, and only to be argued about when the damage had been done.

I also learned a little about the Irish. This was at a time a few years before the troubles began. I admit that I did not come across any bad feeling, although the inhabitants of Northern Ireland must have wondered what on earth was behind our war game. It took just a day for me to begin to receive requests for compensation; payment for loss of sleep because of the noise we were making, for difficulties in completing the early morning milking on time, damage to crops, fences and buildings, and, best of all, for the 'ruptured cow' syndrome. I must have received at least half-a-dozen demands for payment because pregnant cows had been so frightened by our low-flying that they had ruptured themselves trying to leap over fences and hedges. Thankfully, we did not have time to investigate but left the matters in the hands of the Royal Ulster Constabulary.

The next few months saw decided progress in the renovation of the station. A considerable amount of building had been put in hand and the hangars were now all equipped to manage helicopters efficiently. Significant improvements had been made in the Airmen's Mess and in their quarters and the massive refuse pile near No. 72 Squadron's hangar had been dispersed. To my surprise, it was found to fill a considerable pit, and that it's filling must have been going on for a very long time because, almost at its bottom, we found a well-preserved propellor of a World War I BE2c. I instituted a cherry tree planting scheme around the parade square and along both sides of the long entrance road into the station, all trees being paid for voluntarily by officers. The first tree was planted by Air Marshal Sir Gus Walker, the one-armed former bomber pilot. He exacted a reward for so doing by insisting on flying a Wessex which he managed to do by clipping a metal rod to the cyclic from his shoulder in place of his missing arm.

I kept up my physical training, regularly playing football and even, on a couple of occasions, turning out for the station team! To most it must have seemed a strange indulgence for a forty-four yearold, but I was able to rely on some old skills and I conserved my energy by playing hard in short bursts. I became the Transport Command Athletics President and managed to encourage the station into doing very well in the Command Championships, coming fourth overall and ahead of many larger stations. I laid out 6 and 12 kilometer road racing tracks leading out from the station and into the beautiful countryside around Well and Sutton. I practised regularly and so did many station personnel and some from 38 Group.

In July, I received an invitation from my old geography master at the Exmouth Grammar School, now made a Comprehensive, to open the school's new swimming pool. When a pupil there, some thirty years previously, I had seen a Wapiti easily make a forced landing on the playing fields. I had then daydreamed about being the first student to make a decent landing in the same area. I readily accepted the invitation and told 'Pry' Earp, the master, now very long retired, that I would land at the School in a helicopter.

Whilst commanding Odiham I found I had two other officers who hailed from my homeground in Devon. Quite a coincidence

I flew down to Devon in a Wessex, arriving a little late because of the sea-fog that stretched from Lyme Regis way into Torbay, completely blanking out Exmouth. Landing in the little of what remained of the area once covered by the cricket and soccer pitches, I dutifully made a speech and opened the swimming pool. Then I was taken around the school by Mr Earp and was depressed by what I saw. Repeatedly, Earp apologized for changes that were all too evident. The large Latin exhortation, 'Mens Sana in Corpore Sano' had been taken down from the entrance to the gymnasium which had been turned into a restaurant and the former School motto 'Facta non Verba', together with the Honours Board, had disappeared. Almost all the playing fields had been built over and the prefectoral system and school uniform were no longer used; and basic manners seemed lost. Although I was in best uniform, little respect was paid to my standing. At a makeshift lunch, Earp had sternly to ask two badly-dressed pupils to get up from a table to make way for us. What I had hoped would have been a memorable delight had turned into a pathetic non-event. I felt desperately sorry for Mr Earp.

I left in something of a bad temper and this was not helped when the fuselage door fell off as we were passing over the village of Newton Poppleford. Luckily, the crewman saw it flutter down to land in some boggy ground just near the bridge that crosses the Otter. I had to hold the Wessex in the hover for almost five minutes while he got down into the marsh and retrieved the door. The noise of this brought the village to life but, fortunately, the village constable did not arrive on his bicycle until we were pulling away.

Although my responsibilities for the two squadrons in Borneo were confined mainly to the care of the 'headless families', I also had to deal with aircrew replacements and the personal records of the squadrons' personnel. I considered that it was high time for me to meet those on whom I had annually to report and, at the same time, to learn something about how they operated. While I was preparing to leave, I had a distressing interview with the distraught wife of a Flight Lieutenant who was reported to be 'shacked-up' with a Chinese woman at one of the advanced landing clearings in the Borneo jungle. I promised her that I would do whatever possible to disprove what was surely nothing more than a malicious rumour.

Both squadrons operated the Whirlwind Mk 10 from numerous dispersed sites in Sarawak, Sabah, and Brunei. I completed a short refresher course on the Whirlwind at Thorney Island and then, on 15th and 16th August, flew in a Comet 4b from Lyneham to Akrotiri, Bahrein, Gan, and Singapore. Before crossing to Borneo, I made a visit to a Belvedere squadron and flew on a resupply sortie over Johore. The next day, I flew in a Britannia to Kuching, and then on to Labuan.

I began my tour of the squadrons by visiting the detachment based on Labuan and flying with them on what were called Trans Ops up to and along the frontier with Indonesia. On the second of these flights we landed at LZ (Landing Zone) 866, a clearing in dense jungle in which I expected to find the supposed lovelorn Flight Lieutenant and his Chinese girlfriend. The LZ was on full alert, just a few miles from the frontier, guarded by a section of Gurkhas. The Flight Lieutenant was in charge of the landing zone and there was no sign of any Chinese women. He asked me to convey his love and best wishes to his wife and to tell her that he expected to be tour-expired by the end of October.

I next moved to Kuching from where I flew nine Trans Ops, most dealing with the positioning of troops in various jungle clearings. Then I went to Padawan to fly six Trans Ops, and to Bau for another four. The work fascinated me. There was no one firing at us even when occasionally we crossed into Indonesia. Squadron morale was high and their flying was very professional. The only real worry was the possibility of engine failure which would mean disaster if an autorotation had to be made on to the jungle canopy. The primary jungle trees stood almost 200 feet high which meant that a landing at their tops would be followed with a catastrophic vertical crash to the ground. For my part, I had learned a lot and I had met all the officers and aircrew on whom I had to report. I liked most of what I had experienced, particularly the food, the weather, and the jungle. I returned to Singapore on 27th August and, after buying some made-to-measure shirts at Changi, left for Lyneham in a Comet 4b the next day.

My experiences in Borneo had given me an insight into an awkward situation that had developed while I had been away from Odiham. Two flight lieutenants had petitioned not to go to Borneo as replacements for tour-expired pilots. Both were Cranwell graduates, one was the son of an Air Officer and it was expected that each would do well in the Service.

I was advised by Group to proceed carefully. I interviewed both and came to the conclusion that each was in a dead funk, scared of operating over the jungles of Borneo. They talked about the perils of engine failure and the impossibility of autorotating into the jungle. I pointed out that the accident rate on our squadrons out there was very low and that I had found both to be in excellent spirit. I asked them if they realized what would happen if they refused to obey an order to serve in Borneo. Each said that he did but that nothing would change his mind. I formally put the order in writing and from each obtained a refusal to obey. I thereupon charged them both with disobeying an order and put them under open arrest to await Court Martial.

My decisions caused quite a stir at most levels and I received some adverse criticism from one of my seniors but, in the main, it was agreed that no other action had been possible. Both underwent Court Martial and were dismissed the Service.

I felt downcast at another decision of a similar nature that I had to make. An over-aged, unmarried navigator, also petitioned not to go to Borneo because it would mean leaving his ailing bedridden, eighty-five year old mother who was in his care. This time, I felt compassion and tried unsuccessfully to find a volunteer to take his place. In the end, I had to send him. His mother died within a month of his leaving and, a few months later, he was killed with the others in his crew, when his Whirlwind crashed into the jungle after an engine failure.

CHAPTER TWENTY-ONE

On 11th November 1965, Ian Smith made a Unilateral Declaration of Independence (UDI) for his country, Rhodesia, following the break-up of the Federation with Zambia (formerly Northern Rhodesia), and Malawi (formerly Nyasaland). No. 38 Group were immediately briefed on the possibility and plans for instituting an airlift to Zambia for the setting-up of an Air Defence Force to cater for any instability that might arise from the UDI; either from Rhodesia or from the Organisation of African Union (OAU) headed by Idi Amin, the dictator of Uganda.

Air Commodore Ian MacDougall, SASO of 38 Group, flew to Lusaka, the capital of Zambia and, with the British High Commissioner, the Commonwealth Secretary, Arthur Bottomley and Malcolm MacDonald, took part in talks with President Kaunda about the despatch of troops and aircraft to Zambia. The discussions were prolonged by the reluctance of the Zambians to accept ground troops in their country on our conditions. We could not allow them to be used offensively, nor could other OAU countries be allowed to send troops to Zambia without our consent.

While 38 Group awaited political decision to begin the airlift, a force was assembled consisting of No. 1 Air Control Unit, No. 51 Royal Air Force Regiment Squadron from the UK, ten Gloster Javelins from No. 29 Squadron in Cyprus, and signallers and movement teams from Aden and elsewhere. As soon as possible, it would be increased by RAF servicing teams, an Army Field Signals Unit, one troop of Royal Engineers, a British

Forces Post Office, and a NAAFI unit.

I was kept completely unaware of this planning and its possible impact on my station. This was brought home to me with a bang on 1st December when, without any warning, I was called to see the A.O.C. 38 Group and told that I was to leave at once for Lusaka to be Chief of Staff to Air Commodore MacDougall. Wendy was ill in bed with glandular fever and I only had time to pack and explain to her what I thought was about to happen before I was hustled away by helicopter to Lyneham to board a waiting Comet. We flew to El Adem and arrived in Nairobi the next day and there I joined with seven hundred and fifty members of No. 51 Squadron, RAF Regiment and left in a fleet of Argosies for Lusaka. As we approached the Zambian capital we entered the airspace controlled by Salisbury, the capital of Rhodesia, from where, strangely enough, we had to request permission to land at Lusaka. The repartee between us and the controllers at Salisbury was truly comical. The banter included such gems as, 'What the hell is going on?' - 'Have you got that bugger Wilson with you?' - 'We've got a cricket match on at Que Que tomorrow, how about joining us?' - and, 'Best of luck, chums, you'll need it.'

My first few days in Lusaka were pretty chaotic. A Joint Force Headquarters had been set up in the Zambian Defence Headquarters and the general impression of the Zambians was that Britain was about to take military action against the Rhodesians. With the help of British officers of the Zambian Army and Government officials, basic needs were being provided for us. At Lusaka, a university was closed to provide accomodation and at Ndola, rough and ready arrangements were made at a showground in the form of beds, bedding, and field kitchens for the RAF Regiment. We had transportation provided from government sources and communications were made available via GPO circuits.

All too soon we were drawn into politics. We had been given the clear aim of supporting the Zambian Government against any outside influence either from the Organisation of African Unity or from Ian Smith, Prime Minister of Rhodesia. The Royal Air Force Regiment had the airfields at Lusaka, Ndola, and Livingstone, firmly under their control within twenty-four hours of our arrival; No. 29 Squadron had flown into Ndola from Cyprus with their Javelins and had already moved four of them to Lusaka. Air Commodore MacDougall was determined to 'show the flag' but, from the very start, he was beset with problems of handling the Javelins. It was difficult to accomodate them on civilian airports. Complaints were made about noise, fuel spillage, and the burning of tarmac from the twin jet engine exhausts. Worst of all, the Javelins had to be flown within strict limits, imposed by the Middle East Air Force, requiring them to be flown as sedately as the Argosy transports in which we had arrived.

Simon Kapwepwe, the Zambian Minister of Foreign Affairs, went public with the accusation that Britain was cheating and using 'shameful tactics'. He charged the British Government with sending outdated, useless aircraft to defend Zambia in a dangerous game of bluff. He had just returned from a special session of the Organisation of African Unity in Addis Ababa where the meeting had congratulated President Kaunda on the firm stand taken with Britain. We had to do our best to counter his accusation by refuting the claims about the Javelins' capabilities against possible strikes by the Rhodesian Air Force. We said, almost with tongue in cheek, that any hostile action by Rhodesian Canberra bombers and Hunter fighters could be dealt with by the Javelins. Ground radar would give the alert and the Javelin's radar and missile system would ensure a kill without its pilot even having to see the enemy.

However, no sooner had we installed our makeshift Air Defence system than an oil embargo was imposed by Rhodesia. Meanwhile, the Zambian Government had drawn up a contingency plan to deal with such an embargo, all oil movement expenses would be the responsibility of Britain and the necessary types of fuel would be purchased and positioned in drums or other containers at points in Dar-es-Salaam, Mombasa, Leopoldville and Beira. The fuel would then be transported to Zambia by road and by air.

On 19th December, I was sent to Dar-es-Salaam to manage the airlift of oil into Zambia by using two Britannias of No. 99 Squadron. On the face of it, this was a strange order because the Tanzanian Government had banned the use of British military personnel from any activity in their country. This had come about when Tanzania had broken off diplomatic relations with Britain and expelled our High Commissioner after a misunderstanding over the intentions of a British destroyer carrying a cargo of empty oil drums into Dar-es-Salaam. This was never to be a 'show the flag' visit but HMS Dido had entered Dar-es-Salaam harbour at some

279

speed, with a large Union Jack on her prow, whoop-whooping on its siren, and taken up a berth close to shore. A discreet anchorage in the creek would have served its purpose just as well and certainly would have averted the spate of rumours that arose about British intentions. There was a story - believed in some Government quarters - that each empty oil drum contained a fully-equipped Marine commando. President Nyerere and his government had left Dar-es-Salaam for the Highlands and British interests were now in the hands of the Canadian High Commissioner. He had suggested that the 99 Squadron personnel should discard uniform to give the impression that the about-to-start airlift was a civilian matter.

I arrived at Dar-es-Salaam in the third Brittania that was expected to be joined by two others to cope with an expected air lift of up to six or seven sorties a day. As I got down from the aircraft, I was greeted by a motley looking bunch of RAF personnel in civilian garb and a large gathering of International Press reporters. I was bombarded with questions about British military intentions and asked why I had taken the liberty of arriving in Tanzania dressed in uniform. I kept my answers short and to the point. I had simply been instructed to fly the maximum oil to Zambia with the permission of the Tanzanian Government. I was a senior officer in the Royal Air Force and always wore uniform when on duty. Our Britannias were in 'uniform' in any case, clearly marked with RAF insignia. I decided I didn't like the look of the untidy 99 Squadron personnel and insisted they would put on their uniforms at once.

I set up Headquarters for myself and quarters for the 99 Squadron personnel in the plush Hotel Kilimanjaro overlooking the Dar-es-Salaam harbour, hiring local transport to travel to and from the airport. We received no help at all from the Tanzanian authorities and the police clearly went out of their way to avoid us. I spent most of my time at the airport and, now and then, flew to Lusaka to report to Ian MacDougall, now officially installed as COMBRITZAM (Commander British Forces Zambia). The weather was always hot and humid and the 99 Squadron personnel were not suitably dressed for working in such conditions. I bought everyone a white sunhat and a pair of suede 'brothel creepers' from a local BATA factory, the bill for which followed me around the Service for the next two years until finally it was paid by the Ministry of Supply. We worked very hard and gradually built up our sortie rate to five a day until, early one

morning, the black Tanzanian overseer of the locally-recruited work force
that loaded the oil drums into the aircraft, greeted me with the news, 'No
black bastards for you today, boss. It's Ramadam. They won't be back
until it is over.'

We had no alternative but to buckle-to and load the Britannias ourselves. I even lent a hand by operating one of the fork lifts. Unfortunately,
the sortie rate began to fall and I duly reported our misfortune to Lusaka.
I was hard at work on a fork lift one morning when I was called to the
communications point we had set up on the edge of our dispersal area.
Unbelievably, using a Single Sideband radio (a direct radio link easily
monitored by any interested party), relayed through Aden, the C-in-C,
back at Upavon was calling me. I knew that voice well and almost stood
to attention in my working undress as he asked me what on earth had gone
wrong with the sortie rate. 'The work-force is on strike,' I told him. 'What
on earth are you doing about it?' then came the terse retort. 'I have everyone working flat out,' I replied. 'We are all at it.' Then I brazenly added,
'I was just a moment ago working a fork lift myself, loading barrels.'
There was no further discussion in an exchange that must have been heard
by many over thousands of miles.

Very soon major difficulties arose with the state of the Ndola and
Lusaka airfields. Both had single short runway, each no more than 2,000
yards, and there were no taxiways or parking stands. At Lusaka, much of
the tarmac was too weak to accept the weight of fully-laden airlift aircraft;
our first Britannia to arrive at Lusaka had gone through the thin tarmac at
the unloading point. Undue and unnecessary fuss was made of the event
which brought President Kaunda, Simon Kapwepwe, Arthur Wina, the
Finance Minister, and Sir Leslie Monson, the British High Commissioner
to the scene. The Press were there in numbers and much was made of the
mishap which was easily repaired overnight.

After Ramadam, our local work force returned and we regained our
former high sortie rate. In fact Christmas Day was our very best effort
when, working around the clock in temperatures well over 100 degrees,
we flew 21,000 gallons into the Zambian copperbelt town of Ndola, seven
flights in all, made over 800 miles. Soon after, I was told that the airlift
from Dar-es-Salaam would be taken over by the civilian Britannia Britavia
Ltd and that 99 Squadron's Britannias would re-position in Kenya, at

Nairobi. The Canadians joined the airlift with four Hercules flying from Leopoldville and the Americans began to operate two Boeing 707s from the same place.

In the last few days at Dar-es-Salaam we ran into a very serious problem. I was in the Hotel Kiliminjaro one afternoon when I was called to the public telephone. Almost incoherently, a Warrant Officer of 99 Squadron managed to say that he was trapped in a telephone kiosk by hundreds of natives. He had run over and killed a child when returning to the airfield and the natives were trying to kill him. I tried to calm him, telling him to hold fast in the kiosk while we got the police to come to his aid. I rang the Dar-es-Salaam police on an emergency number I had been given but was told by a Captain that there was nothing they could do about a matter that was all of our own doing. I had the CO of 99 Squadron with me at the time and two crews were eating in the hotel restaurant. We set up a task force immediately, found four cars and then, in convoy, set off at high speed, with horns blowing to clear the way, on the road towards the airport.

We had no difficulty in finding our embattled Warrant Officer. I was in the leading car which we drove through a dense crowd right up to the door of the telephone kiosk. The other cars followed and formed a ring around us. I really thought that we would have a fight on our hands and we were, of course, unarmed. Luckily, someone who was probably the headman appeared, together with another elderly person who could speak English. Bit by bit, the hubbub subsided when it could be seen that someone in authority was speaking to their leader. The Warrant Officer was extracted from his prison and driven away. I promised the headman that justice would be done and restitution made to the family of the dead child; we did not argue over who was to blame. The next day, I returned with a sum of money, large by Tanzanian standards, together with a collection of goods and pieces of equipment we had found surplus in our stores back at the airfield. Throughout the whole of this time, we did not see a Tanzanian policeman nor make any contact with the police.

I was not sorry to leave Dar-es-Salaam but first saw 1966 in with a rip-roaring party around the swimming pool at the Hotel Kilimanjaro. No secret was made of the fact that we would soon be on our way and we invited local dignitaries and even the odd Government official who had not taken to his heels after the HMS Dido incident. By midnight, the party was out of control and the swimming pool was the magnet. There were tables in the shallow end with people sitting on chairs, eating and drinking. At the stroke of twelve, almost everyone dived into the pool, a junior Minister in evening dress was pitched, struggling, off the top diving-board and I swam a length underwater in the company of a female reporter of the Daily Telegraph.

There was a dreadful mess to clear up the next day. The manager of the Kilimanjaro was undoubtedly pleased to see us go. He was forgiving of the damage we had done in and around the pool, yet I had to settle many bills. That afternoon, we handed the airlift over to Britavia and No. 99 Squadron left with their Britannias for Nairobi. I flew back to Lusaka in a Caledonian Airways Britannia laden with oil-drums.

With my return to Lusaka, I was able to revert to my true role as deputy to COMBRITZAM. Within the Organisation of African Unity, Tanzania and Zambia had always maintained that a defensive role for British troops in Zambia was wrong and that, at the very least, a token incursion should be made into Rhodesia to show our seriousness in protecting the Kariba Dam. The Zambians could not understand our being stationed in their country, it apparently seemed to them that we were an occupation force. They had kept the British Government under pressure to do something positive about breaking Ian Smith's oil embargo and COMBRITZAM had been warned to stand by for a top-level meeting between our Prime Minister and the President of Zambia. First, however, Arthur Bottomley, the Commonwealth Secretary, would arrive ahead to prepare the way and I was to make arrangements for his arrival at Ndola from Nairobi.

I flew there the next day and I thought it appropriate that the visit of such an important visitor should be matched with a Guard of Honour. After its inspection, he could then make a short speech to the assembled Press, and leave for Lusaka with the High Commissioner. I had time to inspect the RAF Regiment Guard of Honour after making them rehearse in the dispersal area at the end of the single runway, right up against the barbed-wire linked metal-meshed boundary fence where the arrival ceremony would take place.

The welcoming party was headed by the High Commissioner and included some local Zambian officials and members of the British Press. A large crowd of Zambians thronged the boundary fence, many of whom had climbed into the trees to get a better view. The RAF Hastings arrived dead on time and taxied towards us and slewing around to position itself adjacent the Guard Of Honour. The steps were put in position, and Mr Bottomley got down. He paused to shake hands with the High Commissioner and then turned and hurried over to the boundary fence, followed by the High Commissioner and some of the Press. There he stood, looking up at the gathered Zambians, those pressed against the fence and others waving to him from the trees. He acknowledged them with smiles and with words. I am sure that not one of them understood anything about what he had said.

The High Commisioner spoke quietly to Mr Bottomley and I saw them returning towards us and indicated that the Guard of Honour should be brought to attention. I was introduced and Mr Bottomley then inspected the Guard in a most friendly manner. He then went to the microphone and began to speak. I am sure that everything he wanted to say was heartfelt and, by the way it was delivered, it was clear that it was all of his own work and not something from a Civil Service brief. It was however riddled with clichés such as 'standing four-square with our friends in Zambia' and 'putting our shoulders to the wheel' to solve the situation. I cringed when he referred to the locals as 'noble creatures' but didn't actually hear the gaffe that made the British Press when he mistakenly referred to the country as Gambia.

Next I was on parade at Lusaka with an RAF Regiment detachment set alongside a battalion of the Zambian Army when Harold Wilson arrived in a BOAC VC10. As he hurried down the steps from the aircraft we all came to attention, arms were presented, and the Zambian Army band played 'God Save The Queen'. Mr Wilson was all urgency, he clearly did not want to linger. After being greeted by Simon Kapwepwe and our High Commissioner, he rushed away for talks with President Kaunda.

There was an air of great expectancy in our Headquarters where we waited to hear of developments. The African Press had made much of the Prime Minister's visit, they lived in hope that something dramatic was about to happen; maybe some action taken openly against Rhodesia and anything to ease the problems of the oil embargo. We waited anxiously and, in the early evening, Air Commodore MacDougall was called away to a meeting in the High Commissioner's residence.

He returned with news a few hours later. As COMBRITZAM he had been involved in discussions with Mr Wilson on how we might make some sort of meaningful demonstration into Rhodesia. The first, almost unbelievable suggestion, was that members of the RAF Regiment would be flown into Salisbury in RAF Britannias escorted by our weary Javelins. He had no idea what was behind such a proposal or whether it would be with the approval of someone in the Rhodesian Government making it a political *fait accompli*. He had argued successfully that such a warlike demonstration could well lead to disastrous results and had managed to get the Britannias replaced by civil airliners and the RAF Regiment to be carried to be in civilian dress and for there to be no Javelin escort. He confessed that there seemed to be no idea of what would be done once this force landed in Salisbury. I was told to arrange the urgent hirings of five civil airliners or transports to replace of the Britannias and was briefed not to inform their owners of the intended use of the aircraft, nor was I to speak to any of the civilian aircrew. I did however wonder how they could be coerced into flying into Rhodesia, taking part in such a curious exercise of 'showing the flag'.

I spent the night telephoning around Central Africa for aircraft that could be flown at once to position at Lusaka. By dawn, I had three standing by in Dar-es-Salaam, one in Leopoldville, and another in Nairobi. At our first meeting, early next morning, we wondered if it would not be best openly to oppose the idea of going to Salisbury by saying that it was operationally unworkable. Mr Wilson was expected to leave for London that morning and I went with the Air Commodore to the High Commissioner's residence to join in the final discussions of what was to be done. I was privileged to sit at the back of the room to listen to the words of Mr Wilson, Mr Bottomley, Sir Leslie Monson, and my Air Commodore.

When the Prime Minister opened the discussion, it was soon clear to me that the idea of any sort of excursion into Rhodesia had cooled to lukewarm overnight. He said nothing to us about what had been discussed with President Kaunda earlier that morning when he had made his farewells. Oddly, however, he kept alive the concept of a flight to Salisbury and must have discussed something with Mr Bottomley and Sir Leslie Monson earlier. Bit by bit, however, the discussion drifted away from the point, becoming a time-wasting effort right up until the Prime Minister said it was time to leave. By then, he had passed the responsibility for any action to Arthur Bottomley. His last words to the Commonwealth Secretary were to see 'what he could do' and that he would call him from the VC 10 to ascertain what that might be.

We left as a party to see the Prime Minister depart from Lusaka airport, and returned to the communications section of our Headquarters to establish contact with the captain of the VC 10. Mr Bottomley seemed distressed, no doubt like the rest of us he was more than a little bewildered. Then, when the VC 10 was entering the Nairobi airspace, the Prime Minister came on the air. He was in good voice and we clearly heard him ask if anything had been decided and if the Commonwealth Secretary had any fresh ideas. After a pause, Mr Bottomley said that nothing had been decided and there were no new thoughts. With that, Mr Wilson went off the air with the words that he would leave everything in the Commonwealth Secretary's capable hands.

I noticed a despairing look on Mr Bottomley's face, yet sensed a feeling of relief amongst the others in the room. He asked the High Commissioner and then COMBRITZAM what he should do. Without any hesitation they both answered in like manner, 'Drop the idea - scrub it'.

Thankfully, this episode was kept quiet despite the Prime Minister's call from the VC 10 which must have been picked up by anyone monitoring radio telephone transmissions. The Press who had us constantly on our guard did not get an inkling of what amounted to nothing more than pathetic pondering. Usually, they were quick to pick up and magnify a story, often taking delight in promoting quite insignificant problems into national crises. A particular case in point was the supposition that the morale of the Royal Air Force Regiment in Zambia was so low that airmen were deserting and pouring over the border into the more friendly Rhodesia. It was true that we had the majority of them living in unsatisfactory quarters in Ndola, and that their initial task of securing the airfields at Lusaka and Livingstone had long since lost its importance. They were now only partly-employed, with time on their hands, and could be expected, now and then, to 'kick up their heels' but it was no more than that.

Some of the more uninhibited took their pleasures in the local stews amongst the 'bush turkeys' as they were called, despite constant warning of the dangers to life and their sexual organs. Some managed to share their pleasures with white women, a few who lived in the Copper Belt, but also others who came up from Rhodesia and even from as far away as South Africa. The burst of publicity that gave rise to letters on patriotism, desertion, and the defence of the good name of the RAF in the British Press arose over the supposed desertion of three RAF Regiment men who had fled across the Zambezi seeking 'virtual asylum' in Rhodesia. The Rhodesians were quick to make much of the story which they linked with that of six soldiers of the Gloucester Regiment, stationed in Swaziland, who were on the run in South Africa. In the event, our three Regiment heroes eventually crept back into Ndola much the worse for wear. They explained that they had been 'kidnaped' by a pair of wealthy, over-sexed, middle-aged South African women who had taken them to Rhodesia and kept them more or less 'confined to camp'. There they had been made to work hard to pleasure the women until, almost in desperation, they managed to escape and get back to camp.

My next real task was to explore the possibilities of increasing the input of oil into Zambia by using Argosies flying from the Portuguese port of Beira. I flew first to Lorenzo Marques, the Portuguese capital, where I spent two days in negotiations with officers at Portuguese Air Force Headquarters. While in the city, I had considerable time on my hands and was able to explore. At the airport, I was surprised to see three Rhodesian Air Force Hunters that had dropped in to be refuelled. I met the pilots, all of whom had served in the Royal Air Force, and they joked about our efforts in Zambia, expressing their view that we would never come into open conflict with them. If we did, they were certain that we would come off second best. I did not attempt to argue.

Furnished with a good briefing on the capabilities at the Beira airfield, I flew there in a Dakota on 17th February. I could see no difficulties in operating six Argosies from a reasonably well-equipped airfield. The Portuguese were already unloading oil in the port to be sent by road to Zambia and could easily stack the drums on the airfield. Accommodation for the Argosy crews could be arranged in hotels in the town, and we could hire Volkswagens to meet our transportation needs. I stayed at Beira for just a day.

On the way back to Zambia our Dakota developed a fuel leak that was bad enough for us to make an emergency stop at Blantyre in Malawi.

Maybe it was because we were British but we could get no real help from the airport authorities to make repairs. Luckily, our pilot had once been an engineer and he was able to botch a satisfactory repair using a length of metalled hose bound and held by adhesive tape. We were on our way again after a delay of only six hours.

The trip to Mozambique only served to highlight the confusion brought about by too many people wanting a 'finger in the pie'. Feasibility studies and surveys made by staff officers from the UK usually proved to be unrealistic, principally because they looked for the best conditions, with little regard for costs. Unbeknown to COMBRITZAM, a UK-based Wing Commander had already made a sub rosa study of the very problem I had been sent to examine in Beira. His version made much of the housing problems, accommodation for the aircrews would be unavailable and tents, a field kitchen, and marquee Headquarters would have to be flown in. He foresaw great difficulties with transportation with vehicles being brought in from Kenya. Then, to cap it all, Biera airport was said to be dangerously snake-infested. As it happened, in the end, our plans were knocked on the head by Portuguese reluctance to support overt British military activities from their territory.

By mid-February 1966 we had the oil airlift into Zambia under control. There were still problems with the state of the oil drums, many of which were nearing the end of their useful lives. The heavy rubber seal-drums leaked so badly that their use had to be limited to the Canadian Hercules with their large expanse of flooring and open cargo doors. Supply by road had been built up from Dar-es-Salaam and Mombasa along the Great North Road, by rail to Kordoma and then by lake to Mpulungo. Oil was moving by rail from Beira to Elizabethville and on into the Copper Belt. The airlift was running at 5,000 tons a month, and the surface lift at twice that figure. Together, this oil input well exceeded requirements.

There was a feeling amongst us at Lusaka that the job had been done, and it was no surprise to me when, on 25th February, I was told I could return to Odiham. I flew to Nairobi in a Britannia where I caught a Comet which took me first to Aden, then to Muharraq, on to Akrotiri, and back to Lyneham.

CHAPTER TWENTY-TWO

It was simply wonderful to be back at Odiham, especially finding that Wendy and the girls were well. While I had been away, the station had been in the hands of Wing Commander C.S.Hutton, the third Wing Commander Admin since my arrival. He had done very well and had fitted into Wendy's 'fire brigade' that still dealt with endless problems of the headless families. The fund-raising had been continued with a fine event that culminated in a joint Christmas Fayre with the Basingstoke Council that had raised hundreds of pounds for the Basingstoke Old People's Welfare Committee. A new Wing Commander Flying had also slotted in well and there had been no flying incidents or accidents.

I was now well into my last year as Station Commander, secretly hoping that I would be allowed to stay on to complete a third. Everything about the station interested and challenged me. I could fly whenever I wanted to and cherished every day of what was to be the most enjoyable appointment of my whole career.

The 1966 operational exercise season began early in March when we took part in Exercise Spring Fancy on Salisbury Plain. It was remarkable because of the dense fog which kept us on the ground for days on end. I managed to get airborne one morning, intending to fly to Warminster for a briefing. It became necessary to fly at walking pace to find one's way through the fog and, in the end, I had to stop at the edge of a farmyard somewhere near Longbridge Deverill to ask the way. The visibility became even worse forcing me to shut down and to call for transport to pick me up and take me to Warminster.

In mid-April we began the build-up for a big combined exercise with the Army and Royal Navy, code-named 'Lifeline 66'. Some 10,000 troops of the Strategic Reserve were mobilised to take part, together with a half-battalion of the Italian Army. The Royal Navy were to make seaborne landings from their revolutionary new assault ship, HMS Fearless, and provide 'enemy' air opposition with their Sea Vixens. The air operations would be under the control of No. 38 Group who would provide the transport force and two squadrons of Hunters for defence. I was designated Forward Air Commander.

'Lifeline 66' began when 1,300 men and heavy equipment were parachuted from Hastings and Argosies over Thetford in Norfolk. I flew there to witness what was the biggest parachute drop made by British forces since the Battle at Arnhem. On 21st April, operations were moved to the south-western tip of Wales and there the war games began. I flew down to Templeton to set up my headquarters between the airhead and No. 1 Parachute Battalion, and witnessed the first assault of the exercise from their headquarters. As I flew back to Templeton, the heavens opened. The rain came down in torrents and within hours our base was waterlogged. Attempts to channel water away from our tents were useless as the water table was only about an inch below ground. Our airmen were attempting to work in appalling conditions but, at last, we managed to get a drying machine to work, and I authorised a rum issue.

My chief preoccupation became the organization of a display for all the foreign Air Attaches accredited in London. It had to be staged on the hills behind Sennybridges in the most realistic manner we could arrange. The next day, the bad weather continued with low cloud, heavy rain and poor visibility. I managed to crawl a Wessex at no more than 20 knots to Castlemartin to discuss details of the arrangements with General Blacker of 3 Division. The weather became so awful that I was forced to leave the Wessex and motor to the display area with the General in torrential rain, by-passing flooded roads at Carmarthen, only to find it completely enshrouded in clouds. We had no alternative but to return to Templeton where the weather was marginally better.

The display-to-be was now nick-named 'Grandstand' and we attempted a rehearsal on the 23rd at Sennybridges but, without any warning, we had to divert nine Wessex loaded with Italians to land in heavy rain on the heath. Communications went haywire and I had to fly with SASO of 38 Group to Templeton to sort out the confusion caused by the weather. In the afternoon we tried again and did better, even though the rain still poured down. We had little alternative but to press on with 'Grandstand' and I flew to Castlemartin to collect the Air Attaches who included many from behind the Iron Curtain; East Germans, Poles, and Russians. A feature of the flight to pick them up was that I had become so soaked with the rain that steam was rising from my drying clothing in the heated cockpit, so much so that the crewman wondered if there was not something on fire in the aircraft.

I returned to Sennybridges with the Air Attaches and sat with them while they watched our display. The rain had mercifully stopped and the visibility was good under a low cloud base. As a spectacle, the show was a success; as an example of how we might go to war it was another matter altogether. I flew the VIPs back to Castlemartin quite fed up and with 'the bit between my teeth', first buzzing AOC 38 Group and party and then, at very low level and at high speed, plunging down the mountainside with many of the passengers showing some alarm. I got them into Templeton just in time to get under cover before another deep weather trough began to go through.

It rained all day on the 24th and my main preoccupation then was another VIP visit, this time of General Darling of Southern Command, Air Chief Marshal Cross, my C-in-C, and Mr Reynolds, the Army Minister. I visited 1 Parachute Battalion and made contact with 16 Parachute Brigade to plan two heliborne assaults that could be fitted into the exercise scenario. The bonus for me at Brigade HQ was that I was able to take my first bath since the start of the exercise. Leaving HQ at midnight I was in bed in my sodden tent by 0100 hours.

It was early call the next day and airborne at 0530 hours to make a reconnaissance of where we would make the assaults. The VIPs arrived at 0830 hours and spent the day on a conducted tour, attending briefings, and watching the two assaults. Both my C-in-C and AOC 38 Group flew as passengers in the second assault and were well pleased with our efforts.

The next day, I finally got involved in the real business of the exercise which once again highlighted the vulnerability of support helicopters to both ground fire and air attack, and of their continued misuse. The deputy Squadron commander of No. 72 Squadron started the ball rolling with a wretched *faux pas* by misreading the location of a dropping zone (DZ). The first wave of troops was put down 2,000 feet short, and the 2nd and 3rd in entirely different positions. There was much tut-tutting from the Army and I was furious. The scenario was then further confused by the umpires totally ignoring the effects of the air attacks made by the 'enemy' Sea Vixens which strafed the area unopposed within an hour of the arrival of the helicopters. Thoroughly fed up, I injected a well-coordinated night 'spoof' helicopter assault into the proceedings. It partly redeemed our mistakes of the morning and gave me the satisfaction of confusing the umpires.

After a night of driving rain which at times reached gale force and played havoc amongst our tents, we spent a day in support of 19 Brigade. We evacuated a very wet and miserable company of Bersaglieri from the front line and took them to the marginally better comfort of the sodden Sennybridges camp. In the afternoon we made two very good helicopter assaults, both of which were ruled out by the umpires. Yet again they had ignored the powerful effect of air-to-ground attacks. Our supposed failure was brought about by the appearance of four Stalwarts (huge six-wheeled transport vehicles designed to cross rivers and the most inhospitable terrain) on high ground overlooking the DZ just ten minutes after we had put down the troops. The Stalwarts themselves had apparently survived not only shelling by field artillery but also the attentions of four Hunter GA9s armed with rockets. Thankfully, the umpires later allowed us success with a difficult night landing behind 'enemy' lines', made without preliminary reconnaissance.

There was every evidence that 28th April was to be the last day of the exercise. At briefings that morning it could be seen that the 'enemy' was in real trouble and a grand slam would put paid to them. Although the weather was reasonable, the grand finale suffered delay after delay. The postponements made it impossible to knit together or rearrange the essential fighter cover for the helicopter deployments and, as the show had to go on, the helicopters were attacked again and again by the Sea Vixens. The scenario had become a nonsense but it was absolutely exhilarating.

When the Hunters got into the act they pitched into the Sea Vixens but most of the time we were theoretically being 'hacked to pieces' partially because we were unable to waste time by taking evasive action due to the exercise timetable. These antics must have gone on for at least three hours with every one of our helicopters being shot down at least a dozen times. Nonetheless, the net closed around the 'enemy' and, at 1600 hours, they called for a timely truce.

I flew to Templeton in a Scout to arrange the withdrawal of the airhead and then back to Sennybridges to be caught up in what must have been one of the fastest ever striking of camps. To a man, all wanted to get away from that rain-soaked muddy swamp of that part of Wales, back to the comfort of home.

At the 'Lifeline 66' wash-up meeting, I made a stand for better and more realistic umpiring of exercises. I had not known until the last day of the exercise that there was not a single RAF officer in the umpiring team. My point was taken, but then submerged in the counter-argument that an exercise had to run its course, elimination of component parts of the war games because of tactical errors would mean an early stop. I had to agree of course, but made a plea for a better understanding of the role of a support helicopter, it could not be expected to fight its way to a DZ, even with fighter cover. In time, I suggested, there might be such aircraft as assault helicopter and they might well play a vital part in limited war. In the meantime, it should be realised that something like a Wessex was extremely vulnerable and could not be expected to be used as anything more than a tactical load-carrier.

It took us some time to recover from 'Lifeline', what with the piles of damaged and still sodden tentage to be repaired and dried, and quite a number of airmen down with colds and respiratory illnesses. I was glad when asked by the Chairman of the RAF Escaping Society if I would help by arranging a pick-up of a party of Dutch and Belgian helpers and fly them to London for a week's holiday. Alistair Steadman at Lyneham made a Comet available and I flew to Valkenburg, near Maastricht to collect the party. You can imagine my delight when I found my old friend, Father Marcel, who had hidden me in the Couvent des Carmes in Namur in 1942, had been included in the bunch of escape route veterans

The helpers were in a fine mood and delighted at about to be flown to

England in such a fine aircraft as the Comet. I naturally paid particular attention to Father Marcel whom I had not seen since the end of the war. I sat alongside him and when he expressed a wish to see the business-end of the machine, I took him forward to meet the pilot and crew. He shook hands with the stewards, engineer, and then the co-pilot. As he lent over to speak to the pilot, the flashing and sounding red alarm signals came on indicating trouble in No 3 engine. He drew back and clutched my hand and I assured him there was nothing to worry about, a Comet could easily function on three engines. He calmed in an instant, put his hand on the pilot's shoulder, and blessed him with the 'Sign of the Cross'. We went back to our seats, saying not a word to anyone. As expected there was no problem in landing on three at Northolt.

There was a respite from exercising with the Army during May and June and we had a reasonably good AOC's inspection, as well as doing well in the Command sports. I settled back into my walking fitness training and decided it was time to make another visit to Nijmegen to celebrate the 50th Anniversary of the Marches. I surprised many by saying that I intended to lead a team from the Station. The news went around the Command like wildfire. There was no shortage of volunteers and, when we started training, other stations took up the idea; Odiham then became a road-marching focus. During a long weekend in early July, I hosted 250 airmen, 50 ATC cadets, and 30 WRAF who marched with our Station team 26 miles a day, carrying the required 25 lbs of equipment on their backs as a final practice for Nijmegen. I led the Odiham team of 30 airmen and was joined by Lieutenant Colonel Len Thacker, a 38 Group RASC officer.

At this time, I became involved in another RAFES (RAF Escaping Society) visit, this time of my own instigation. I was still a Committee member and regularly attended Society meetings in the Duke of York's Headquarters in Chelsea each month. I had the three most famous women in escape route history, all former members of the *Comète* Line, invited by the Air Board to spend a few days in England where they would meet dignitaries and as many of those they had helped to escape as we could bring together. The heroines were all holders of the George Medal, Mlle Andrée de Jongh (*Dédée*) Mme Elvire de Greef, (*Tante Go*) and Mme Micheline Ugeux, (*Michou*). They first visited the Ministry of Defence and met the Chief of the Air Staff, Air Chief Marshal Elworthy, and other

Bryan Wharton

Mlle Andree de Jongh (centre) meets one of the men she helped to escape

'The best travel agency ever'

By Jeremy Bugler

ON THE surface, it was a strange meeting—the group of emphatically British R A F men who spoke "English French" and the three middle-aged Belgian women. Yet, they met in London last week for good reason—a reception to meet men they helped to escape.

The three were Mlle Andrée de Jongh, Mme Elvire de Greef and Mme Micheline Ugeux, all George Medallists and key figures in the famous Comété route along which 817—mainly R A F—airmen escaped to fly again. The group consisted of members of the R A F Escaping Society who went down the line which one ex-gunner, shot down over Belgium, described as "the best travel agency there ever was."

The Comété line, which ran from Belgium to the Pyrenees, had an extraordinary network of helpers throughout France and Belgium.

Inspiration of the line was Mlle de Jongh (Dedee), who works now in a leper colony in the Cameroons. She and her father put the Comété into operation. In her work ("It wasn't always want to stop") she crossed and recrossed the Pyrenees 33 times, swam the Somme to avoid German patrols, and spent the last two war years in Ravensbrueck and Mauthausen.

Mme de Greef (Tante Go), was described by one escaper as "the rallier." When the line was betrayed and broke, she got it back into action.

Mme Ugeux ("Michou") was at 19 handling the despatch and reception of aircrew, and helping to re-establish the line after betrayal in 1944.

A strange occasion, with conversation going from the light-hearted ("Remember that bloke who replied 'Don't mention it' to the German who said 'Danke schoen?') to be serious.

Sunday Times 8/1/1967

A cutting from the Sunday Times dated 8th January 1967. Dédée is in the centre talking to a former evader. When the Comète line was broken by the Germans and many of the operatives captured or killed, Dédée was among those that were to spend two years in the horror of the concentration camps at Ravensbrueck and Maulthausen

295

members of the Air Board. After lunch at the Royal Air Force Club, they were taken to Battersea Heliport where I had arranged for them to be picked up by Wessex and flown to Odiham. On arrival they were met by the AOC and SASO of 38 Group, shown around the Station and then taken to the Officers' Mess to meet scores of those they had successfully helped to escape. They then attended a Guest Night. Far too many speeches of thanks to the ladies were attempted by RAFES members; yet it proved to be a memorable occasion.

I flew to RAF Laarbruch in Germany on 24th July with my marching team in a Beverley from RAF Abingdon. We were housed in Royal Netherlands Air Force barracks at Nijmegen and made very welcome and comfortable. The Marches were completed in fine style without a single dropout I believe that I was the first Group Captain ever to complete the course. It was certainly a surprise for the officer taking the salute, C-in-C, RAF Germany, when I marched past at the head of the Odiham team.

We flew back on 30th July, the day of the World Cup football final. The slowness of the Beverley made it possible for me to listen in to the whole England versus Germany game between the take-off at Laarbruch and the landing at Abingdon. I heard the commentary of the playing of extra time on the set in my staff car as I was driven back to Odiham, and was just entering the Station when the famous, '...they think it's all over' comment was made.

In August we took part in a series of small exercises with the Army at Sennybridges, Keevil, and Otterburn. We finished the month with a much larger one on Salisbury Plain where, once again, we became embroiled in Exercise 'make believe'. It was a scheme devoted to the use of helicopters, both the Army's Scouts and our Wessex. I was again the Forward Air Commander. The three-day exercise was planned to finish with a mass helicopter approach with troops attacking to finish off the enemy who had become boxed-in around Sidbury Hill near Ludgershall, a dominating feature that overlooked every possible avenue of activity for about ten miles around. The Brigadier commanding the attacking force wanted the best part of a battalion put down in broad daylight almost at the base of the hill. We had good information of enemy defences from Scout reconnaissance helicopters and knew that there were tanks on the hill and that our intended DZ was within rifle and machine gun range. I argued with the Brigadier that there was no dead ground we could use between our forming-up area and the DZ; that once on our way we would be in full view of the enemy and, lastly, that in any case we were already too close to the hill to camouflage our preparations. Once engines were started, the noise would be heard in the enemy forward positions. I told him that his plan made little sense and that, if we were really in action, I would certainly not sanction its implementation. He argued fiercely that the troops had to be flown and doubted my ability to 'read the ground' as a soldier would. I still refused and he reported my views to his superior. In the end, I was asked to proceed '...for the good of the exercise'.

I flew in the leading Wessex, loading the troops about 10 miles from Sidbury Hill, out of earshot of the enemy because the wind was blowing briskly away from the hill. Fully loaded we waited with engines running for almost ten minutes while the enemy were theoretically shelled on the crest and slopes of the hill. The order to move off came through on open radio and we set off in two waves, flying at no more than fifty feet and doing our best to hide our approach. Unfortunately, we were in the open for the last two or three miles as I led 36 Wessex towards the DZ which I could now clearly see in two open fields at the bottom of the hill. The noise the Wessex were making must have been deafening as we thundered in to the DZ. I chose the top right-hand corner of the first field coming in at speed and flaring into the hover. The troops began to unload quickly but not before a Centurion tank broke through the hedge and almost stuck its gun into our cockpit.

At the wash-up, my views on exercise nonsense were supported by more than one Army officer and we had at least got the attack and support helicopter argument right out into the open. I believe that my point struck home; that the best person to judge the effective use of the support helicopter was the airman on the spot.

We were only marginally involved in the 1966 Farnborough Air Show in early September with a static display of a Wessex and its role equipment. It was there that I heard the welcome news of our purchase of a number of American Chinooks to replace our aged and inadequate Belvederes and dramatically to increase our carrying capabilities. On the final day at Farnborough I was told that a Chinook would be visiting Odiham the next day for us to see and to speak to the pilots. There was a fine turn-out of No 38 Group officers and almost every Odiham pilot on the sports field waiting for the Chinook to arrive. We heard it long before we could see it, travelling at high speed because we could hear much blade-flapping from the twin rotors. It came into view low down just a mile to the east of the airfield and the pilot began an almost 45 degree flare as soon as he saw us but, because of his speed, careered across the airfield, tail down, and only reduced to approach speed some distance away on the other side. We were able to look over the machine and listen to the enthusiasm of both the Boeing Vertol test pilots. Without any argument, the Chinook was a helicopter the RAF badly needed.

In October, I was asked by the Chairman of the RAF Escaping Society to help with the arrangements for the annual visit to Brussels which ended with a Solemn Requiem Mass for Belgian helpers in the Koelkelburg. I flew in a Hastings to Evere with a party of about 20 RAFES members and a chosen group of airmen and airwomen from Odiham. With the permission of the Belgian Air Force, our group was privileged to line the steps into the cathedral, and to pay respects to members of the Belgian Royal Family.

That month I was injured in a football match. I still played the game regularly and very much enjoyed doing so. This time it was a game between Flying Wing and the Sergeants' Mess; somewhat on the rough side but in good humour. Just before halftime, I was badly tackled. A big chunk of flesh was kicked from my left knee cap and, more seriously, damage was done to my right leg which I thought had been broken. I was carried away to sick quarters to be stitched-up and happily to be told that nothing had in fact been fractured. I had to walk with a stick for a week or two, somewhat upset with the prognosis that I would most likely have trouble with my legs, possibly for the rest of my life.

CHAPTER TWENTY-FOUR

While still hobbling around and not being able to fly, my next appointment was given to me almost overnight. There had been an emergency of some sort in the Operational Requirements Department of the Ministry of Defence (Air). I was told that within three days I would have to take up the job of DDOR7. It was an almost immediate 'down tools' for me at Odiham. I only met my replacement, Bill Martin, on the day I left and was unable to make the customary farewell calls in the neighborhood and in Basingstoke. Regretably there was no time for a dining-out evening or for me properly to take my leave of the staff with whom I had worked for two years. On the plus side we were between lettings with our house in Tadworth and were able to repossess our home at once.

DDOR7 had the responsibility for the operational requirements for all transport aircraft and the helicopters. The fixed-wing requirements had been agreed for some time; the slow, aged, and uneconomical Hastings were to be replaced with the American C130 Hercules; VC 1Os were in service replacing the Britannias and Comet 4s and one squadron of Belfasts was dealing with the heavy lift requirement, while Andovers were taking over from the Argosies. The only fixed-wing remit I had was the little Beagle that was being considered in the communications role.

On the other hand, there was much to do with the helicopter requirements. An order had been placed for twenty Chinooks that were being bought direct from Boeing Vertol. The augmentation of the Wessex force, the replacement of the Whirlwind and Scout, and the possible introduction of an assault helicopter for the Army and a general purpose version for the Royal Navy, were all wrapped up in what was labeled the 'Anglo-French helicopter package'. It had three component parts: the purchase of the Sud Aviation 330, the Puma, and the production of a new batch of aircraft for the RAF by Westlands; the development of the Sud Aviation Alouette 3 for communications work in the RAF and for training in the Army; and the design and development by Westlands of a multipurpose helicopter, the Lynx, for the Army, Royal Navy, and the French.

Much had already been done by the time I arrived to take up my duties. The Ministry of Supply had already signed contracts with Westlands and the French for all three projects. In early December, I went to Marignane, just outside Marseilles, to see the SA 330. I gained a dramatic first impression of this beautifully designed support helicopter in one of the first production models for the French Air Force. I flew with M. Cottignot, the Sud Aviation test pilot who did things with this heavy helicopter that I thought were impossible; maximum speed runs of over 200 mph followed by vertical climbs with an upside-down rollout at the top, almost as though the machine had been looped. I found that the SA330 handled better than the Wessex but I could sense that it was not as robust. When I returned, I submitted a short list of what I thought would have to be done to the machine to bring it more into line with our expected operational requirements.

I also flew in the Alouette 3 which was to be renamed by us the Gazelle. Again, dramatically, Cottingnot showed me a problem in the development that was facing the French. He took the light helicopter up to its maximum permitted speed at that time, 90 knots. Without any real warning, the machine began to shake alarmingly, the vibration being so severe that the instruments could not be read. *'Pas de probleme,'* he said, and so it was. Within a month the Alouette 3 had broken through its vibration barrier and development was speedily completed.

In the New Year's Honours List, I received another unexpected surprise when made an Ordinary Commander of the Most Excellent Order of the British Empire. I was duly reminded not to forget to return the insignia of the OBE just as I had done with the MBE.

The senior staff of my Deputy Directorate included a Wing Commander specialist in all types of transport aircraft, apart from helicopters, and an

Army Air Corps major with the sole responsibility of dealing with the Lynx requirements. The Anglo-French helicopter package dominated our work, although we naturally kept watching briefs on everything developing in the transport field. I concentrated on the helicopter side and, happily, found myself drawn into demonstrations and being offered flights. I flew in the gigantic Russian MN 10 from Gatwick, amazed at its capability yet surprised at the lack of sophistication in a machine that could lift a loaded motorbus and yet required the pilots to use television cameras to see what was below and behind them. I enjoyed myself in a Huey Cobra at Middle Wallop, my first experience of an attack helicopter. It was extremely fast, very maneuverable, and a delight to handle with its small computerized cyclic and control levers. There were regular trips to Marignane where Cottingnot demonstrated the progress being made with both the SA330 and the Alouette 3. I flew the Scout, Jet Ranger, and Fairchild Hiller 1100. Bill Martin at Odiham, helped me whenever possible, by letting me fly a Wessex when making staff visits. I would telephone him the night before and, next morning, there would be a Wessex landing at Headley Court, the RAF Remedial Hospital, just four miles from where I lived, ready for me to fly.

This arrangement with Bill was to save my life. We were involved, together with the Queen's Flight at RAF Benson, in monitoring the production of two special Wessex to replace the Whirlwinds that carried the Royal Family. I regularly flew to Westlands at Yeovil, always in a Wessex provided by Odiham. I was at work in my office in Whitehall one afternoon when I received a call from Benson telling me that the Captain of the Queen's Flight would like me to join him at Yeovil the next day when he hoped to accept the first of the two special Wessex. I rang Bill Martin only to be told that he had no spare aircraft at such short notice. I telephoned the Queen's Flight to say that I would have to motor down to Yeovil and the Commanding Officer said he would be flying a Whirlwind to Yeovil with the Captain and that there was a spare place available which I could take; I readily accepted. Then, just as I was about to leave the office, Bill Martin called with the news that he had found a spare Wessex for me and that it would be at Headley Court early the next morning. I quickly telephoned the Queen's Flight and canceled my seat in the Whirlwind.

I took off from Headley Court about twenty minutes after the time the

Whirlwind was expected to leave Benson. I called their Whirlwind on the way but received no answer and when I landed at Yeovil I was shocked to learn that the Whirlwind had crashed soon after taking off from Benson, killing everyone on board, including the Captain of the Queen's Flight.

In July I made a very interesting visit to Washington, reporting first to the British Joint Services Mission and then going on to Philadelphia to fly in the first Chinook of the batch that had been ordered. I was allowed to fly it around the city and to practice approaches, hoverings, and landings on the Boeing Vertol airfield. My appreciation of this first-class helicopter was shattered when I landed and was handed a telegram telling me to return to London because the Chinook order had been canceled. This dithering by the Government was to cost £25 million in cancellation fees and yet the same Chinooks were reordered a few years later.

Being in London gave me more opportunity to help with fund raising, particularly on behalf of the RAF Escaping Society. I had been a Committee member, off and on, for fifteen years. The Chairman was my old navigator, Scottie Brazill and my former rear gunner, Bob Frost, was another Committee member. The Society was in its hey-day, fully engrossed in charitable work, most of it on the Continent. I was able to arrange flights to visit helpers and for our members to attend reunions both at home and abroad. I became involved in a series of fund-raising events on behalf of the Society and other similar charities in Belgium and the Netherlands

Perhaps that was why I found myself with a new challenge one day at the Royal Air Force Club. One lunchtime I was talking to my friend, Group Captain Dennis David, about plans I had for a national raffle to raise funds for the Benevolent Fund when I must have been overheard by Marshal of the Royal Air Force Sir Dermot Boyle who was standing nearby; he was clearly interested in what I was saying. Dennis David introduced me to him as a long-standing friend who had a knack for fund-raising. Well I remember Sir Dermot's words, 'Well done, but you have not raised a penny for the Royal Air Force Museum, have you?'

I had to confess that I had not and, furthermore, that I knew absolutely nothing about a Museum project. There was a tut tut from Sir Dermot who then openly asked me if I would try to support the Museum as best I could. I was impressed to be spoken to in such a friendly manner by such a great man and listened to his every word as he described to all around what had to be done to build a long-overdue memorial to the Royal Air Force. He was the Chairman of the Trustees of the Museum-to-be, and his words struck home personally when he finished with a direct appeal to me. 'I would be most grateful if you would lend us a hand, Randle.'

That afternoon I went to see Group Captain Levien, a former bomber pilot, who had been appointed the Museum's Appeals Director, and who had an office in High Holborn. He explained how he was employing the traditional ways of raising money, begging letters to commerce and industry, one to each station commander in the Royal Air Force outlining various ways in which the station could help, and fund-raising schemes almost all of which were identical to those I had been using. If I was to be of any help, then I would have to come up with some new ideas.

I simply could not admit defeat, really working on various ideas, all of which would have made little impact in reducing the rather large amount of money required. Sir Dermot's exhortation began to bother me, I did not want to tag myself as a failure. Then, one night, as I was reading in my bath, as was my habit, I stumbled upon what was to prove a real money-spinner. I was browsing through an illustrated book on Portuguese Army uniforms that I had bought a while before in Lorenzo Marques during the Zambian oil airlift. Most attractively, the author had portrayed the evolution of the uniform, step by step, from the 17th century to the present day. In an Archimedian flash of invention, I believe I even muttered 'Eureka', I saw a way of doing something similar with the history of the Royal Air Force, and turning it to financial account. The next day I began to seek advice from various experts in the souvenir business. I switched from thoughts of illustrated postcards to something which was new in the collecting world, an illustrated envelope made into a commemorative postal cover.

I had collected stamps when young and had since become a compulsive collector of anything attractive and within my financial bounds. I began work from the premise that whatever I produced would have to be something that I, myself, would want to collect. The history of the Royal Air Force was a treasure house of notable events and anniversaries, so there would be no difficulty in finding the subject for a cover. The envelope had to be pictorially attractive and drawn by a good artist, preferably someone with a distinctive style. Joe Levien had shown me some striking illustrations he was about to use for an appeal brochure for the Museum that had been drawn by Tony Theobald, an artist working for Trident Artists in Carnaby Street. I told Tony what I had in mind and he quickly sketched a design for a cover, it looked better than anything I had hoped. He was my immediate choice and, for a small fee, designed my first venture, a simple cover showing the Cenotaph and the flags of the three Services, that I intended to issue on 11th November, 1968, to mark the 50th Anniversary of the Armistice.

I kept my plans very much to myself and discussed them only with Wendy, my wife, because we were about to gamble with our own money. I had 1,000 envelopes printed by a small firm in Southampton, Bittern Press, managed by a former German parachutist who had been a prisoner in England. He had liked the country so much that he had married an English girl and decided to stay. To my surprise, the covers sold themselves, almost all were snapped-up by stamp dealers and I managed to make a small profit which I reinvested in the next step. That had to be how best to become accepted in the philatelic collecting field.

I turned to a stamp dealer for advice, Melville Brown of Stamp Publicity, Worthing, who schooled me in the nature of commemorative hand stamps, how best to advertise and sell them. He thought I would benefit if I worked through the British Forces Postal Services, thus giving an official status of sorts to my work.

Together with Melville Brown, I produced a cover dealing with the history of the Royal Air Forces Escaping Society. This did well and produced an even better profit. The problem was that I was dealing only with stamp dealers and knew that, if I were to realize full profit, I had to get into the retail market and bring the individual collector under my control. I decided to produce the covers in series, handle my own advertising, and to add interest and value by having everything flown in RAF aircraft.

I achieved the breakthrough I wanted with a cover marking the 50th Anniversary of the Inauguration of Regular Passenger and Cargo Services that had been made in DH4As of No. 1 Communication Squadron of the 88th Communications Wing from Hendon on 10th January, 1919. I gambled with a production of 7,050 covers which were flown by the Metropolitan Communications Squadron from RAF Northolt to

Villacoublay, Paris, over the very route taken in 1919. I did not waste money on advertising, there was just a notation made, free of charge, in the Post Office Philatelic Bulletin, unfortunately giving my address as Tidworth, not Tadworth. Within hours of the publication of the Bulletin, orders began to pour in from both individuals and stamp dealers. It was a great success and I had learned a lot. The price of the cover was too low at 5 shillings; the stamp dealer demand was so considerable that it would be sufficient to pay all production costs; and I had completely underestimated the workload involved.

On the positive side I was able to hand over a cheque for the Royal Air Force Museum Appeal Fund for £797 pounds and 5 shillings to Sir Dermot Boyle. I told him that I thought I had discovered a new way to raise funds and, in answer to his question about its viability, I said that if I could get properly organized, it might well produce a lot of money over quite a number of years. He telephoned Sir Robert Craven, the Air Member for Personnel and arranged an interview for me. From this, AMP agreed that I could make formal representation to all Station Commanders to help me to produce a series of covers throughout the Service, and for me to be recognized as head of what would be called the Royal Air Force Philatelic Consortium. There was an immediate favourable reaction to what I had proposed. Within the Operational Requirements Department, Wing Commander John Davis volunteered to help, and I soon made a start on the regular production of commemorative covers which has produced millions of pounds for Registered Charities, and is still doing so, today.

In the meantime I still had a full time commitment to my job in the RAF. The Anglo-French helicopter package was by now well under way. Eleven modifications of the Puma had been incorporated as a result of our own particular support helicopter requirements. These were mainly associated with the strengthening of the aircraft and making it more adaptable to the carriage of troops. The Alouette 3, now named the Gazelle, had completed development and was under production at Yeovil. Westlands were proceeding with the development of the Lynx, but experiencing difficulty in the design of the rigid rotor and it looked as though they would have to seek help from the French. On the fixed-wing side, we were happy to rest with the Hercules and VC10 although the Americans were trying to get us interested in the CS Galaxy. This enormous carrier did not fit into our plans at a time when we were beginning to cut back on our international commitments and had almost shut the door on our overseas policing by withdrawing from Aden.

One of the perks of being in the Operational Requirements were the invitations to inspect aircraft developments at factories and air displays. I particularly remember being at the Paris Air Show in 1969, sitting with Alan Bristow of Bristow Helicopters, watching McDonald, the Fairchild Hiller test pilot, perform a most spirited display of the 1100. I mentioned that I had flown in that very machine with McDonald, but not in what I judged to be a potentially dangerous fashion. I thought that if he didn't ease up there might be trouble. I put my cine camera on the helicopter and was filming his quite remarkable manoeuvres when disaster struck. The transmission of the 1100 must have failed and the helicopter exploded.

It was while I was there with Alan that he told me one of his Wessex was about to fly all the way to Australia, a remarkable first-ever. In a flash, the idea of it carrying commemorative covers came to me. Alan was puzzled at such a suggestion, but agreed while saying that he thought it could not be done because the Wessex would be leaving Redhill during the afternoon of the next day. I could see considerable value to our fund-raising programme if, somehow, we could manage to get envelopes on board. I called John Davis from Le Bourget and asked him to buy 500 envelopes and 500 copies of the Ross and Keith England to Australia flight stamp; then to make up the envelopes, take them to be cancelled at the Redhill Post Office the next day, and load them aboard the helicopter. It worked like a charm and, a few months later, we sold all the covers for a handsome price.

Another coup was made during the Daily Mail Transatlantic Air Race when we had 6,500 covers produced. The majority were flown in the Victors that refuelled the Harriers over the Atlantic but some 250 were packed under the ejector seat of Harrier XV744 that won the race by flying from a pier in Manhattan to the coal yard at St Pancras Station in London and, again, a good profit was made for the Museum.

The long-term effects of my past physical misadventures were now beginning to come home to roost. I knew that my advancing years had something to do with it but I was no longer physically active in my work and I was putting on weight. I began to suffer acute pain in my chest at the point of a former fracture of the left collar bone where peculiar blemishes were appearing in the skin. In the end, I was put under treatment at the Central Medical Establishment who regularly made cortisone injections, and, eventually cured the trouble.

The next stage in my physical decay occurred when my right leg gave way. I became very distressed because I simply couldn't move, the slightest jolt gave rise to excruciating pain. I was taken to the RAF Hospital at Halton where badly torn cartilages were removed from above and below the right knee cap and, for good measure the left knee cap had something done to it before it was stitched up. I stayed at Halton for eight days getting used to the pain which was so intense at night that I could only sleep when sitting upright in a chair. I then spent more than a month at the RAF Remedial Hospital at Headley Court working on the restoration of the use of my legs. While there, the doctors gave me a thorough overhaul. My medical category was downgraded because I was becoming deaf, chiefly because I had flown jets in the Fifties wearing a flying helmet instead of a bone dome, and had broken both eardrums. More serious was the discovery of why I could not turn my head fully to the right. An X-ray revealed that sometime in the past I had actually broken my neck or at least badly chipped a vertebra (almost certainly at Lossiemouth when the Wellington exploded). It must have healed itself but was becoming arthritic. Thankfully, they decided best to leave things well alone.

I had been away from my post for more than two months and went back to work knowing I had much to do to catch up in what remained of the final six months of my tour. Unfortunately, within weeks, I made a bad mistake in handling staff matters. The Americans had invented a device that could estimate the rate and degree of a crack developing in helicopter blades. It was called the Blade Inspection Modification (B.I.M.) - each extruded blade could be filled with nitrogen under pressure through a gauge that monitored any loss. The average period of the development of a crack in the blade from start to destruction was put at four hours. It therefore followed that if the B.I.M. was inspected after each flight, the average being about an hour, a developing crack could be spotted in good time. To me, B.I.M. seemed a salvation at a time when most fatal helicopter accidents were due either to rotor or rotor-blade failure.

I readily agreed with the Ministry of Supply that B.I.M.s should be installed in all RAF helicopters having extruded blades. I did not consult the Royal Navy or the Army, assuming that the Ministry of Supply would have done so. My mistake was not to tell my superiors of the decision I had taken.

This error was uncovered at a meeting of the Defence Research Policy Committee when ACAS(OR) was asked about B.I.M., something on which he had never been briefed. I was properly called to account and spent the next few months sorting out the muddle I had caused. The matter was eventually discussed by the Defence Research Policy and the Operational Research Policy Committees, and the order to install B.I.M. was ratified by the Minister of Defence. When all had been resolved, I appeared before the Deputy Chief of the Air Staff, Air Marshal Sir Peter Wykeham, and was formally reproved.

Not long after, my tour at the Ministry of Defence came to an end. I had not done well and naturally wondered what was in store for me as a next appointment. At an interview with my friend, Dennis David, then in the Air Secretary's Department dealing with Group Captain appointments, he confirmed that it would be difficult to find me a job of any importance. I knew that I was about to get what I deserved when told that I was to be the next President of the Cranwell Board at the Officers and Aircrew Selection Centre, RAF Biggin Hill.

CHAPTER TWENTY-FIVE

I was not at my best when I arrived at Biggin Hill, I had put on a lot of weight, my digestion was in a mess, my legs still gave me trouble and I was not very happy with a posting to the 'Elephant's Graveyard'. That was an expression based on the belief that aged and played-out elephants were, in the end, left to themselves to wander off into the distance with nothing more to do but to lie down and die. I had no reason to complain, knowing that I had got what I deserved. I had been extremely lucky with my career until then; promotions and good appointments had come about unexpectedly. I was forty-eight years old with the guarantee of another seven years of service. It didn't worry me that there would be no further promotion, I just hoped that those years would be spent industriously.

The Officers and Aircrew Centre had Air Commodore Peter Seymour as Commandant, and three Selection Boards: Cranwell, Aircrew, and Ground - each under the control of a Group Captain. The Centre had been purpose built alongside the Battle of Britain Memorial Chapel. There was no Service flying at Biggin Hill, the Station existed only to administer the Selection Centre. The airfield had been taken over by the Bromley Council which allowed some civil flying, mostly done by flying clubs.

I was given a short course on interrogation techniques before taking up my duties. The candidates were examined in batches of about twenty aspirants at a time. The process of selection for the RAF College at Cranwell began with an interview of each by me. I made a first assessment before the candidate was passed on to one of the three Wing Commanders who controlled examination boards. They were then aptitude-tested and moved on to the main part of the testing where, in teams of five, they were given initiative and command tests conducted under the careful scrutiny of the Wing Commanders and their staff. All findings were then evaluated and written up, and decisions were made. Seldom did we have a divergence of opinion.

In most cases, I found that the grading I had made at the first interview coincided with that finally awarded by the Board. I suppose that a lifetime of growing up with airmen and dealing with flying personnel's problems had given me an instinct easily to spot the good from the mediocre. I remembered the way the Air Vice-Marshal had dealt with me back in 1941. A youngster's genuine desire to make a career from flying always shone through, those I classified as 'seconds' were either looking for security of employment or a good standard of living. First impressions meant a lot. If a candidate could not take the trouble to present himself smartly dressed or be on the tip of his toes during the interview, I instinctively marked him down. One day an Air Marshal's son appeared before me dressed in a multi-coloured floral shirt, dirty and badly-worn trousers, together with long, unkempt shoulder-length hair. In reply to my first question, he muttered that his father thought it would be a good idea for him to join the RAF. I passed him on to the Board with a zero rating. After some aptitude testing, he simply gave up and walked out the Centre the next day.

What I enjoyed most was the regular visit I had to make to the RAF College at Cranwell where the selections we had made were gone over in discussion with the Commandant, Air Vice-Marshal Desmond Hughes. We usually dealt with the business in his office where I went through the findings on each successful applicant in detail. He had a fine sense of humour and his questions to me were always telling. Not once, however, did he disagree with what we had found.

It had not taken me very long to settle in and take the measure of my workload. I soon found that I had much spare time on my hands. I made this clear to the Commandant and asked if there was anything further that I could take on. The Air Commodore gave me the task of monitoring the work of a squadron leader and a flight lieutenant who had been attached to plan the annual Biggin Hill Battle of Britain Display. He also appointed me as the Display Controller. He then asked me to have a look at the possible structure of the Selection Centre in the light of pending cuts in Defence expenditure now that we had given up the imperial policing role. This was a straightforward exercise. I based my paper on what I had culled from an interview with Dennis David who was still at his post with the Air Secretary. It seemed logical to disestablish the Air Commodore Commandant and the three Group Captains, and put a Group Captain in charge of three Wing Commander Presidents. Much more important was the removal of the Centre to a large active station, even Cranwell itself. There would be considerable savings because the closure of RAF Biggin Hill would have to follow. I often wonder if this paper was kept on hold for the next twenty years, because the Centre is now at Cranwell and RAF Biggin Hill was closed in 1992.

Air Commodore Seymour retired and was replaced by Colin Baker. He quickly understood my attitude to work and became interested in what I was doing to raise funds for charity, in particular, the blossoming philatelic programmes. The arrangements I had made with AMP's Department now meant that fund-raising project officers were standing-by on most RAF stations. At Biggin Hill there were many enthusiastic volunteers to help me and, for a change, RAF aircraft flew into the station to pick-up or deliver covers. As a result I was able to bring much of the philatelic work I was doing at home onto the station.

The immediate effect of this was remarkable. Communications with RAF stations dramatically improved. Ministry of Defence (Air) were bombarding the stations for financial help to complete the RAF Museum, and many station commanders saw my philatelic programme as a way of making their particular contribution. This made it easy for me to introduce a series of covers that linked forty stations with particular aircraft that had been flown or used by them. I made a start with RAF Upavon with a cover showing the B.E.2 that was flown from there in 1914. It was then flown in Concorde on a development test flight with Brian Trubshaw at the controls. The series quickly developed and became financially self-supporting. The money began to pour in and I knew that I was sitting in a fund-raising gold mine.

I soon began to learn something about the cut and thrust of commercial competition. Many stamp dealers realised that I had opened a new collecting market and began to copy my work. This included a couple of self-seeking individuals in the RAF whom we tried unsuccessfully to stop. The Army commissioned a stamp dealer to produce not one but six series of commemorative covers that ranged over battles, regiments, regalia, personalities and medals. I had to fight to keep my ideas and programmes under wraps and, continually, to stay ahead of the competition by finding ways of improving our product. I had a head start in being able to fly covers in RAF aircraft and, to this, I added the attraction to the autograph collector of a limited number of each issue being signed by important people. This happily brought me into contact with many great people either by letter or by personal visit. Within months, there was a quantum leap in the value of our fund-raising as a result.

Those who signed covers for us included Marshals of the Royal Air Force, Lord Portal of Hungerford, Sir John Slessor, Sir Arthur Harris, and Sir Dermot Boyle. On the fighter side, Air Chief Marshal Sir Keith Park, Air Commodore Al Deere, Group Captains John Cunningham, Douglas Bader and Wing Commander Bob Stanford Tuck. On the bomber side, Air Chief Marshal Sir Ronald Ivelaw-Chapman, Air Vice-Marshal Ivor Broom and Group Captain Leonard Cheshire. Of a general nature, Sir Francis Chichester, Brian Trubshaw, Sir Barnes Wallis and the World's Aerobatic Champions, Igor Egoriv and Sonia Sanitsaya. Also I enlisted four former members of the RAF Schneider Trophy teams, Air Vice-Marshal S.N. Webster (1927), Air Commodore D'Arcy Greig (1929), Air-Vice Marshal F.W. Long and Group Captain L.S. Snaith (1931).

This extraneous work in no way interfered with my primary duty of President of the Cranwell Board, now renamed the University Cadetships Board. I drove to Biggin Hill each day from my home in Tadworth and, steadily, I began to regain my health. I made a point of walking each day at least a mile or so and, when there was time to spare, all the way around the perimeter of the Biggin Hill airfield, a distance of 3.85 miles that could easily be covered within the hour. I extended fund-raising for the Museum by setting-up an annual raffle within the Service. Tickets were sold on every station where there was a RAF Philatelic Consortium project officer. The first prize, the first time, was a brand new Mini, donated by a car dealer in Sevenoaks, to be won by whomsoever could guess the actual distance, to the second decimal point, that could be covered by the Mini using exactly one gallon of petrol. I drove the car at a steady 30 mph, in fourth gear, around and around the airfield until it came to a stop. The RAC measured the Mini's performance at 61.85 miles to the gallon, and the car was won by an elderly lady who had never driven. The second car raffle was for a second-hand Jensen, donated by a classic car fanatic. The winner was not too happy when he saw his prize. We therefore sold the Jensen for him and gave him the cash.

Almost two years had passed and I was now serving under my third Commandant, Air Commodore Ian Allan. The fund-raising was going very well and had become well-organised. An annual meeting of Station RAF Philatelic Consortium members had been instigated and more than £100,000 had been handed over to the RAF Museum Appeal Fund. The first annual fund-raising luncheon had been held in the RAF Club where station commanders or project officers gave the money they had raised for the RAF Museum to Sir Dermot Boyle.

I got wind of my probable next appointment just after I had managed my second Battle of Britain Open Day airshow in September, 1971. It seemed likely that I would be offered the post of Deputy Director of Public Relations at the Ministry of Defence(Air). I was not at all happy with the news. I was 50 years old with perhaps another five years to serve before retirement and did not relish spending my remaining time in relatively uninteresting jobs. My time in the Royal Air Force had been rewarding, sometimes exciting, and always interesting. I had never been overly ambitious, promotions and rewards had always come as a surprise. I knew that I had reached my peak at Odiham, and that all that had followed since had been downhill.

Once again there was a surprise in store for me. The cuts in Defence expenditure that had come about after we had left Aden and given up 'bandit bashing' were now affecting the RAF career structure. There was an overbearance of more than fifty Group Captains and a redundancy scheme - not a Golden Bowler - was announced offering any group captain premature retirement. I did not hesitate, most likely my name went to the top of the list. My request for retirement was accepted and I had not the slightest doubt that I had made the right decision. The powers-that-be had opened the door for me to leave and to make a start on a second career.

I well remember my last day in the Royal Air Force. There were deep regrets saying goodbye to a an organisation in which I had spent thirty years of my life. I knew that I would miss the comradeship, the fellowships I had shared with some of the best people in our country and the unexpected thrills that often came from not knowing what next was to happen. I had put these thoughts together in the preparation of the speech I had to make at my dining-out in the historic Biggin Hill Officer's Mess. Unfortunately, much of what I had prepared was usurped by the Commandant and used in his introduction for me to speak. I was not in the mood to extemporise and proposed the toast to the Royal Air Force after making a very poor effort of saying goodbye. I didn't stay long after the dinner, making my excuses to the Commandant and rescuing my little MG Midget from the hallway into which it had been carried. I left in a very downcast mood and this was not helped by my being stopped at the Purley crossroads by the police who asked me what was doing and where was I going. It was just before midnight and I was dressed in full mess kit, complete with decorations and wearing my Service cap. I was not disposed to be helpful and retorted by asking them why on earth had they stopped me. 'We're looking for some burglars,' came the reply. I simply could not be bothered to answer them. I engaged gear and drove away wondering just how many burglars in the Purley area went about their business in a Group Captain's uniform.

There was little doubt that the two undemanding years spent at Biggin Hill had made it much easier for me to get ready for a return to civilian life. Much of my charitable work had brought me into contact with business firms and professional fund-raising organisations and, of course, the emerging Royal Air Force Museum. I had given little thought about what I would like to do for a second career, I just hoped that I could find something that would keep me close to aviation matters.

There was a resettlement scheme for officers leaving the Service. Instructional courses could be taken in a wide range of subjects, accounting and book-keeping, business studies, home maintenance, even how to fill in the time when left with nothing to do. The most popular of these by far was bricklaying but, for some reason that I do not remember, I chose a four-week stint in the Language Laboratory, Boscombe Down, hoping to put a finer edge on my knowledge of French. I drove there and back in the

MG Midget, each day from my house in Tadworth and, at the end of the course, could honestly admit to having made some progress.

During the course, I foolishly accepted advice from another Group Captain who had also taken early retirement on what to do with my money. Although we were comfortably off and had no financial worries, he convinced me that I should commute my pension. I had become impressed with my friend's ability to play the Stock Exchange which he said had been the source of considerable additional income to him in recent years. He offered to advise me how best to invest the lump sum I would receive from the commutation and, after discussion with Wendy, I went along with his ideas. The sum of £28,000, quite a considerable amount in those days, bought what I thought in my ignorance was a fascinating portfolio. All too soon, I was in dead trouble. It was 1972 and the market was collapsing, the portfolio fell apart. I was to see my investments lost one after another, until I pulled out in desperation, four years later, rescuing just over £4,000.

Outside my own personal financial catastrophe, I still had control of the philatelic fund-raising programmes. They had become so much my personal responsibility that, when I retired, I was not disposed to hand them on to anyone. I had a 'tiger by the tail' and, in any case, I had promised Sir Dermot Boyle that I would help the RAF Museum for as long as it took to write off the Appeal Fund. I had become well known by the Trustees of the Museum and had met its Founding Director, Dr John Tanner, on many occasions. The programmes were well founded in the RAF and, with proper management and inspiration, they could be made to work for many years to come. Before I had finished my language course at Boscombe Down, I was asked by Sir Dermot whether I would like to join the team engaged in the setting-up of the Museum. I accepted the offer at once, and duly signed a contract, not as a civil servant, but as an individual working directly under the Director and being responsible to him alone.

The Royal Air Force Museum was in its final year of preparation. It was being built on the north side of RAF Hendon where two very large Belfast-trussed hangars had been joined together. The airfield had been closed for more than a year, the last aircraft to land there had been a Beverley, now permanently parked in the open, close to the hangars. The

RAF station was contracting in size, the airfield had been sold and was being developed into the Grahame Park housing estate. The Station's sole responsibility was to house and manage the new RAF Computer Centre that had been purpose built near the old Officers' and Sergeants' Messes.

I knew that my appointment had been made to ensure that the philatelic schemes continued to the benefit of the RAF Museum. I reported with the title of Public Relations Officer, surprised to find myself the only ex-RAF officer there. John Tanner, the Director, was the museum's leading light and inspiration. His former job had been Chief Librarian at the RAF College, Cranwell, where he had spent years working on plans to create a lasting testimony to the RAF that should have been constructed decades ago. His right-hand man was Jack Bruce, the renowned aviation historian, the best authority on the history of aircraft, particularly those flown during the Great War, that I have ever met. The Chief Designer was Ray Lee whose flair and ability was to mark the Museum as the very best of its kind. Up to a point, I was left on my own to find my place in the scheme of things and to develop responsibilities other than those of a philatelic nature.

I soon met a very strange challenge. The Museum complex included the World War I Grahame White hangar, still in reasonable repair, about four hundred yards from the Belfast hangars. It had been empty for years until it was brought into use to house a Short Sunderland flying boat that would find a permanent resting place when the second stage of the Museum's development could begin. I was extremely annoyed when I first saw it in a state of absolute neglect. Hundreds of pigeons that had made their homes in the hangar roof and had encrusted, almost submerged it, with their corrosive droppings. Some effort had been made to protect the machine by spreading newspapers over the wing and fuselage but this had only compacted and increased the enormous weight of excrement on the machine. The white covering paint was decaying due to the acid of the droppings; something had to be done, and done quickly. With the help of some volunteers from RAF Hendon and the local Air Training Corps squadron we tackled the cleaning of the Sunderland by first removing hundred-weights of the droppings. These had to be pushed and scraped off the wing and fuselage and then shovelled into a lorry and taken away. It took the best part of a month, working at weekends, to remove this mess and get rid of the stink. We then took the law into our own hands and attacked the pigeons managing to drive them away and closing their means of entry with wire netting. The Sunderland itself was then thoroughly washed down and cleaned.

My place of work was an office on the first floor of the Museum, near to that of the Director and next to Geoffrey White's, the Museum Secretary; a very happy arrangement because he was an accountant and soon took an interest in the financial aspects of the philatelic schemes.

One tedious problem, however, was that of getting daily to Hendon from Tadworth and back. There was no public transport that made any sense; I had little alternative but to commute by car. I chose to avoid the congestion on the roads at rush hours and set-off each morning by six o'clock, aiming to be over Kew Bridge and on to the North Circular Road by seven. By arrangement I left the Museum between three and four, o'clock in the afternoon, ahead of the going-home rush. I got rid of my tiny MG Midget and bought the bigger and speedier MGB GT.

I watched the Opening of the Royal Air Force Museum from the balcony overlooking its entrance. It was a grand occasion and went without a hitch. I could see John Tanner's evident satisfaction as he escorted the Queen around the Museum, he must have been thrilled at achieving a lifetime's dream. He had reversed our habit of turning our backs on our national military history, the unthinking way in which so many of our aeronautical treasures have been carelessly cast aside. I remembered that some time ago, we had everything required to form a national aviation museum. In the early 1920s, almost ninety different aeroplanes used by the British, French, Germans, and Austro-Hungarians in the Great War, had been put on display in the Agricultural Hall at Islington. In the few years that followed all these machines were either destroyed or sold abroad for want of interest, money and space in which to exhibit them. I watched Her Majesty regarding our small display of World War I types, just four examples, and two of them replicas.

John Tanner was an ambitious man and the Museum at Hendon was just a start. If there was to be the best possible exhibition of the history of the RAF then much more had to be done. The collection at Hendon, supported by a reserve collection at Cardington, was just a beginning. There was a wealth of material that could be found to be put properly on display.

Room for this to be done, and money to pay for it, had to be found.

There was some extra space at Hendon, by the end of the 1970s the Dermot Boyle Exhibition had been added to the main building, the Battle of Britain Museum, and a serve-yourself restaurant was functioning in a purpose-built hangar across the car park facing the main Museum. A second Museum had been housed in hangars at RAF Cosford and there were plans to add an extension to the main Museum to serve as a Bomber Command Museum.

The Grahame White Housing Estate was now fully developed and thankfully divided from the Museum complex by a main road. RAF Hendon was under threat of closure and when the day came there would be inevitable further encroachment on the Museum's area as the vacant land would be sold and no doubt built upon. There were some, including myself, who wished that the Museum had been built somewhere else. Other aviation museums such as the Imperial War and Fleet Air Arm had been set up at airfields, Duxford and Yeovilton respectively. My choice for the RAF Museum would have been Biggin Hill and, as things have turned out in recent years, it would have been a better way of keeping alive the memories of our past, as Hendon, bit by bit, disappears under concrete.

My part in John Tanner's plans was to find as much money as possible to help pay for them. The backbone of our fund-raising was still the philatelic scheme that continued to flourish throughout the 1970s. It guaranteed an annual income of at least £100,000. I opened a small shop just inside the Museum front door in my first year. This did well and gradually expanded into the lucrative business that can be seen there today. I turned my hand to anything that could produce a profit. I designed or had designed, collections of commemorative medals working with John Pinches Ltd, now the Franklin Mint. I had collections of RAF badges and emblems produced, together with tokens, souvenirs, and car stickers. I helped with the promotion of sales of Fine Art prints of paintings by John Young and Frank Wootton and headed fund-raising teams at most every Air Display in the country. There we sold goods, souvenirs and commemorative covers. All this kept myself and Wendy extremely busy, while, at the same time, we enjoyed ourselves.

I believe that the greatest benefit I derived from my work at the Museum was the contact I made with truly great people. As the only ex-RAF person in the place I acted as a magnet that attracted questions and problems from visitors and particularly former members of the RAF. I soon built up a heavy workload that filled in all seven days of the week. My original title of Public Relations Officer had Education Officer added to it until it became absolutely necessary to recruit someone to concentrate solely on trying to educate the young. I sat in on the Civil Service Selection Board which happily agreed with my choice of the man, Wing Commander Bill Wood who had been one of my deputies at the Selection Centre at Biggin Hill. Then, one day, John Tanner brought a smartly-dressed mounted policemen to my office and told me to find him a job within my domain. That was Michael Fopp, now the Director General of the RAF Museum, who had been forced to retire from the Metropolitan Police because of injuries sustained during the Grosvenor Square anti-Vietnam riots. Another welcome addition to my staff was Wing Commander Bob Stanford Tuck, the famous Fighter Command veteran. Bob had been retired from the RAF for some time and had experimented with various stunts such as chicken battery-farming, and mushroom growing.

I got to know Bob well. Our friendship held until the time came for him to leave and retire to his house at Sandwich. I used to visit him regularly until he broke his heart over the death of his wife, she died in his arms. A few months later, I attended his funeral.

Bob was invaluable in making contacts for me in the fighter world, and for coming up with answers to tricky problems that had still to be sorted out in the history books. I still had much to learn about the glamorous side of the RAF, that of Fighter Command. Bob was a gentle person and seldom entered into argument. He was a bit of a romantic and once surprised me with his belief that there had been chivalry in the air shown between the fighter pilots of the *Luftwaffe* and the RAF. He had a close friendship with Adolf Galland, Hitler's General of Fighters. One day, Bob arranged for me to meet Galland. He introduced me as a former Bomber Command pilot whom the Germans had shot down. At once, I could sense the mutual dislike between us and when, over coffee, the conversation turned to chivalry in the air and the respect there was supposed to be between each side, I could not contain myself. I told Bob and Galland that they were talking rubbish. As someone who had endured the London blitz and had been dubbed as *Terrorflieger* for dropping bombs on Germany, I could not accept that there was any friendly feeling of any sort between the Germans and ourselves. My outburst brought an end to the conversation. Bob apologized to Galland for what I had said and, afterwards, said that he thought I had been very rude and thoughtless to an important Museum guest.

With Bob Stanford Tuck, a close friend

There were many other personalities that stand out in my memory. Perhaps chief amongst them at that time were Leonard Cheshire and Douglas Bader, both of whom had enlisted willingly in my fund-raising schemes. I was to regard Cheshire almost as a saint. His operational career had been without parallel, but it was what he had devoted his very existence to since the war that amazed me. The Cheshire Homes for the aged and the infirm that he had created were a veritable lifeline for so many. The effort that had gone into the many projects was prodigious, and it was all due to the incredible ability of just this one man. I felt honoured and humbled whenever we met, he helped me considerably with my fund-raising for the Museum and I did my best to help him build more homes.

Douglas Bader was of course another legend. I first met him through Bob Stanford Tuck at an Air Show for the RAF Benevolent Fund at Greenham Common. He had a reputation for being sharp and abrupt, not suffering fools gladly. I suppose that it was because we were both trying to raise money for charity that we found common ground and I am sure I was the one who benefited most. Bader was known internationally, and his signature was valuable. He willingly signed hundreds and hundreds of covers, perhaps thousands. We often met, usually to discuss fund-raising. He paid regular visits to the Museum and I was often the person who dealt with his queries. He used me as a sounding board for his ideas and usually as a provider of historical information. I grew to respect him, and valued our meetings.

Douglas suffered at least two heart attacks but refused to slow down. He kept his incredible drive and enthusiasm right to the end. On the day he died, I received a telephone call from him in his house at Ascot, quite early in the morning. He wanted my opinion on a speech he was to make in the Guildhall that evening. He read some notes to me, asked me a question or two about Bomber Command, and I confirmed that the speech was absolutely correct. He then drove from Ascot to Northolt from where he was flown to RAF Finningley in Yorkshire, officially to open the Battle of Britain At Home Day show. He flew back to Northolt in the late afternoon and, after a brief rest, drove himself to the Guildhall where he made a good speech. After dinner, he set out to drive himself back to Ascot but suffered a fatal heart attack on the way.

There are many other personalities that come to mind. In his failing days, I helped Edgar Percival, the aircraft designer, with the cataloguing of his many trophies and artifacts at his flat in Cumberland Place. I met the charming Jean Batten, the pre-war record breaker, on many occasions. Together we produced a fine money-spinner in the form of a commemorative cover marking her record-breaking flight to Australia. She usually came over from her house in the Canaries to visit the Museum. I regularly kept in touch with her by letter until my letters were returned, 'Addressee unknown'. Much later, after extensive enquiry, I was told that she had moved to Spain where she had lived in very straitened circumstances. She had died and had been buried in a communal pauper's grave together with many other people. Our efforts to get her a fitting burial came to naught. We were informed there was no way that her remains could be indentified from amongst all the others if the grave was opened.

The Museum was also a place where many non-entities, daydreamers, and downright rogues turned up to impress family and friends with false stories and make-belief. Again, I was often the one that had to deal with their antics. I made every allowance that many old men cannot remember accurately and, in their limited experience, and ignorance, misread the past. The 'chip-on-the-shoulder' syndrome was often there, together with the ignorant other ranks belief that, '...them officers didn't know a thing.'

There was one person who was a classic, he regularly made visits and always sought me out. About seventy years old, he avowed to having been an Imperial Airways pilot before the war and served during the war as an RAF pilot on special duties. He claimed that he had been awarded the DSO, CGM, DFC, AFC, and had been recommended for an award of the George Cross. He usually carried with him the miniature versions of these decorations. Our investigations of his claims and supposed exploits soon showed that they were figments of his imagination, there was no record that he had ever served in the RAF or had flown with Imperial Airways. We did not tell him we knew he was false, just humouring him as a harmless eccentric.

One weekend, I was managing my fund-raising stall at an air show at West Malling when, to my surprise, this hero, who was being conducted around the stands by the air show organizer, was brought to my stand and introduced as Squadron Leader so and so, a very important person of whom I may have heard. He was wearing his miniature medals pinned on to an RAF sports blazer with the RAF badge on the pocket. With a straight face I said that I had not had the pleasure, and I kept my hands clasped behind my back; after an awkward silence he was led away. I was too busy to waste time in spoiling his masquerade but knew that he now realized I had known him to be a fraud. I never saw him again and I am sure he never returned to the Museum. I did however get a letter from his widow about eighteen months later asking if the Museum would like to acquire his miniature medals and a written account of his eventful life.

In 1974 I was elected Chairman of the Royal Air Forces Escaping Society. The Society was in good shape, contact with helpers in nine different countries was excellent, and the finances were in order. The

President was still Air Marshal Sir Basil Embry but he had retired to live in Western Australia, leaving his duties in the hands of the Vice President, Air Chief Marshal Sir Ronald Ivelaw-Chapman. I enjoyed my three-year stint as Chairman, dutifully attending every monthly Committee Meeting, and the annual major function, the weekend spent with the *Comète* Line in Brussels that always finished with an impressive Solemn Requiem Mass in the Koelkelburg. Looking back, I think the most important thing I did was to co-operate with Sir Ronald on the drafting of a paper on the closure of the Society. Together we wanted to avoid the distressing problems that would arise if the Society were to be allowed just to fade away. We had been born out of the RAF Benevolent Fund and our paper explained that when the day came for the closure, then the Benevolent Fund would take over all residual funds and responsibilities.

A year later I became a Governor of the Royal Star and Garter Home for Soldiers, Sailors and Airmen on Richmond Hill just across the road facing the entrance to Richmond Park. My reputation as a fund-raiser had grown. Marshal of the Royal Air Force, Sir Denis Spotswood, a former Trustee of the RAF Museum and now Vice-President of the Board of Governors of the Royal Star and Garter Home, wanted me to set up a fund-raising organization in the Home and to ensure that it worked. I had no idea of what was involved or whether I had the capability to manage such a task. My masters at the Museum were not at all happy with Sir Dennis's suggestion but, after paying a visit to the Home and seeing for myself the wonderful work done to help desperately ill and often neglected ex-Servicemen, I was more than happy to accept the appointment. I would now be able to see more of my fund-raising efforts devoted to the real need of people rather than to the inanimate objects of a museum.

It did not take me long to realize that it would be almost impossible to add very much to my already heavy workload at Hendon. I could foresee the establishment of something similar to that which I managed at Hendon, but it would have to exist under the control of someone especially selected. As the Governor responsible, I would then be able to advise and monitor the work.

We advertised and received fifty-two applications for the post of fund-raiser. I was allowed to winnow these down to a short list of six who appeared before a Selection Board of three Governors, including myself, and the Commandant of the Home. We were unanimous in the selection of the one I liked best, ex-RAF, just turning thirty, physically active, and ambitious. We worked well together and within weeks we had a fund-raising programme agreed by the Board of Governors. In the first year more than one million pounds was raised by a combination of what I called 'passive' fund-raising - the writing of begging letters to all and sundry, together with 'active' fund-raising along the lines of the outdoor work I was doing at the Museum. I was able to leave the fund-raiser very much to his own, he needed no encouragement from me. However, in the last year of my first three-year stint as Governor my hero resigned to take up a similar appointment with an organization prepared to pay him £10,000 a year more than he was getting from the Royal Star and Garter Home. It was back to the Selection Board again and, luckily, this time, we found a good replacement with not such an ambitious eye.

It was during 1977 that another door of experience was opened for me. I met the television producer, Gerry Glaister, a former RAF photo-reconnaissance pilot, who had made his name in a big way with a series on the Colditz prisoner-of-war camp. He had plans to match this most successful account of escape attempts with a series dealing with the other side of the coin, evasion from capture, dwelling of course on the history of escape routes. He contacted me as Chairman of the RAF Escaping Society for information on how the escape routes operated. I attended a meeting at the BBC Television Headquarters in Wood Green where I met him and his principal script writer, John Brason. I must have impressed them with my knowledge because, soon after, I was asked to consider becoming Technical Director to a series, called 'Secret Army'.

Again, I had no idea how this additional work might impinge on my duties at the RAF Museum. One of the satisfying things about my duties there was that I was left to make my own speed. I now and then appeared before the Trustees to report on progress with fund-raising. My immediate boss, John Tanner, to whom I owed my loyalty, never hindered me in trying to do my best. I told him that any work I did with the BBC would be unpaid and that much of it would be done at home in my spare time. He raised no objections, indeed he encouraged me, believing that it might well, one day, lead to some worthwhile benefit coming to the Museum.

Up until then my only previous contact with the television industry had been a couple of visits made to the Elstree film studios with my good friend, Group Captain Hamish Mahaddie, during the filming of the 'Pathfinders' series on which he was the Technical Director. I went with him believing that his job was to make sure that facts and figures were correct, and that no mistakes were made during filming. I sat with Hamish at the edge of the set both times, noticing that he was never asked a question. I once pointed out to him that a pilot's DFC ribbon was being worn upside-down. 'Quite right,' he said, while trying to attract the Director's attention, but the filming continued. 'You should have told me that before shooting started,' shouted an irritated director. 'It's too late now - there isn't enough film time left.'

That recollection was very much in my mind at my first duty outing, the filming of some background scenes in a field near High Wycombe to be used for publicity purposes. I was with John Brason and we had no script. I was struck at once with the poor acting that was far removed from reality. The extras playing the parts of Germans didn't look right. Too many had their long hair stuffed inside steel helmets that wobbled as they moved. Some looked so frail that they would never have been accepted in the *Wehrmacht*. The little dialogue I overheard was cliche-ridden and modern in style. From this, I learned one very important thing; if I was to do my best as a Technical Director then most of my work had to be done before the cameras rolled and that would be at the scripting stage. My contribution could not be left until the Director called 'Action', when valuable money and time would begin to be spent.

From the very start, John Brason, the principal scriptwriter and coordinator of other writers' work, provided me with scripts in final draft form. The first four episodes of Secret Army contained scenes based on what happened to me and my crew in 1942. I found it fascinating to follow the pen of a master script writer, and easy to spot and explain where there could have been an error or even how an improvement could be made. I worked on the scripts at home, often well into the night, and always returned them, with comment where necessary, within twenty-four hours. Most of the filming was done in studio at the BBC Television Centre. I had ample time before shooting to check costume in detail in the dressing and make-up rooms. I then sat throughout the day's filming in the company of Gerry Glaister and John Brason, seldom having to make comment.

Sometimes I worked on location in the countryside around Peterborough, other times on RAF airfields.

I actually took part in a short series, 'Behind the Scenes', where I explained the duties of a Technical Director. This led to a part in a children's programme where I reviewed a selection of children's books. I appeared in a couple of 'After the News' excerpts on Bomber Command, once with Air Marshal 'Mickey' Martin and once with Air Vice-Marshal Don Bennett, the former A.O.C. of No 8 (Pathfinder) Group. The best perk of all, however, was the setting up of a 'Secret Army' display by BBC Enterprises in the Royal Air Museum.

The display took up the whole ground floor of the Dermot Boyle Exhibition Wing. A visitor was able to move from set to set, almost as though making a visit to an escape route. Against a background of the dramatic 'Secret Army' theme music, time could be spent learning about the exploits of Bomber Command aircrew, *Luftwaffe* night-fighter crews and the incredible people who ran the escape routes. There was a replica of a room in a 'safe house' which contained examples of forged identity documents, passports, clothing and food coupons. A walk along a darkened corridor took one into a mock-up of a Lancaster fuselage where the crew could be seen making the final approach to the target amidst the noise of bursting flak. There was a Gestapo office from which anti-escape route operations were planned, and hundreds of photographs of actual helpers taken during the war. This display attracted tens of thousands of visitors to Hendon before it was dismantled in 1980.

The 'Secret Army' television show ran for three years, thirteen episodes a year. It was judged a success and remembered as being fundamentally realistic and accurate in detail. My wish to finish the series by doing an 'Alfred Hitchcock' by appearing in just one scene, was granted in the 36th episode when I was allowed to play the part of a German infantry officer, *Oberleutnant* Rath. I was given just two words to utter - 'Mortars fire!', shouted after putting down binoculars when peering at an advancing company of Coldstream Guards. I was positioned in the open-ended loft of a barn on the edge of a farm. It was intended that as the Guards stormed into the farmyard directly underneath me, I would be killed by a blast from a Sten gun, and would fall forwards, out of the loft, down on to the hard ground below. I managed to avoid this potentially dangerous manoeuvre for an almost sixty year-old by convincing the Director that half-a-dozen bullets from a Sten would knock me backwards, not forwards, and so, right out of camera. In the event, the demise of Rath was filmed downstairs. I fought to the last, wildly firing my Luger and urging my men to die bravely. I reacted to the burst of Sten gunfire by flinging myself violently backwards against the barn wall, and slowly collapsing into a bed of stinging nettles.

The infamous Oberleutnant Rath in the series
'Secret Army'

My career as a Technical Adviser to the BBC continued for just another year. I worked with Gerry Glaister and John Brason on a six-part series called 'Fourth Arm', a story about the training of agents in the Special Operations Executive. Again we got the atmosphere and detail right, basing much on the training of Commandos at Lympstone in Devon, and agents in Imber village on Salisbury Plain. The in-studio shooting was done in Scotland which meant a couple of days, every fortnight, away from the office while I travelled overnight to Glasgow, spent a day in the studio and returned, again overnight, to London. This intriguing romance with make-believe finally came to an end after I had technically checked two films on Fighter Command, one dealing with a day during the Battle of Britain.

CHAPTER TWENTY-SIX

In the first ten years of its existence, the Royal Air Force Museum had established a world-wide reputation for its excellent displays and presentation. The only limit to its steady improvement and expansion was the lack of space and funds. No charge was made for entry to the Museum, all running costs were met by a vote from Ministry of Defence (Air). The main Museum and the adjacent Battle of Britain Museum at Hendon were full, as was our Midlands museum at Cosford. John Tanner, our Director, was well aware that more could or should be done particularly to cover the early days before the formation of the RAF in 1918 and, perhaps more pressing, to bring into focus the history of the biggest and most controversial part of the Royal Air Force, Bomber Command.

Towards the end of 1981, he concluded that the next step forward could best be made by an expansion of the Museum at Hendon and that it should be devoted to the story of Bomber Command. He had plans drawn up to build a large annex alongside the main building, big enough to house a Lancaster, the remains of a Halifax that had been raised from the bed of a fiord in Norway, a Wellington that I had made more warlike by buying and having fitted a Fraser Nash two-gun front turret, a Vulcan, a Mosquito, a D.H.4 day bomber of the Great War, a Flying Fortress B17 that would have to be flown across from the United States, a Mitchell B25, and other machines that might become available in time. We all wanted to see something of the Stirling, Whitley, Hampden, Fairey Battle and Bristol

Blenheim, knowing that such riches, if they could ever be found, would be matters for the very distant future.

The plans for what became known as the Bomber Hall were approved by the Trustees who agreed that work should proceed within a certain financial limit and that attempts to raise the necessary funds for construction should begin at once. The foundation stone was laid by Marshal of the Royal Air Force Sir Arthur Harris, our wartime Commander-in-Chief. He stood motionless and erect as it was lowered into position just a few feet away from him by a Puma helicopter from RAF Odiham. This was the first time I had seen 'Bomber' Harris or 'Butch' as he was fondly known by most of us who had served in Bomber Command. He had been unique among commanders during the war because he hardly ever saw or talked to the men who were carrying out his orders in the skies over Germany. He was not an aloof and uncaring man, but the simple fact was that he was too tied down to meet the crews of Bomber Command. Unlike other commanders - land, sea or air - who would fight and then take time to regroup, Harris had a major battle to fight nearly every night for fully two years.

From that point on my efforts were directed towards raising money to pay for the building of the Bomber Hall. All too soon, an adverse reaction set in against our proposed expansion, driven along by hand-wringing liberals similar to the Labour Party politicians who had raised doubts about the area-bombing policy of the War Cabinet at the close of the war. No Appeals Director was commissioned, as in the case of both the RAF and Battle of Britain Museums. We were asked by the Trustees to do our best while feeling that perhaps they had made a mistake in committing themselves to the building of a Museum before the necessary funds had been found.

I was quick to learn something about what certain individuals had been doing to keep alive the comradeship of Bomber Command. During a rain-swept Open Day at RAF Abingdon, I had sheltered my fund-raising team under the huge wing of a Vulcan. Across the perimeter track from us was a short row of stalls under dripping lime trees. The largest of them was labelled 'Bomber Command Association (1939-1945)' and manned by five very sorry-looking men of my age.

I introduced myself to them as a former member of Bomber Command and someone who was about to become concerned with the building of a

Bomber Museum. I shook hands with Harry Pitcher DFM, Ray Callow, Ernie Cummings DFM, Cyril Ainley, and Doug Radcliffe, a true Band of Brothers, who had been working together for some years developing an organization to keep the wartime spirit of Bomber Command alive. I had to admit that I had heard nothing of them and was flabbergasted when told that a Bomber Command Reunion was held every year in the form of a Dinner at the Grosvenor House in Park Lane and that it was always organized by Ray Callow. They went on to explain that the Association needed recruits which they touted for every weekend there was an air show, that was why they were at Abingdon. I joined there and then, paying the modest sum of £1 for my membership. I returned to my fund-raising stand wondering how it was that a bunch of former NCOs had so well-organized themselves when the rest of us had been content to let matters take their course.

The building of the Bomber Hall went ahead well and, very soon, the roof was in place and we began to assemble the aircraft and associated equipment. Some little progress was made with the appeal for funds but, in the main, unlike the success of the Royal Air Force and Battle of Britain Museum Appeals, there was a noticeable lack of interest shown by commerce and industry.

I was personally gratified to be involved in the creation of a museum that would serve as suitable recognition of Bomber Command's incredible history. I knew that the feeling would be shared by many thousands of veterans and, in particular, the Wellington crew I had flown with during my tour of operations over Germany. I had kept in touch with them over the years but we had not seen ourselves as a group since that fateful night of 16th September, 1942, when we were shot down. I managed to convince them all that they should attend the Opening planned for 12th April, 1983. Wally Dreschler, Norman Graham and their wives agreed to fly over from Canada. I did not forget our 'passenger' that night, the American, Dal Mounts who said he would fly from California with his wife. Scottie Brazill and Bob Frost were of course living almost on the Museum's doorstep and agreed to help me make arrangements for the others.

The Bomber Hall was opened by Her Majesty, Queen Elizabeth the Queen Mother. The principal attendants were Marshals of the Royal Air Force Lord Cameron, our Chairman of Trustees, and Sir Arthur Harris; Dr

John Tanner was in charge of proceedings. I had been given a privileged position for myself and crew, near the Wellington, from where we could easily see the progress of the Royal party around the Hall. That had been timed to the second and would finish with speeches by the two Marshals of the Royal Air Force and the Queen Mother, after which she would officially open the museum.

We must somehow have attracted the attention of Her Majesty as she drew near to the Wellington. I saw her questioning Dr Tanner who then came across to us and asked me to line everyone up because the Queen Mother wanted to meet us. I was the first to be introduced and was asked to introduce the others in turn. She asked a wide range of questions and was particularly interested in our stories of how we evaded capture. She had to be reminded to move on and, later, I was told that the diversion we had caused had set back the Opening by eight minutes.

The next day was spent deep in nostalgia, the Commanding Officer, RAF Hendon set aside the Ladies' Room of the Officer's Mess for a special luncheon. We were given a first-class meal, carefully served by stewards, and eaten against a background of the music of the Forties that included the crew's favourite, 'Blues in the Night' and 'I Don't Want to Set the World on Fire'. After lunch, my crew and I set out in a convoy of three cars up the A1 to Dittington to visit the scene of the devastating crash I made in the fog one night in June 1942. I led the crew to the village but could not recognize a single feature. Drawing up behind an elderly man walking his dog I asked if he knew anyone who could remember a Wellington bomber that had crashed in Dittington forty years before. His eyes opened wide and he leaned down to peer at me through the opened window of my car. 'Were you that bastard?' he asked.

Our newly-found friend had been asleep in a house not far from the farm we had almost demolished. He remembered being awakened by the explosions of our fuel tanks and oxygen bottles. He took us to the farm that had been completely rebuilt and introduced us to the new owners. We then drove on to RAF Wyton where we visited the sick quarters in which we had spent two days pulling ourselves together after the crash.

Soon after the Opening of the Bomber Hall, I was appointed Director of Appeals and given the thankless task of dealing with the debt that had accumulated during the building and endowment of the museum. It seemed a daunting job yet, although I was pleased to be thought worthy of such responsibility, I had the foreboding that I was about to tackle the impossible. There had been little success so far and it was difficult to see how any of the traditional ways of fund-raising could prevail against the growing unpopularity of Bomber Command. I was, however, well aware that there must be thousands of 'old lags' like myself who might be induced to help. Bomber Command had been the biggest single specialized unit during the war. Many organisations had been set up to remember the old days and I was quick to find that the most progressive of them was the Bomber Command Association (1939-1945); the principals of which I had met at Abingdon. Harry Pitcher was its elected Life Chairman and there was an Executive Committee set up to serve until further notice.

My former crew back together once more. Pictured here outside the medical centre at RAF Wyton where we were taken following the disastrous crash on the village green at Dittington.

Left to right: Norman Graham, Bob Frost, myself, 'Scottie' Brazill, Wally Dreschler

I concluded, wrongly at first, that the Bomber Command Association (1939-1945) could be expanded and developed into an all-embracing Bomber Command Association. The idea found little support at first, largely because the Executive Committee members, all of whom were ex-NCOs, did not believe that there would be any higher-level support forthcoming. The Association depended largely on the drive and initiative of Harry Pitcher, ably assisted by his wife; and he was the leading sceptic.

Progress was, however, made at a meeting in the Royal Air Force Club on 28th July, 1984 when representatives of all the Bomber Command associated organizations and the leaders of the Bomber Command Association (1939-1945), Bomber Command Register, Aircrew Association, and the Bomber Command Federation, met to decide on a new President of the many organizations of which Sir Arthur Harris, who had just died, had been leader for so long . It was also hoped to discuss the way ahead, hopefully under the coordination of one single organization. The meeting unfortunately proved inconclusive. Mr Pitcher was, however, asked to call his Executive Committee together to determine whether the Bomber Association (1939-1945) could extend its charter sufficiently to undertake this coordinating function. Unfortunately, Harry Pitcher died the next day.

Control of the Association was taken over by the Deputy Chairman, Ernie Cummings. He convened a meeting at the Royal Air Force Museum on 17th November, 1984, attended by 127 members of the Bomber Command Association (1939-1945), together with Bomber Command squadron and affiliated organizations. I acted as Secretary and, after dealing with the accounts and some residual business of the 1939-1945 Association, we moved on to elect Air Vice-Marshal D.C.T.Bennett as President in place of Sir Arthur Harris. In his acceptance speech Don Bennett said that the present Association was limited in its charter, finances, and ability, and was in no position to accept the challenge of becoming a true sounding board and focal point for all Bomber Command matters. After considerable discussion, it was agreed that the Bomber Command Association (1939-1945) should be wound up and that the Bomber Command Association should take over its assets and become established as a Registered Charity. I was elected to an Interim Committee and asked to draft the Constitution of the new Association and to deal with the Charities Commission over its charitable status. My draft constitution was ratified at the first meeting of the Interim Committee at the Royal Air Force Museum on 16th December, 1984, when we appointed a full-time Secretary and Marshal of the Royal Air Force, Sir Michael Beetham, Air Chief Marshal Sir Hugh Constantine, Air Marshal Sir Augustus Walker, Air Marshal Sir Harold Martin, and Air Commodore John Searby as Vice Presidents.

The criticism of Bomber Command's offensive against Germany increased with the Opening of the Bomber Hall. That there should be continuing protests from some of the Germans who found themselves in the path of devastating 1,000 bomber raids was no surprise. What I found sad and extremely distressful was that the criticism also seemed to be gathering pace at home. Worst of all were the persistent attempts to heap blame for the conduct of the area bombing campaign on the shoulders of Sir Arthur Harris. Critics depicted him as a cold, hard man who deliberately bombed civilians. Others went further and actually accused him, and by implication, all members of Bomber Command, of war crimes.

I was naturally caught up in this controversy. My attempts to raise money by open appeal were confounded by the bitter comments that seemed to come, sometimes misguidedly, from many quarters. The bombing of Dresden was pushed to the front as a callous British atrocity. Certain parts of the media did their best to rewrite history by inferring that Harris alone had decided to erase the city, whilst in reality he had believed the bombing of Dresden to be a mistake. He had voiced his objections to Churchill before the attack, but was overruled.

To the end of my days, I shall cherish the memories of my liaison with this great man. He was, of course, vitally interested in the progress of our appeal for funds and I was privileged to make regular visits to his house in Goring-on-Thames to make reports. At the same time, I took every advantage of using his autograph to increase the sales and value of a wide range of souvenir items; he never raised an objection. He had just turned ninety and, although becoming physically frail, his mind and wit were still razor-sharp. He soon set a routine for my visits, I would arrive in the early morning, just after he had eaten breakfast. Over coffee, I told him about matters at Hendon and answered his questions. Then we got down to the fund-raising business. In the time I spent with him, he must have signed a few thousand items for me. I remember a batch of 850 Fine Art prints of Terence Cuneo's 'Last Halifax', six batches of 250 special versions of commemorative postal covers, numerous photographs, and many appeal letters. He always used his full title when signing, ten words in all, yet his rate of signing was 250 pieces an hour. He spoke as he signed, his only stipulation being that I placed each item before him and removed it after signature.

I was always invited to stay for lunch which was often prepared by Sir Arthur himself when Lady Harris was away. The menu seldom varied, roast wild duck, garnished with cherries, always served with South African wine. He never spoke to me about the past nor did we discuss the continual vilification of Bomber Command. Like me, he was a collector of many odds and ends and we also shared a keen interest in gardening, flowers and fauna.

If the weather was clement, he usually took me for a turn around his fine garden, before returning to the house for his afternoon nap. One day, I happened to say how much I admired an old-English single-petalled pink rose that stood as a well-tended column at least ten feet high near the garden entrance. He said that it was an Elizabethan variety of considerable age. I asked if I could take some cuttings and so add it to my collection of unusual roses. He laughed and said that it was not possible to propagate his rose in that way but I could try. I took half a dozen cuttings and when back at Tadworth put them out to strike in the usual way. They didn't take and I had forgotten about them until Sir Arthur asked me about them six months later. I had to admit that I had been unsuccessful but would like to try again. 'By all means, take as many cuttings as you wish,' he said. 'But it will be the same story again, of that I'm sure.'

This time, I took fifty cuttings which I bound tight together, left them soaking in water for a week, treated with a hormone growing paste, and then planted them firm in a tub of mixed sand and loam. The tub was sunk in the rose garden until, one day, to my great delight, I noticed that two cuttings had struck. Before I could relay the news to Sir Arthur, he died on 5th April, 1984. I now have two fine bushes in my garden of what we call the 'Bomber Harris' rose.

I did my level best as Director of Appeals but made little headway. I worked seven days a week and was helped by many good people. In the autumn, I simply had to take a rest and went with the family on a holiday to the South of France. There, one day, I fell asleep on the beach at Cavaliere while sun-bathing and awoke with my chest badly sun-burned. I did not know then that I had set in motion a disease that would almost cost me my life.

On Boxing Day, 1985, while shaving myself in the bathroom, my daughter Beverley, a scientist researching in carcinoma at Bristol University, saw reflected in the mirror, an enlarged mole bleeding on my chest. She knew at once what it was. Our local doctor was called and within the hour I was on my way to Roehampton for an operation. It took some hours to remove a malignant melanoma and to cover a six inch-long cavity in my chest with a skin-graft from my leg. I recovered consciousness in a women's ward completely unaware of the seriousness of my condition. Beverley again came to the rescue. She convinced the specialist surgeon who had removed the tumour that I would do better if taken home where she would nurse me. She collected me that afternoon and drove me to Tadworth in a complete daze and put me to bed. When I had got my wits about me again, she told me that the specialist had confided his hope that the malignancy had been removed in time. He was certain that if the melanoma had been left for a few more weeks then it was most likely it would have been too late to stop the cancer spreading throughout my body.

Lying in bed, brooding away at home, I become well aware of my mortality for the first time. For more than forty-five years I had given little thought about how my days would end. I had seen action in two wars, survived crashes and explosions, and suffered fractures to many parts of my body. I had grown used to the idea that when fate decided it was time for me to go, the end would be sudden and swift.

As I began to mend, I found it impossible to regain my former 'devil may care' attitude. I could not put aside thoughts that I might already be on the road to a slow and painful death. When the cage-like bandage was removed from my chest after the skin graft had knit, I underwent the first of a series of examinations to determine whether the melanoma had been completely removed and that there were no signs of the spread of cancer. Physically, I was making good progress, mentally I was in turmoil. After the second examination, I was cleared fit to return to work and told that I would have to report for examination every three months.

337

I had been away from the Museum for more than two months. During that time, drastic steps had been taken because of our inability to raise the funds for the building of the Bomber Hall and, more importantly, because we were no longer able to pay our way with the management and upkeep of the enlarged Museum. The only significant income was from my fund-raising programmes and what we achieved at air shows and exhibitions. The Ministry of Defence had taken over the debts and, at the same time, put the Museum under new management, insisting that in future it was to be self-supporting. This meant a stop to further expansion, the introduction of admission charges, and the early retirement of our Director. I did not know, nor was I ever approached to be asked or told, but it had been written into the new organizational plan that I would stay in the employ of the Museum to raise funds.

I was greatly surprised to be faced with a massive audit of my fund-raising organization immediately upon my return to work. It took Price-Waterhouse almost a month to complete. Their findings confirmed its viability and did more than enough to confirm steady future income. They did however observe that success depended entirely on my ideas and the amount of help voluntarily given from within the Royal Air Force and by my band of helpers. They suggested that my future work should be supported by the Ministry of Defence and that Key Insurance cover should be taken out on me to the extent of £500,000.

My relationships with my Director and the Trustees began to suffer from this point on. I felt that I no longer fitted into the scheme of things. The Ministry of Defence was approached to see if my work could better be undertaken by a limited company under their direction. I attended meetings in AMP's Department where I tried to explain that the success of my work depended very much upon voluntary help and that, if they were to employ people to raise funds, then the profit margin would be inevitably reduced. In the end, the Ministry of Defence agreed and the idea of going commercial was dropped. However, by now, the happy atmosphere I had enjoyed at the Museum ever since my arrival there fifteen years previously, had all but disappeared. I was 65 years old, completely unsettled and, as far as I knew, possibly on the verge of terminal illness. I submitted my resignation as Director of Appeals and it was accepted. I left the Royal Air Force Museum on 15th December, 1986.

In April, 1987, the period between my regular cancer checks was extended from three to every six months. Steadily, I began to recover my peace of mind and, with that, my former restless urge always to be trying to do something. The Royal Air Force Philatelic Consortium had been disbanded on my retirement but its products had been left 'in the air' possibly just to wither and die. In the year before my illness, I had discussed ways whereby the various schemes could be kept going, particularly if the interest base could be broadened to include the Army and the Navy. With this in mind, it took little urging for me to decide to get back to work.

I formed the Joint Services Charities Consortium during that month. I took on the chairmanship of a group of like-minded retired personnel from the three Services devoted to raising money for deserving charities. I looked around for a suitable organization to which I could anchor the organisation and fortunately was able to choose the Royal Air Forces Association, operating from its headquarters in Chiswick under the direction of its Secretary General, Air Commodore Mark Tomkins. Soon work had started on schemes similar to those I managed when at the Royal Air Force Museum - philatelic programmes, fund-raising at Air Shows, Exhibitions, military tattoos, and gatherings. Together with the RAFA and Frank Wootton, the renowned aviation artist, we did very well with a trio of Fine Art Prints, signed by the famous of the Royal Air Force. I was thoroughly enjoying myself, now back on my feet and my own master. I was doing better than I had done at Hendon.

The period between my cancer checks had been extended to a year by 1990. I was certain that the disease would not return. Then, one Saturday afternoon, while watching the football results on television, without any warning, I suffered a heart attack. I thought that my time had come. It was a truly frightening experience that left me writhing on the floor fighting for breath while trying to alert the family's attention to my distress. An ambulance was called; the paramedics sedated me and gave me oxygen. I then fell unconscious, coming to in the intensive care ward of the Epsom General Hospital.

Yet again, luck was on my side. Two days later, I was recovered well enough to be moved into a bed in a single room. I could just about stand and was able to shuffle a few steps. I was very weak but my brain was alert, so much so that I was able to telephone Mark Tomkins to tell him that I would be unable to attend the fund-raising luncheon at the Royal Air Force Club planned for the morrow, but that Wendy would be posting him the cheque I had intended to present to the President of the RAFA, and that the luncheon should surely go ahead.

I was kept in hospital for three weeks. It took all my effort to manage the walk from the ward to Wendy's car; I had spurned the use of a wheelchair. The time spent in bed had wasted the muscles of my arms and legs but happily had reduced my weight by 25lbs. Although I was to be kept under observation for some time, the doctors told me there had been no lasting damage to my heart. I was therefore determined to get well and so set up a personal remedial programme. It began with walks and attempted push-ups, first in the bedroom and then in the lounge. I marked out a walking track around our long garden. Little by little, I forced myself around this circuit, increasing the number of laps completed each day. I recovered the use of my legs and arms and, when I tackled the treadmill test at the hospital after three months, I passed it with ease.

I was soon back in full flight and counting my blessings. In both cases of illness I had been given timely warnings; first to stay out of the sun and not to irritate any of my fine collection of moles on my body and, second, to make sure that I did not put back the the heavy load of fat that I had lost. I was able to undertake and maintain a far better workload than before because I was feeling so much better. I gave up flying but was able to continue my indulgence in driving fast cars. I began to write books and, fortunately, found a publisher. I disciplined myself to early rising and writing regularly for a few hours each day before breaking off to tackle the fund-raising business that still went well. Furthermore, I am so well supported by my dear wife Wendy who, in fifty-seven years of marriage to an eccentric like me, has had to put up with so much. I still have the bit between my teeth, knowing that there is still much to be done and enjoyed. What I firmly believe, above all, is that having retired from work twice before, there is no intention of my retiring a third time.

INDEX

ALSO NEW FROM INDEPENDENT BOOKS

'SHARK SQUADRON PILOT'

By Bert Horden

'Shark Squadron Pilot' is a graphic illustration of the realities of the air war in the Western Desert. Bert Horden joined No. 112 'Shark' Squadron early in 1942 and was soon initiated into the ground attack role of the 'Kittys'. With their garish shark's mouths painted on their aircraft No. 112 Squadron wreaked havoc on the German Afrika Corps as the war in the Western Desert rose to its climax. Inflicting terrible damage with machine gun fire on soft skinned targets, like convoys of trucks, and causing significant damage with their under-slung bombs on the hard skinned Panzers, the aircraft of '112 Squadron soon became well known to Rommel's troops.

Using his diary and flying log book to preserve the accuracy and immediacy of the events Bert Horden has written a superb account of desert flying . In places extremely graphic and throughout well illustrated, *'Shark Squadron Pilot'* will be an important contribution to the recorded history of the Second World War.

ISBN 1 872836 45 3

UK Price: **£16.95**

ALSO BY BILL RANDLE:

Kondor

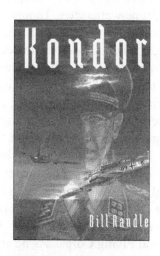

This exciting book is largely based on fact, and on the first hand experiences of Bill Randle who, as a young Sergeant Pilot, was shot down whilst flying a Wellington bomber in 1942. What followed forms the basis of this story; Bill, however, has chosen to tell it from a unique perspective.

As the RAF stepped up its bombing campaign in Germany and the Occupied countries, more and more aircrew were falling victim to the steadily increasing number of flak guns and to the nightfighters hunting under the cloak of darkness. Those airmen who survived often managed to evade immediate capture and were able to make contact with the Resistance. Gradually, more and more Allied aircrew were successfully 'processed' and passed down a carefully prepared escape line to a neutral country and eventually back home to fly again.

Acutely aware of this, the Germans strove relentlessly to destroy these lines, together with the courageous people who ran them. This is the fascinating account of one such operation, code-named Kondor: although a novel, the blend of fact and fiction is such that the reader may find difficulty in differentiating between the two...

ISBN 1 873836 25 9

287 Pages UK Price: **£14.95** (plus £3 towards p+p)

'BROKEN WINGS'

Opening in 1914, 'Broken Wings' introduces Bill's new character, Thomas Ebdon. Fascinated from an early age with the embryonic science of flight, Thomas resolves to become a flyer. However, his humble beginnings in rural Devon dictate that he must serve King and Country in the Infantry and from his idyllic country life he is pitched into the charnel house that is to be the beginning of the First World War.

Fighting in the mud and barbed wire he sees the early bombers and fighters wheeling overhead and yearns to fly, to take the fight to the enemy in the open halls of the sky. At first discouraged because 'only gentlemen fly' he persists and is eventually accepted for the Royal Flying Corps. As he enters the realms of the 'twenty minuters' (the average life expectancy of a new pilot and observer) he finds he is a natural flyer and manages to outlive many of his peers. But as the pressures increase and the armament of the aircraft becomes steadily more deadly how long will he survive?

Calling upon his extensive knowledge of the First World and of early aviation Bill has created another masterpiece historical novel which will keep readers engrossed to the end. 'Broken Wings' is a must for anyone with an interest in the First World War, in aviation or anyone who likes a good story well written.

ISBN 1 873836 35 6

224 Pages UK Price: **£14.95** (plus £3 towards p+p)

**Independent Books, 3 Leaves Green Crescent,
Keston, Bromley, BR2 6DN
Tel: (UK) 01959 573360
Fax: UK) 01959 541129
e-mail: mail@independentbooks.co.uk**